WILDFIRE DAYS

A Woman, a Hotshot Crew,

and the Burning American West

Kelly Ramsey

SCRIBNER

New York   Amsterdam/Antwerp   London
Toronto   Sydney/Melbourne   New Delhi

Scribner
An Imprint of Simon & Schuster, LLC
1230 Avenue of the Americas
New York, NY 10020

Names and identifying characteristics of some individuals, firefighting crews, and geographic locations have been changed. Some dialogue has been recreated.

For the boys

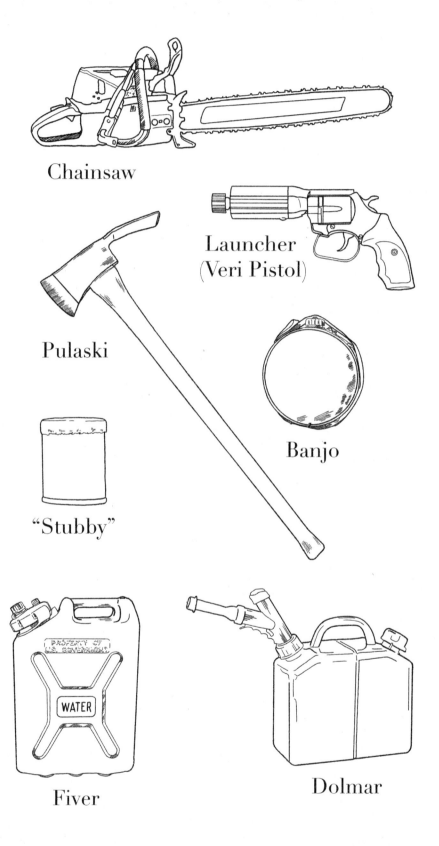

Chainsaw

Launcher
(Veri Pistol)

Pulaski

Banjo

"Stubby"

Fiver

Dolmar

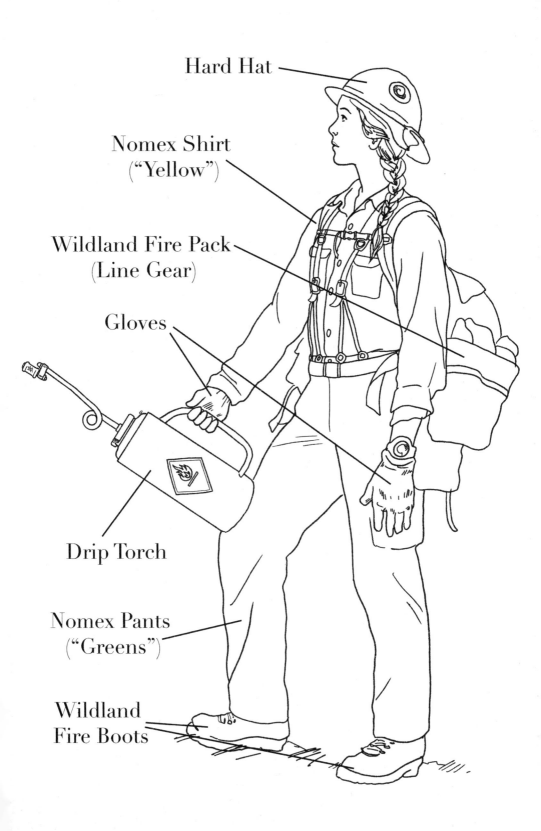

Hard Hat

Nomex Shirt
("Yellow")

Wildland Fire Pack
(Line Gear)

Gloves

Drip Torch

Nomex Pants
("Greens")

Wildland
Fire Boots

What is to give light
must endure burning.

—VIKTOR FRANKL

Labor Day

They had warned us about the wind. Every briefing for the past week had mentioned the front, a freak weather system, a real watch-out situation: the East Wind Event. Calling a threat an "event" was funny to us. Somebody made the joke, and we snickered, arms crossed over our chests, feet toeing the dirt. Dust covered the ash on our boots, and chew spit fell into the circle as Van discussed the day, the work. Saliva lay in bubbly pools until the dirt swallowed them, leaving dark spots near each man with a chewing tobacco pout or a nicotine pouch in his upper lip. Sometimes I'd try a Zyn, which set my gums on fire. If you did it all the time, the guys said, it didn't burn.

We looked up—the wind had come in howling. Pines bent under its invisible force, and someone muttered again, *Here's the big event*, and we laughed. Van said, or said with his eyes, "This is serious, guys. Come on."

The lot where we briefed was a dozer push near the intersection of two dirt roads. You had to traverse a mound of earth and torn-up bushes to find a private pee spot. Or I did—the guys pissed wherever they liked in gleeful arcs. I crouched in the thicket and made my own puddle, the urine steaming in the chill wind before it sank into mud.

Back at the buggy, I placed my hairbrush on the bumper. Every surface collected dirt, from the floors to the rims of the taillights, no matter how often Keller swept. The dirt on this forest bothered us, fine and soft as sifted brown flour. Walking, we sank shin-deep into loose soil. Dust filled our mouths and nostrils and lungs, and we coughed and choked and spat.

I poured a bottle of water over my head. We made fun of Bao for doing that, what we called his "birdbath," but this was day fourteen, and my hair was a stiff helmet of ash, so I'd take the ridicule. The water coated my scalp and drenched the collar of my yellow shirt, which would stick to my neck until sun or flames dried it. By then I'd be soaked with sweat anyway. One thing they don't tell you about fire is how wet you'll be.

I asked Wink, "Hold my phone?" Then used the camera as a mirror.

Wink looked away toward the engines lining up for shift. Green engines, red ones, yellow trucks, our crew and two others in green buggies—everybody was here. Men yawned, drank coffee. Slowly cranked themselves up to the capacity for emergency.

"Thanks, Winky," I said. "How's it look?"

He hunched into his bony frame, blinking. "It look g-good."

"Gotcha!" Eddie hooted, waving his phone. The *one* time I groomed myself, captured for posterity?

I groaned. "Let me see."

He showed us the video: Wink with the phone, me parting my wet hair. Behind us, the green forest, and a column of smoke beginning to bloom above the tree line.

I punched Eddie and told him to fuck himself. He laughed and went away chewing. But I had a cold feeling. It was too early in the day for a column like that. Something bad was coming.

PART I

Season One

How can I explain that you feel safe at this war,
knowing that the people around you are good people?

—MARTHA GELLHORN

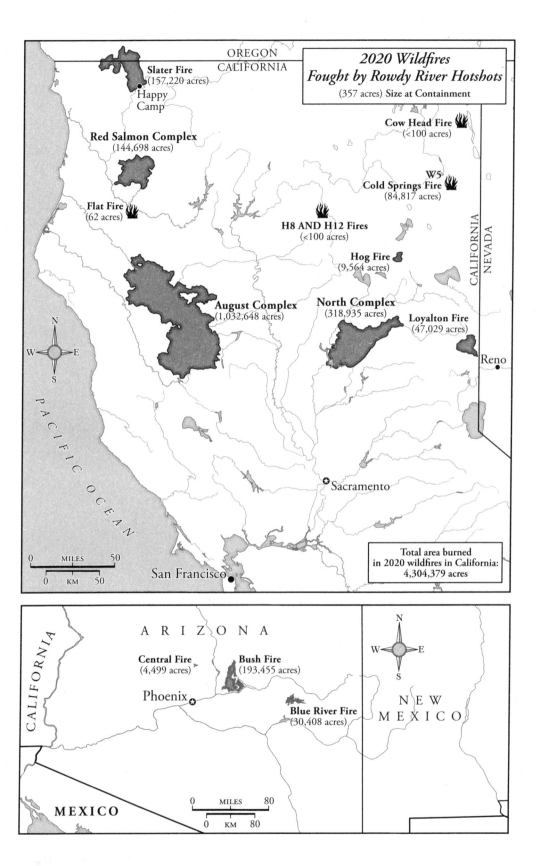

ROWDY RIVER HOTSHOTS

2020 Roster

<u>**Superintendent**</u> (**"Supt,"** pronounced *Soup*): Samuel "Van" Van Allen

<u>Alpha (A-module, or "A-mod")</u>
Captain: Benjamin "Benjy" Rose
Squad Boss ("Squadie"): Andrew "Mac" Macaluso
Senior ("Lead"): Scotty Castaldi
Senior ("Lead"): Shane "Wink" Winkler

Temporary Seasonal Employees ("Temps"):
Ryan Edwards, 3rd year
Julian Hayes, 2nd year
Blake Haines, rookie
Beryl "Barrel" MacCrum, rookie
Miguel Rosario, rookie

<u>Bravo (B-module, or "B-mod")</u>
Captain: Rob "Salmon" Salomon
Squad Boss ("Squadie"): Matthew "Fish" Fisher
Senior ("Lead"): Thatcher "West" Westbrook
Senior ("Lead"): Ishmael "Bao" Bayabao

Temps:
Luke Dawson, 6th year
Edward "Eddie A." Ahacic, 4th year
Eli "BJ" Jones, 3rd year
Alexander Trevan, rookie
Shaun Keller, rookie
Kelly Ramsey, rookie

Chapter 1

The Lime

Most of my stories begin with going over a mountain, and this one is no different.

It was May. I drove a pass we called Grayback, named for a peak it skirted but never saw. The winding road threaded the Siskiyou Crest, a string of lonesome mountains marking the farthest northern margin of California. These were primeval woods, deepest green, an ocean of wall-to-wall conifers huddled so close they seemed to be whispering secrets or harboring fugitives. Mushrooms sprouted from the pine litter; salamanders sheltered in damp rock shadows. Black bears and mountain lions rustled the brush, watched by owls you'd hear at dusk but never see. People whom solitude had rendered nearly transparent lived in canyons carved by glassy streams—Clear Creek, Elk Creek, Indian Creek—that rushed headlong into the Klamath River, the forest's throbbing heart. It ran high and cold in spring, carrying snowmelt home to the Pacific.

Despite all that water, the place was sun-drenched, hotter by the year, and the land burned. Fire had this country by the throat. Fire was the reason I climbed the mountain.

I lived in a town called Happy Camp. Yes, that's a place. This was the *real* Northern California, not the Bay Area, thank you very much. If the Golden State is a bent appendage, its swollen forearm bearing LA like a red boil, my California lay above the elbow.

The flat where Indian Creek riffled into the river was a natural settlement for the Indigenous Karuk people, who thrived there for tens of thousands of years. They found jade in the shallows, hunted deer and elk, burned the brush from the hills each winter, and fished Steelhead and Chinook from the Klamath's deep eddies—until, in a familiar story, white Europeans struck gold.

The forty-niners maintained an office—they do to this day, the New 49'ers Prospecting Club—in the center of Happy Camp. Now and then, potbellied white-haired men drifted into the sun, squinting mole-people still hoping for their big break. *Keep dreamin'*, I thought.

What little gold there had ever been was gone, and half the riverbed with it, piled in pebbly mounds called "tailings" along the Klamath's meandering course. During the rush, the town was so marked by violence and cultural clashes that it earned the nickname "Murderer's Bar." Later, it became a timber town, then a weed town. Hidden in the hills lay marijuana grows, covert farms siphoning creek water through PVC pipes.

In a lesser-told story, the tribe held on; the town was more than half Karuk, and the tribe saved the community after each extractive industry's collapse. In the absence of a municipal presence, in one of the state's poorest counties, the tribal government *was* the government.

Still the town—once home to ten thousand people—shrunk and suffered. About a thousand scrappy souls remained when I arrived in 2018. A grocery store, post office, pizza shop, and liquor store lined the streets near a single blink-and-you'll-miss-it intersection, although the prominent Bigfoot statue was hard to overlook.

Wildfires had ravaged the Klamath mountains for decades, worsening each year since the '90s. In a world rising to a rolling simmer, fire in California was a biblical crisis, and here was its hellish heart, a forest so hot, steep, overgrown with brush, and strangled by poison oak that it was notorious among firefighters, who made their feelings known on a popular T-shirt: *Fuck the Klamath.*

For the right person, though, the Klamath was paradise, its beauty reinforced by its difficulty. To stay, you had to be pretty stupid, very tough, just plain poor—or so in love with the forest you couldn't tear yourself away. I might've been all of the above. The local itinerants, who camped under the Indian Creek bridge, shuffled along the highway, shaking their fists at invisible foes. Meth had taken their teeth; now it was after their minds. Yet in the water, salmon defied the dams (a contested issue, with a bumper sticker: *Un-dam the Klamath!*). They swam to the ocean and ran upstream each fall, seeking their ancestral creeks to spawn and die. At dawn, fishermen stood waist-deep in the muscle of the current, casting their flies.

Grayback Road lost county maintenance near the crest; through winter the route was buried, but in spring, locals with souped-up trucks plowed a single, perilous lane through the snow. That April had been warm, and I felt lucky to encounter only patches of melting ice as I followed Indian Creek's green canyon north out of our forest, over the spine of the crest, and down the other side into the damp, heady woods of Oregon.

Near the top of the pass, a faded wooden picnic table slouched at an overlook. On my first day with the Forest Service, a couple years before, we had stopped there and piled out, looking across the valley. I took in the sea of trees, crevasses spilling into deeper canyons, ridge upon ridge; a vast, rippling quilt of green earth darkening to blue where the mountains met the horizon. Over a million acres of forest.

"Welcome to your office," our boss, Jeff, had said. "Sucks, doesn't it?"

As I navigated the pass, I wondered: *How the hell did I end up here?*

I was born 2,500 miles away in a small town that had outbid other cities to become the capital of Kentucky. My father, Bob, was a lanky dropout from Louisville who built houses, a smoldering Marlboro loosely glued to his sweet-talking lips. His father had been a traveling salesman who abandoned the family early on, his mother a clerk or possibly a high-class prostitute. My dad grew up poor, hated by an older brother who saw him as the favorite—not that this kept him safe from their mother's acid tongue. Even in her later years, after she turned born-again Christian, my granny was a severe woman whose gifts of Bibles and angel figurines felt like unspecified threats.

Before he left school, my dad had been the star quarterback. He'd done a stint on a commune, knew a few chords on the guitar, and could build anything out of wood. His catchphrase, stolen from a book about a psychic, was: "You create your own reality."

My mother, Cindy, was a petite, serious girl from Pennsylvania with an art history degree. A stranger in Greenwich Village once told her, "You have a look of eternal virginity about you," and she did, with dark curls haloing a doe-eyed face. She grew up in a subdivision that bordered a golf course, wearing socks that matched her skirts. Her father worked in advertising; her mother, who had been a gifted dancer, raised five children. Reared in a home where someone might vacuum a spill from the front lawn, my mom grew into a meticulous, determined woman who was in the right almost as often as she believed she was.

A dreamer and a doer, my parents had little in common except the naïveté required to fall for one's opposite—which is exactly what happened when my dad sauntered into the architect's office where my mom worked. They were married six months later in a field of yellow grasses and settled in an apartment inside an old tobacco barn on a friend's farm, which lay at the end of a gravel drive off Devil's Hollow Road. Cross the creek, pass the pond, you can't miss it.

I thrust my dark head into the world in a Lexington hospital during a rare November cold snap. Snow dusted the highway and, car running in the lot with my mom inside, my dad cut the line at Burger King, saying, "My wife's in labor."

You could say two nice things about my parents' marriage. They were in love once, at least for a while. And they chose to have a child. Beyond that? Disaster. Engine failure. Goat rodeo. And my favorite: dumpster fire. My parents together were kerosene and a match.

Six years later, I flew to visit my father in Massachusetts. He'd been gone since I was two years old, and though he'd come to visit, he still felt like a stranger. I was nervous.

My dad waited outside the airport, cigarette in hand, eyes squinted at some invisible concern in the distance. Boston was covered in snow. He and his new family lived in a rambling, drafty, two-story house set back from the road on a wooded lot. Inside, the rooms were warm and messy and full of people: my new stepmom, Renee, a tall blonde with a brassy Detroit accent; her sister, Carol, a belly-laugher; my dad, impossibly tall and handsome and cool; and my new six-month-old sister, Courtney. The Christmas tree had a bulbous lump at the base, damp and earth-smelling. My dad explained that this was the root ball, and in spring, they'd plant the tree in the yard.

"Come with me," he said, and I double-timed to catch his loping stride. We pulled on boots and crossed the yard. Snow lay in drifts against the buildings. Inside the barn, in the glow of yellow lights dangling from the rafters, stood dozens of machines: saws and lathes and grinders, drills and presses. The air smelled like wood chips and oil. I could tell by how he showed me every corner that his workshop was his joy, his retreat. He was himself here.

"Let me show you something," he said. He picked up a slab of wood, a square foot of inch-thick cedar or pine.

"For me?" I asked, because carved into the tablet in elegant script was a single word: *Kelly,* the name my parents had chosen for me, which meant "warrior" or "wood." He ran a long finger over the letters and said with that warm sweet accent we shared, the softened sound of the mid-South, "Yeah, silly! It's a sign for your room. Keep all the critters out."

I giggled. "There's no critters, Daddy!" I hugged his leg, and he lifted me into his arms. I'd been told I was too big to carry, but not for him. His beard scratched my forehead. His flannel shirt smelled like tobacco, sawdust, and whiskey—forever after the dark perfumes of love.

On Christmas morning, I lay on a quilt with Courtney, whose muddy-green eyes watched my every move, her wisp of blond hair pale as a summer whitecap. I made faces until she giggled, seizing my index finger in a tiny plump fist, squeezing me tight. She wouldn't let go, and I hoped she never would. My *sister.*

Here was all I longed for under one roof. Which is to say: a family.

"Family," in my experience, was an unreliable concept, an abstract that never quite cohered before dissolving entirely.

Thirty years later, I sat on the porch of a farmhouse in Fentress, Texas. The phone rang, and I looked at the screen, shocked by the name that appeared there. I could count the times he'd called in three decades on one hand, and still I could guess what this was about. I picked up anyway.

"Dad?"

"Hello, little daughter of mine."

Tripping over my words, I split the difference between asking him how he was, and where.

My dad was homeless. A severe alcoholic, he drank until liquor was the lone star by which he navigated a world he was darkening himself, glass by glass. He had abruptly left my stepmom and their four kids years before. He drank until he could no longer work, then stayed with friends or girlfriends until they kicked him out. He lived with each of my sisters, who eventually were forced to boot him too. Finally, he slept in his truck, until he crashed into a concrete post and couldn't afford to get the vehicle out of impound.

Now he was just . . . out there. Like an animal in the cold. He sometimes scored a bed in a shelter, sometimes slept on the street. This was a shelter phase, I thought; you had to be sober to get in, and he sounded lucid.

"Madeleine got me a few shirts," he was saying. My youngest sister, who often took care of him. "Courtney brought me some underwear and socks. It's hard when all you got is a backpack."

My nostrils burned. I blinked back tears. I'd been right; he was asking for money. But I no longer cared.

"What do you need?"

He said, matter-of-factly, that he could use a second pair of pants. That way he'd have something to wear while he washed his first pair at the Laundromat. I tried to imagine a life reduced to two pants, dirty and clean. I tried not to wonder how filthy he was.

I told him I'd send money to Courtney, who would get him the cash. He might spend it on whiskey, I knew that. But I was helping him for my own sake. To comfort myself.

"Thank you, my beautiful daughter," he said warmly.

My ear held and squeezed the sound of that "you," spoken as only a man from Kentucky could, like the tree that grows wild along riverbanks, the species they say cures cancer. *Yew*. He could still make me feel like the only "you" on earth.

But the image woke me at night: My dad curling up to sleep on a sidewalk in the cruel midwestern winter. His body a lump under a blanket, under a tarp—like someone who might have already died.

It was almost too much to bear. So I didn't; I pushed my feelings down. Or rather, I sweated them out. I began to take long hikes, usually alone. I backpacked into the Grand Canyon, scaled a fourteen-thousand-foot peak in Colorado, jumped from a high bridge into a Guatemala river. I trudged desert dunes, crossed islands, and scaled volcanoes. With relief, I learned that a certain level of physical exertion—call it "exhaustion"—would silence sadness. About ten miles in, there lay a quiet place, a wide-open pasture in the mind. I pushed myself there again and again.

Despite all this effort, I sensed grief, like a relentless predator, gaining on me. So I ran.

Less than a year after hanging up the phone on that Texas porch, I ended a relationship, shoved my things into a storage unit, and drove to California. There, I found that the outdoors could be more than an escape; you could make a life out there, even a career. The volunteer position I took on a trail crew soon became a paying job as a wilderness ranger. Happy Camp and the U.S. Forest Service took me in.

Over the next two years with the Klamath National Forest, I learned the difference between a ponderosa and a Jeffrey pine (it's in the bark texture—"Gentle Jeffrey, Prickly Ponderosa"). I could distinguish the hoot of the aggressive barred owl from that of the reclusive northern spotted owl. I could navigate the Marble Mountain Wilderness by feel, buck a log with a crosscut saw, replace a trail sign, dig a new trail, or rescue a lost hiker. I could read water well enough to float Class IV rapids in an inflatable kayak. I knew the cry of the red-tailed hawk, the secret swimming holes on every creek, and where to pick blackberries when they ripened in July.

My second summer on the Forest, I lived in a government barracks with female firefighters, ladies who could do hundreds of push-ups and run a six-minute mile. They came home from assignments reeking of woodsmoke, faces smudged with ash. Though they claimed to be exhausted, they were lit up, as if brought to life by fire. I had dated a firefighter my first summer out there, and I'd admired his chiseled physique, but seeing the women was different.

As we held pull-up contests in the kitchen doorway, and as I watched them come and go, muscular and unapologetic in heavy leather fire boots, I was smitten with a new vision of what a woman could be. In a word: strong.

That summer I got Red Carded, or qualified as a wildland firefighter. Doing so required online courses in firefighting methods and successful completion of the Pack Test, a three-mile walk wearing a forty-five-pound weight vest to be finished in under forty-five minutes. Since I'd been backpacking all summer for work, a six-foot cross-cut saw (like the old, two-handled lumberjack saw) balanced on one shoulder, I blitzed through the Pack Test, hardly breaking a sweat.

All season I begged to be taken on a fire. But it was a slow summer, with few fires in Northern California; the local crew went to Canada, and I was devastated not to be picked up as a fill-in. Finally, in late August, an engine needed an extra body to tag along on a lightning strike, and I hopped in a truck with two guys I'd never met.

We hiked to the top of a peak called Tom Martin. It was less hike, more hand-and-foot scramble over bear-sized rocks. We carried our line gear (firefighters' version of a backpack) and a hand tool, plus bladder bags, which are yellow satchels holding five gallons of water. You attach a brass hand pump to the bladder for spraying out hot spots on a fire.

All told, we carried seventy pounds apiece. Weighed down, the bladder sloshing, the climb was painfully hard, but I grinned the whole way up the hill. Doing something that difficult felt like a high.

At the top, the "fire" was a letdown. Lightning had struck a single ponderosa pine, blackening its trunk. By the time we arrived, the day after a lookout spied the inky smudge of a new start on the horizon, somebody had already cut the tree down. Now it lay on its side, a corpse smoldering in a pale cloud of smoke, hints of red flickering poker-hot under the armored plates of bark.

We grabbed our tools and made quick work of scraping away the burning bark, cooling the log with water as we did so. At six thousand feet, the peak's vantage point offered panoramic views in three directions: the green swale of Seiad Valley to our west, the pink crests of the Red Buttes Wilderness to the north, and to our right, the hills of Oak Knoll, the eastern district of the forest, where timber gave way to scrubby chaparral.

"Whoa," said Dakota, a bearded first-year firefighter on the engine. He was gazing at the horizon.

I stood and looked. "*Whoa.*"

While we'd had our heads down working, something had happened to the east. I'd overheard the noise on the radio, an evolving incident: the Lime Fire. Through the early morning hours, the fire had lain quietly in the shade. Now it awakened, climbing a brush-packed slope on the far side of the valley, flames licking upward. The Lime began to put up a column, meaning that all the threads and tendrils and wisps of smoke rising from every burning bush and tree and blade of grass braided together, billowing and twisting, climbing the sky, forming a pillar of smoke that tied the earth to the stratosphere.

If you've ever seen a photo of the mushroom cloud from an atomic bomb, a fire column is a little like that. Goose bumps prickled my arms. I blurted, "We need to get over there!"

Chris and Dakota laughed.

Chris explained that the three of us wouldn't be top of mind in this critical moment. Sure, that reasoning made sense, yet I had the strangest feeling. At the sight of a smoke column, most people feel a healthy hitch in their breath and want to run the other way. You should. But all I wanted to do was run *toward* the fire.

Sign me up! Put me in the game, Coach. The sight of smoke made my skin tingle and my arm hair stand on end, but not with dread. With excitement.

Back at the station, my supervisor threw back his head and laughed. "You got the bug! You're hooked."

"Nah." I played it off, but it was a known phenomenon: getting bitten by the fire bug. Once fire got you, they said, there was no going back.

Tony teased me for doing push-ups on the line that day and said, "You know where you might fit in? There's a crew nearby; they're a lot of fun. Rowdy River Hotshots."

I figured *why not?* and applied.

Okay, the process was a little less casual than that. I applied through the federal government's labyrinthine online system, made several phone calls, and finally drove over the mountain to meet with Benjy and Mac, two men on the crew's "overhead" (leadership team), to whom I made my case. I *really* wanted to join *this* crew, I swore, pledging to train all winter.

I'd been told that nobody got hired onto a hotshot crew by submitting a résumé or sending a polite follow-up email. You had to court them, woo them, flatter them, promise that this module was your top and only choice.

In truth, Rowdy River *was* my top choice, though mostly by default. You had to live within a certain driving distance of a crew's station, because during fire season you'd be on a "two-hour callback."

In that time, I could reach several crews' headquarters: Klamath Hot-shots, Salmon River Hotshots, and Rowdy River. But an ex-boyfriend who I may have low-key stalked worked for Klamath, so they were out. And I'd heard unpleasant rumors about Salmon River, whose station perched along one of the sketchiest roads in the region—no, thanks. Rowdy River it was.

I remember what I wore to visit the station: skinny jeans, Chelsea boots, a puffy jacket. My hair hung to the middle of my back. I felt exposed in civilian clothes. The small office smelled like feet and die-sel fuel, and the two men remained sitting in the only available chairs, so I towered above them while shrinking under the scrutiny of their gazes. Both were bearded; one blond and narrow-bodied (Mac), and the other dark haired and barrel shaped (Benjy). The latter's liquid brown eyes strayed down the length of my body—not sexually, per se. I knew the look; he was assessing my physical fitness. I cursed myself for not having a shape that looked more obviously sporty. Stupid hips.

"You been hikin'?" he asked gruffly.

They called in January and offered me the job. Would I come? I emitted an elated and possibly squeaky yes, then hung up, feeling sick. *Oh god.* Now I had to actually *do* this. So began a phase of daily training—and continual anxiety.

Hotshot crews are physically and operationally intense. They're often referred to as the "special forces" of wildland firefighting (although any hotshot will roll their eyes at those words). These crews tackle the most difficult and remote parts of wildfires, doing the hardest manual labor and hiking deep into the wilderness to places other crews can't or won't go. All wildland firefighters are tough, but hotshots have a reputa-tion for being among the toughest.

To prepare for the rigors of the work, you had to achieve certain physical standards (as formally defined in the Standards for Interagency Hotshot Crew Operations, or SIHCO, also the name for a governing body that ensures adherence to said rules): a 10:30 mile-and-a-half run, five pull-ups, twenty-five push-ups in under a minute, and sixty sit-ups in sixty seconds. But that was the bare minimum. You also had to complete strength circuits, six-mile hill runs, wind and hill sprints—all of which were peanuts compared to the hiking. And only the hiking really counted.

I trained with my friend Paige, who would also be joining a hotshot crew in the spring. We rose in the dark to hike. Often, we hit the top covered in sweat as the first pink light streaked the sky. The more we trained, the more excited I became. Something in me not only tolerated but *loved* this kind of challenge. As it turned out, I liked to suffer, and the depth of one's suffering directly correlated to the degree of one's euphoria at the top.

Paige left that winter, and I kept training on my own, hiking fire lines (imagine a trail, but instead of having switchbacks, it goes *straight up* the mountain) three times a week with the required forty-five pounds. My heart rate hit 188 and stayed pinned there for an hour as I gasped open-mouthed up hill after hill. I ran sprints, lifted weights, practiced pull-ups until I could squeeze out a few. Did thousands of sit-ups and planks. Still, I didn't feel ready.

Not only was I anything but a natural athlete—okay, I wasn't a weakling, though my childhood sports had been ballet, summer swim team, and *figure skating*—but I had almost no experience as a firefighter. Most people who came to a hotshot crew had a few fire seasons under their belt; I'd be the only rookie to both the crew and to fire. Scariest of all, while I had hoped the crew would pick up another lady or two, I learned that I'd be the sole woman and the first in nearly a decade. To many of the guys, I'd be the only girl they'd ever worked with.

Just me and nineteen men who were probably faster, stronger, and more knowledgeable than I was. No big deal.

So here I was, driving a mountain pass to keep a date with doom. I mean destiny.

I pulled over to get a breath of the cool mountain air. The oxygen felt clean, filtered by the parapet of conifers. I loved stopping at this pullout, which marked the edge of a stand of rare trees: the Brewer spruce, also called the "weeping" spruce, an evergreen whose boughs made a distinctive sagging swoop, as if sadly shrugging. The weeping spruce was endemic to the Klamath Mountains, meaning it grew there and nowhere else, and the tree's range and numbers were dwindling, thanks to climate change and fires. This slope above Indian Creek supported one of the largest continuous stands in the world.

I glanced up.

What do you think, guys? Will I make it?

The trees rustled in the wind, maintaining their diffident shrugs, as if to say, *Maybe, maybe not. Does it matter?*

Oh, it mattered. It mattered a lot.

For one thing, I needed the money; I'd spent the last few years working trails for a pittance, and I was fifteen thousand dollars in debt. As a hotshot, you'd get close to a thousand hours of overtime, which could add up to a decent living.

I also needed to impress these guys. I didn't even know them, but I wanted to show them how hard I could work, how tough I was. I wanted to earn their respect—or better yet, their love.

It didn't exactly make sense. I already had a boyfriend, Josh, and a wonderful house in Happy Camp that we shared with four dogs, a cat, and a goat. Well, the goat lived in the yard and bellowed a needy "Mehhh" from dawn to dusk, but you know what I'm saying: a comfortable, regular life. Josh, also a firefighter, was talking about marriage, even kids. Such a partnership was everything I claimed to want. Yet the most excited I'd been in months was the moment the crew called to offer me a job. I couldn't wait to get into the thick of it, to hoof up some terrible hills.

Still, after a winter of struggling to get as strong and fast as we were supposed to be, I was afraid I wouldn't be good enough. What if this was a crazy idea, a terrible mistake? They'd probably pull me aside on the first day of work and gently inform me that, *Sorry, you're just not a good fit.*

Unfortunately, the first day was tomorrow. They were expecting me, and I was my mother's child: responsible. You don't take a job and not show up. You don't let people down. You are *nice.*

The breeze that ruffled the spruces sent a chill up my arms, but the familiar trees were a comfort. No matter what happened, I thought, my forest would be here. I could always come home.

With a farewell glance at the green valley, I hopped in the truck and swung onto the road over the mountain.

Chapter 2

Day One

Welcome to California.

My stomach executed a small, clumsy somersault at the sight of the blue and gold sign. How stupid—I'd just *come* from California, crossing a sliver of Oregon to reenter the Golden State. But I had wanted to live here for so long, and how could you feel anything except astonishment about a place that contained the Sierras, the Mojave Desert, the redwoods, the Pacific Coast, the glacial lakes of the Trinity Alps, and the severe, desolate mountains of the Klamath? Country of wilderness, elk, and condor. Wildflower super-blooms visible from space. Not a state so much as a world.

The road, Highway 199, barreled through a tunnel and emerged into a blinding canyon. Conifers covered the ridges. Cliffs plunged to a gorge where the Rowdy, the only river in the state that had never been dammed, flowed freely in a narrow turquoise channel. I handled the curves with care as the highway followed a narrow ledge above the water.

The hamlet of Baudelaire sat astride the confluence of the Middle and North Forks of the Rowdy River, anchored by a convenience store/post office building and a Forest Service station. I had admired the station's white buildings with green trim, the stone fences and handsome lawns. As I pulled between river-rock pillars to enter the parking lot, a guy standing by a truck camper waved.

"You must be Kelly." He grinned.

"Yeah," I said, confused, until I remembered: just one girl. Of course they'd know my name.

"I'm Eddie! People call me Eddie A."

His large hand made mine seem small and cold. A mustache and dimples framed his smile, and his warm dark eyes were fringed with the kind of eyelashes girls pay good money for. His hair, long enough to curl around his ears, was dark brown, almost the same shade as mine. It was hard not to stare at his biceps. Weirdest of all, he was friendly and at ease, as if we'd known each other for years. I thought of an eddy, the slow swirl below a rapid where you pulled out of the current to catch your breath.

"Wanna flip around and follow me? I'll show you where you're gonna be living."

Jogging ahead as I followed in my truck, Eddie led me across the compound to the edge of the woods. I parked beside a two-story white house, and my stomach lurched. Two or three boys—really, they looked like young boys—were shooting hoops in the driveway. They looked so athletic. Jesus, I didn't look like that.

"Hey," said a six-foot blond kid unloading bags from his Prius. "I'm Shaun."

"Kelly." I shook his hand.

Shaun (who would go by his last name, Keller) was twenty and looked like an overgrown Danish child. He uttered a soft "Nice to meet you," hoisted a duffel and a fishing pole, and disappeared into the building.

"You Kelly?"

I shook the hand of a stocky Black man who flashed a beautiful smile. His upper body was a wedge of muscle. His name was Eli, he said. "But you can call me BJ. Everyone does."

"Why's that?"

Eli Jones's mom was Indigenous Yurok, his dad African American. Father back East and mother deceased, he'd lived as a teenager with his Yurok cousins. As the second Jones in their school, he was called "Black Jones," or BJ.

"Sounds kinda racist," I joked.

"It's fine. That's what I've always been called." He shrugged and followed us in.

Inside, the building was like all barracks: run-down, with a distinct suggestion of Hantavirus risk, i.e., mouse-infested, but kind of cozy, too. Like summer camp (or so I imagined—we'd never been able to afford it). We passed a narrow, sunny kitchen and crossed a living room with stained carpet, pleather couches, and a flat-screen TV. At the foot of the stairs, a door opened into a large room with built-in shelves in the corners. What had been an open doorway to the kitchen was jerry-rigged shut, a sheet of plywood screwed into the doorframe.

"This is yours. It used to be the dining room." Eddie laughed.

Another boy came thundering down the stairs.

"Hey," he said, taking off huge, mirrored sunglasses with the brand name Heat Wave on the temples. "I'm Ryan."

Nineteen, golden-skinned with brooding eyes, he wore a crop-top sweatshirt that read *Tove Lo*.

I thanked the boys, and they took off. I dropped my bag on the floor. Twin bed, dresser, old couch. A window overlooked the forest, while another faced the driveway. I fingered the paperbacks past hotshots had left behind: Peter Matthiessen's *The Snow Leopard*, a true crime book about the Manson murders, a war novel.

I tacked a map of the Siskiyou Wilderness to the doorway plywood. On the other side, Keller and BJ were talking about fishing. I liked hearing their voices. I liked the room, *my* room. I would live here during the week and go over the mountain to Happy Camp on weekends, at least until we started rolling to fires.

Living out of a few bags was liberating, and I noticed that along with anxiety about the next day (terror, it would be fair to say), I felt peaceful here, a mountain range from home. Comfortable, in other words, by myself.

As I stacked my clothes in the dresser drawers, my thoughts returned to the first home I could remember and the first thing I believed about life: that I was on my own.

My parents, whose marriage was a ship in shallow water by the time I learned to walk, tried for a fresh start in Florida. *Florida*, of all places. Needless to say, it didn't work. My dad went somewhere else after that, maybe Texas. My mom filed the papers, and the two of us drove home to Kentucky, belongings piled into a pale yellow Subaru hatchback.

We rented a place on Old Dailey Avenue, near downtown Frankfort. The house gazed across the highway at the Sour Mash bourbon distillery, where I sat on Santa's lap to submit my material requests each December. I remember my mother reading to me, the shape of my bedroom, the cold, curved edge of the clawfoot bathtub, the cabin in the woods where my best friend lived—and very little else about those first few years.

When I met my dad for the first time I can recall, I was five. The tall man leaned against our fence, smoking a cigarette. He didn't look like a dad, just a guy. But he brought me Andes mints, a treat I'd never had before, two wafers of milk chocolate sandwiching a layer of green creme de menthe. He wore Lee jeans and leather loafers, and he claimed that the chocolate was soft because he'd brought it inside his shoes. I believed him, ready to accept anything he told me. Then he was gone.

Our street wasn't fancy: a working-class neighborhood with some rentals like ours, a few retirees' well-kept ranch houses, and several trailer folks. The neighbors had a daughter my age from whom I contracted head lice, and my mom couldn't *believe* they didn't take their kids to a dentist, yet there were the parents watching TV from a satellite dish. "Somehow they can afford *that*."

How did anyone afford anything, I wondered, when they always talked about the money they didn't have and how much someone didn't send in child support? He was late again. He was usually late, if he sent a check at all.

We moved to Pennsylvania when I was seven because my mom took a job with my uncle's computer consulting startup—and, I think, so my mom could have help from her family. They were wonderful: my gentle, indulgent Nana and whistling, yarn-spinning Opa, the aunts and uncles and cousins, all of whom gathered for Sunday dinners and crowded family holidays.

That summer, I flew to see my father again. Dad took me to one of his job sites, where he taught me to caulk a bathtub. He'd done this a thousand times, and the action was sure: with one long finger, he smoothed the white paste into the channel between tiles. When I tried, I made a mess and smeared caulk on my MC Hammer pants. Mom wouldn't be pleased; the smell of cigarette smoke I brought home in my suitcase was bad enough.

But I was proud of the white smear, confirmation of time spent with my dad. After I outgrew the pants, I kept them folded in the back of a drawer. I hated to let anything go, and I hoarded small mementos, from ticket stubs to birthday cards to the wing-shaped pins the airlines gave me for flying alone between parents. Anything could be evidence, proof of life.

Yet nothing seemed to prove I wasn't alone. In our apartment in Pennsylvania, I lay awake at night, watching the headlights that shone through the blinds and raced across the ceiling. I could hear Clarence, the elderly man whose duplex backed up to ours, snoring heavily. I wiped my wet cheeks and prayed for someone to rescue me.

But who? My dad was far away and never called. The Christmas gifts were labeled in my stepmom's handwriting. My mom slept across the hall, but I couldn't tell her how I felt. She only wanted me to be happy and to hear otherwise would wound her. If I shared my real feelings, she would only stiffen and say that everything was going to be fine, when as far as I could tell, that wasn't true.

Childhood, anything or anyone I had been before—all was forgotten as the sun rose over the station and the sleeping hamlet of Baudelaire, light snagging on the cold river surface. I could think of nothing but what I might face on my first day as a hotshot. *Aspiring* hotshot.

By first light, I stood at the edge of the crew bay. I tried to keep still, as if doing so could render me invisible.

There were so many men. Boys on dudes on bros, everywhere I looked, male forms moving in all directions with their muscles and deep voices and bow-legged struts. They talked loudly, took up space without a second thought. They ate and joked, messed with chainsaws, drank coffee with loud slurps, laced their boots with calloused fingers that moved nimbly over the leather. Men who hadn't seen each other all winter hugged or slapped hands with a *'Sup, man. Good to see you, brother.*

They asked how the offseason was. They said, with affection: "Bro, you got *fat.*"

Imagine a woman saying that. I almost snorted.

This was one of the first times I had been in a space devoid of women. I felt the absence of their softening presence, their warm voices and laughter, breasts and hips, compliments and hugs, how we would have whispered, *This is scary*, and, *Who do you think's the hottest?*

The firefighting crew I'd subbed onto for several months at the end of the previous season, Crew 2, had included five women. Now I saw that I'd taken that experience for granted. Even a few girls could tip the scales, and the balance of men would self-correct, subtly softening their language, their jokes, even the way they spat. Not here. The bro show was in full effect, and I realized with horror that not a person in sight could loan me a tampon.

Many of them wouldn't even look my way, but a few shook my hand, uttered names I forgot, and showed me around, explaining how to get my gear dialed in. They had given me something to do, which I desperately needed. Everyone else was busy, or pretending to be, and I could tell you shouldn't be caught otherwise.

We weren't the only resource headquartered at the Baudelaire district station. Across the lot, a barnlike building housed two firefighting engines, and two office buildings under the trees accommodated all the usual Forest Service departments: recreation, timber, fuels, biology, botany, hydrology, and so on.

"The bay" was our crew's dedicated facility: three joined garages with roll-up doors, customized by the guys using planks they'd hand-milled from redwood, cedar, and Douglas fir from the nearby forest. Wooden cubbies labeled with our names covered one wall, and a slab Redwood bench provided seating nearby. Beneath a storage loft at the back of the bay were rooms for supplies and uniforms, hand tools, and chainsaws. The central area was arranged with a workbench, folding tables and chairs, and a woodstove. Deer and elk antlers hung from the rafters, and above the door to the saw room dangled a taxidermy raccoon. His name, someone said, was Skittles.

The bay had the cozy masculine feel of a clubhouse or hunting lodge. You felt special just to be permitted inside.

Finding the cubby labeled with my name, I pulled out its contents: a gray hard hat with the crew logo and my name; a Mystery Ranch fire pack; and a black North Face duffel bag—the personal gear, or "PG" bag—with a sleeping pad and tarp already inside.

I knelt on the concrete, watching from the corner of my eye as one of the long-term temps laced his boots. The men on this crew wore extra-tall boots, sixteen inches ("sixteens") covering their calves, whereas firefighters elsewhere wore eight- or ten-inch boots. Most guys on our crew ordered an extra-high two-inch heel, called a "double stack," which gave you better purchase on steep slopes. The boys even laced their boots with a proprietary technique, holding both lace ends in one hand and swishing in a Z pattern, grabbing multiple hooked eyelets at once. They had a *lace* flex? Jesus.

The boot brand mattered, I learned too late. If you were cool, you had Nicks, Clemons, or a new brand, JK Boots. I wore a lowly pair of White's, purchased off the shelf for two hundred dollars as opposed to the five to seven hundred you'd shell out for custom Nicks. Mine were flat-soled, smooth, eight-inch black leather. Wrong in every way, or "bagger," as in trashy. If the guys hadn't already, they'd soon say, "What are those, *White's*?"

As new temps, our first task was to meet with Wink, a hunched man with a stutter, to finish collecting our gear, from fire shelters to sleeping bags, first aid kits, and government issue Meals Ready-to-Eat (MREs). I'd consumed only one MRE in my life, and I didn't poop for four days afterward. I shuddered at the memory.

Wink would also distribute our Nomex, the fire-resistant clothing in which we'd live this summer: dark green pants with oversized cargo pockets ("greens") and a thick, collared shirt the color of French's mustard (the "yellow"). Greens and yellows were drawn from a central cache, so you wore the pants or shirt another person had worn in year(s) past, sometimes finding their patches and handsewn hems. We wore yellows only on an incident; donning your yellow any sooner than the seconds before entering the fire was also "bagger." The standard uniform in station was boots and greens with a gray cotton long-sleeve shirt, crew logo embroidered over the left breast.

Rowdy River nurtured a quirky style: knee-high boots, slightly cropped pants to show off said boots (or, in Benjy's case, pants "bloused," with the legs tucked in), and hand-crafted suspenders. I knew they prized being tough, but the look was *adorable*.

Wink waved the gear checkout forms at Eddie A. "You never gave back your sleeping bag last year, so you don't g-get one now."

"It was filthy. You said to throw it out, remember? C'mon, Wink. Please," Eddie whined.

"No way. You is s-sleeping on the ground this year. Sorry." Wink shrugged.

"Hey," said Van, our Superintendent, popping his head into the bay. "We're gonna gaggle outside."

"Gaggle," the guys called to spread the word. "Gaggle by the trucks!"

"Put on your masks," Van added. "And get six feet apart. The District Ranger is big on that stuff. He's from New York."

With a shrug that said no one could be expected to understand New Yorkers, he stepped into the sunlight, and we hastened to follow him. The rest of the world was in lockdown, trying to prevent the spread of a deadly virus, but things were different for us. Wildfires didn't stop burning in a pandemic, so we couldn't stop fighting them.

We stood in a spread-out circle in the parking lot. You had to shout to hear someone on the other side, which made for a tough meeting. As we went around introducing ourselves, I studied Van. He was close to six foot, broad-shouldered. Everything about him was tidy, trim. He held his shoulders hunched up toward his ears, as though bracing for impact. The guys had told me he used to be tremendously fat, and they still called him a variant of "Dozer" behind his back, but he'd lost all the weight. He had pretty hazel eyes, but they were squished between his forehead and cheekbones, like someone had tried to smush him.

Van was friendly, fastidious, long-winded, and did everything (except talk) in a hurry. His smile appeared with a violent flash, then vanished, as if he'd had the thought, *I should smile now*, followed by, *Well, took care of that.*

"Normally, we'd have three or four weeks to get prepared for our readiness review," he said. "But with coming on later due to the Covid thing, our timeline is gonna be shorter. Our review is scheduled for next week, and we're hoping to go available just after Memorial Day. So I'm going to need every one of you, and especially you rookies, to get up to speed fast."

Yikes. I wasn't even sure what "go available" meant. But I knew I was a rookie and that I should be afraid.

My fear redoubled when a man named Fisher, a Goliath in wire-rim glasses, barked at us after lunch: "Gear up to hike! We're doin' French."

The boys rushed the saw room. I didn't. That was my first mistake of the day, though hardly my last. I knew they were grabbing chainsaws so they could do the hike with extra weight, a good way to prove yourself. But I reasoned I was already at enough of a disadvantage. The men were huge. With the exception of a guy named Ishmael, they were all larger than me and draped in muscle. For this first hike, it couldn't hurt to carry the ordinary forty-five-pound pack and a five- or ten-pound tool. I'd stick with that until I saw what I was up against.

The line gear was a technical pack designed specifically for fighting wildfires; Mystery Ranch was top-of-the-line, i.e., the only acceptable brand. The pack featured a bucket-like central compartment with a drawstring closure, a cube at the bottom that held the fire shelter, two large side pockets for water and fuel bottles, a front zip pocket, and a top zip pouch, the "brain," for smaller or quick-access items. Unlike a regular backpack, the line gear's weight rested almost entirely on your hips, leaving the arms unencumbered, and the shoulder straps came to a T over your back—all to allow freedom of movement while digging or running a chainsaw.

What we were required to carry was listed in our "crew organizer," the small booklet of reference material we called the "handy dandy." We carried:

6 quarts of water minimum (most of us carried 8 liters, or 2 gallons, which alone weighed 16 pounds)

Fire shelter

File and sheath

Shroud (a scrap of Nomex that attaches to your hard hat to protect your neck from heat)

Leather gloves

Headlamp

1 case of batteries

2 rolls of flagging

1 roll of fiber tape

Eye protection (safety glasses, goggles, or sunglasses)

Ear plugs (2 pair minimum)

4 Fusees—yes, that's *fusee*, not a misspelling of "fuse" (stick-shaped flares used in firing operations)

Food sufficient for 2 meals (usually 2 MREs)

Individual first aid kit

2 Sigg bottles of fuel or bar oil

50 feet of P-cord (narrow rope)

4 Glow sticks

Wedges (for sawyers and swampers)

Red Card, your firefighting qualification card

Incident Response Pocket Guide (IRPG), "which shall be on
   your person at all times."

The IRPG, Red Card, emergency contact card, Sharpie, and lighter could most often be found in a canvas-and-Velcro pouch we called the "man purse," which we carried in one of the deep leg pockets of our greens. Certain items were so critical, you needed them on your body. I carried the man purse in one pocket, a knife in the other.

Optional items included: watch, knife, pen, notepad, lighter, compass, signal mirror, Avenza or other mapping app on your phone. I already carried, and would gradually expand my arsenal of, gender-specific necessities: tampons and panty liners, toilet paper, wet wipes, and ziplock bags to pack out used tampons and TP. Out of paranoia, I stocked lady supplies everywhere: line gear, PG bag, hotel bag, bin on the buggy. Most of us also carried a poncho or jacket and a tarp, because you never knew when you'd get stuck out there for twenty-four-plus hours.

I slid into the pack and fiddled with the straps, trying to shorten the line gear to my body, which was clearly half the size of whoever had carried this pack before. Mystery Ranch had begun making small and female-specific packs, but the slimmer guys had snatched up the extra smalls already, so I was stuck with a medium. It draped over my ass, and I felt like a child in her parent's clothes.

Mac, one of the Squadies, approached me. He was tall, early thirties, and slender, almost effete, with wispy blond hair, a thick beard, and blue eyes that sparkled as if he liked you a lot, was mocking you— or maybe both? He was hard to read.

He sidled over, a Dolmar in his hand. A Dolmar, or "dolie," is a red plastic jug that holds several gallons of fuel, with separate compartments for saw gas and bar oil. We hiked these into fires so the chainsaws could easily refuel on the line.

One of these jugs weighs twenty pounds. He dropped it at my feet.

"Hey Kelly. Wanna hike this dolie?"

New as I was, I could see it wasn't a question.

"Sure," I said, trying to shape my face into a game grin.

He smiled and walked off. I slid my Pulaski—a wooden-handled cutting and digging tool—through the handle of the Dolmar, hoisted it onto my shoulder, and almost cursed aloud. The dolie nagged my shoulder blade and sloshed against my back. The pack hung down past my butt and thumped against the back of my thighs. Everything was oversized, awkward, and heavy—sixty-five-plus pounds altogether. I started to panic.

Meanwhile, the guys emerged from the bay carrying chainsaws with thirty-six-inch bars. Between the power head, fuel and oil, and the bar, the average saw weighed twenty-five pounds (on top of the forty-five-pound pack). Yet they strolled into the lot like they were carrying nothing, joking and smiling as they lined up for the hike.

For a fleeting second, I wished desperately that I were a man, with a man's body. Then I rebuked myself for the thought.

"Hey Kelly." Ryan waved me over. "Scoops?" I lowered the dolie and joined them in the bay.

"Scoops" was crew-speak for pre-workout powders full of caffeine and mystery supplements that made your lips and hands tingle and supposedly improved athletic performance. I'd experimented with a mild pre-workout called C4, but Ryan's was a harder variety with a name like War, Gorilla, or Cannibal. Ryan, BJ, and Keller, my barracks buddies, were all doing it. So I figured, *why not?*

"Sure, let me get some water." Normally you'd pour a scoop of the powder into a bottle of water, shake it up, and sip on it for a while.

"No, dawg. We're dry scoopin'."

I watched what they did and followed suit, dumping the powder directly into my mouth, then washing it down with a single swig of water. I burped up a little blue cloud, and the boys laughed.

"Hell yeah, Kelly! Took it like a champ." Ryan gave me a fist bump. I grinned.

"Line out," Van called.

My heart was a jackhammer only I could hear. I hefted the Dolmar and rested it against my back, then followed the guys as we formed a line. I started out as close to the rear as I could, adjusting my hard hat. I always forgot that the smallest thing—training bareheaded, then hiking with a hard hat at work—could add a few ounces and another minute element of discomfort.

Van got in front. "Let's go, boys!" he said. Then he glanced at me, looked uncomfortable, and added, "Uh, and girl."

I smiled nervously and gave a shrug to let him know it was cool. Call me a boy, whatever, let's get this over with.

Turning, he called out, "Moving!"

As we began to walk, one by one, we repeated, "Movin'!"

"Moooooove-ing!"

"Moving!"

Like a line of ants, we walked through the lot, left the station, and crossed the street ("Crossing!"). On the opposite side of the highway, we filed into the entrance to a hiking trail with a sign that read, FRENCH HILL. Van stopped.

"This is our crew's most basic hike," he said. "While the standards for hotshot crews in terms of running and everything else do apply, doing this hike successfully is the main requirement for staying on the crew. It is mandatory for being allowed to go on a fire assignment. I'm not sure if we'll go all the way up today, but if we do, it's three miles, and crew time is under an hour."

My heart was beating so wildly, I was surprised my shirt didn't pulse. Three miles an hour meant a sub-twenty-minute mile. That's a reasonable pace on flat ground, or with just one's body weight. With seventy pounds, up a steep hill, that pace is *hauling ass*. I thought I might hyperventilate, drop dead before we began. And perhaps that would be best.

"I'll set a reasonable pace," Van said. "Keep up, don't gap out, and close the gap if there is one."

He turned, pressed a timer button on his watch, and called "Moving" as he began to walk (speed walk) up the trail.

We began to climb through an open-canopy forest littered with ferns. I pushed myself to keep pace as the boys fast-stepped and the hill began to rise. I was soon huffing for air, the Dolmar swinging and thumping and the pack thudding, tripping up my legs.

By the second switchback, as we stepped over a small creek, I was starting to fall behind. You were supposed to keep no more than two feet between people; any more was "gapping out," which gives the person behind you license to pass. The gap between Keller and me yawned, and I watched his gangly body begin to pull away—three feet, four feet, five—

"Pass her!" somebody behind me yelled.

"On your left," a man grunted as he powered by me, falling in between me and Keller.

"Stay on him, Kelly," a voice said.

I tried to. I watched the boot heels of the man in front of me, and I huffed and puffed, my heels digging into the earth, the Dolmar pressing down, trying with all my might to keep the two-foot spacing. But I couldn't make my legs go any quicker; they were lead. It began to happen again—four feet, five—

"Close the gap!"

Six feet—

"On your right!" Another man, brushing past me.

"On your left!" Another one, breathing heavily.

Before I knew it, I was in the back. Everyone had passed me except Benjamin, that day's "drag," the one who comes last and picks up the stragglers. *Fuck.* Benjamin, or "Benjy," was a barrel-chested Indigenous Hoopa man with dark hair longer than mine and a beard to his belly button. A twenty-year hotshot, a legend, he was also the person who'd taken a chance on me and suggested I be hired—in other words, the last guy I wanted to let down.

By now, the switchbacks were tightly stacked. I could see the main pack above me, one or two switchbacks ahead, a line of men with chainsaws balanced on one shoulder moving at an effortless clip up the steep slope. Between me and the pack were a few others who had also gapped out—Keller, another rookie named Miguel, somebody else. But that wasn't comforting. Not only was I very last, but the interval between me and the next person continued to grow, until I lost him every time he went around a corner.

I huffed, I gasped. My heart and lungs felt like they were being put through a meat grinder. I tried to will my body to WALK, SPEED UP, but my legs just *wouldn't.* My quads screamed. My calves seized. All my worst fears were coming true, and I might be having a heart attack too. The scoops had been a bad idea.

Finally, I realized that we were hiking alone, me and Benjy. He had snuck up behind me and was quietly hiking on my heels, his pace just fast enough to make me feel pushed. I couldn't see anyone ahead of us.

"Thought you trained this winter," Benjy said gruffly.

"I did. Just not like this," I gasped.

"Thinking you shoulda trained a little harder, huh."

I said nothing.

"Thought you said you were hikin' a saw."

"Sometimes I did."

"Sometimes?"

"I'm sorry," I said. "I'm really sorry." I fell silent. Breathing was enough of a struggle. Sweat poured off my face.

We climbed in silence for a while. The longer I went without seeing someone ahead of me, the worse I felt. I started to picture how I'd be fired at the end of this. "Just not a good fit . . ." Or maybe I'd resign. The crew had quite literally left me in their dust. I figured it was a good time to give up, apologize, and walk off this hill forever.

But just then, Benjy started to coach me. "This is the last steep pitch," he said. "Hang in, keep it steady up this stretch, and you'll get a little break."

"Okay," I breathed. I came to the top of the hill, and he was right. The trail flattened slightly as it passed through an open stand of timber.

"Good," he said. "Now, you're gonna come around this switchback here, and the trail's gonna flatten out through a kinda saddle. When you hit that, pick up some speed. That's where you can gain on 'em."

We came around the switchback, and he said, "Go! Push!"

I did, scurrying my legs as fast as I could manage, almost jogging across the flat. Benjy effortlessly kept pace with my burst of speed and said, "Good! Now you've got it."

We neared the end of a mild hill where the trail leveled off as it crossed a brush field.

"You're almost there," he said in my ear. "You can't see 'em yet, they'll be kinda hidden. But you're close. Start pickin' up speed now, and when I say run, you run, okay? Run as hard as you fuckin' can. Finish strong."

"Run?"

It was a hill.

"I'm not jokin'."

"Okay," I breathed shakily and dug in, speeding up marginally. As we left the timber and entered the open slope, I saw a few hard hats, somewhat obscured by bushes maybe forty yards out. Oh god. They were going to watch me coming. The last one. The slow one. The *girl*. It was a big, shamey show. What if—

"RUN!" Benjy bellowed.

And, not believing it was possible, sure I had nothing to give, I broke into a sprint—or as close as I could get under all that gear. Pack bouncing against my tailbone, quads pulling, calves cramping, Dolmar thumping and shifting dangerously on my shoulders, I ran up the last stretch of hill between me and the crew. I ran like my life depended upon it. And who knows, maybe it did.

As I got close, the guys began to yell. To my surprise, it wasn't insults or jeers. Instead, like a sports team, they were cheering for me.

"Yeah, Kelly!"

"Hell yeah!"

"You're almost there. Push!"

"You got this, Kelly!"

Through the din I saw Van. "Just get to me," he said. He was standing, arm extended, acting as a finish line. I sprinted the last ten yards, the boys screaming, "YEAH, KELLY," and when I got to Van, I stopped short and low-fived his hand, letting the Dolmar slide to the ground. He was wearing a huge grin, one that lingered.

"*Hell* yeah," he said.

The guys went back to talking, gathering their stuff for the hike down. I could barely stand. I was heaving, soaked in sweat, and thought I might vomit. I put my hands on my knees, willing the puke back down. I took off my hard hat and mopped my face with the sleeve of my yellow. Benjy, coming up behind me, cuffed me on the shoulder.

"Nice work."

"Um, no," I gasped. "But thanks. Thanks for sticking with me."

"I've seen worse." Benjy shrugged.

Van addressed all of us. "Alright, boys. Er—guys. Alright, everybody." He laughed self-consciously. "Well, first hike, and that wasn't too bad. Now you know what you're up against. We definitely have room for improvement. Some people were gapping out, and our time at the front wasn't great."

Oh, fantastic, I thought. *The* front *was too slow?*

"Some of you," Van said. "Seemed to be phoning it in. You looked like you were *walking*. That's unacceptable. I don't care if you're first in the pack or dead last. I want to see you going as hard as you can. Look at Kelly."

He pointed, and they looked. I froze in horror. I couldn't see myself, but I could *feel* myself: a hot mess. My face turned beet red with even the mildest cardio, so I knew it was flaming.

"That's what you should look like when you get up here. That's the effort I want to see."

I shook my head and rolled my eyes, like *Oh, trust me—nobody wants this*. I was humiliated. But how nice of Van to say that. It was really, really nice, and I never forgot it.

At the end of the day we stood in a circle in sweat-soaked shirts. Benjy spat loudly, his arms crossed. Van thanked us for a great first day, said we had a lot of work ahead and that he was happy to have all of us.

Then he held his right index finger up in the air. I didn't know what was happening.

"Daaaaaaaaaaay—"

"DAY ONE!!" The crew yelled, thrusting a number one into the air triumphantly.

I thought this ritual would change by the day—day two, three, four—but no. When we were in station, every day was "day one."

In the barracks that night, I sat in the living room with the boys, who tried to tell me my hike wasn't so bad.

"I've seen worse than you, Kelly," Ryan said. "Way worse."

"Oh yeah," BJ agreed. "One year, we had a guy who stopped at the water tank."

The tank was a quarter mile into the hike, barely three switchbacks up.

Ryan started laughing. "Oh my god, yeah, and Benjy said he was slapping himself."

"He was hitting himself in the fuckin' face! What did he say?"

"'I'm not worthy! I hate myself!'"

"Oh yeah, and Anderson—"

"He threw up like a thousand times and couldn't even finish."

"Did they wash?" I asked. This was my fear: "washing out," or being asked to leave.

"Nope. That one guy quit. Other dude was a hotshot for two years."

"It's not as hard to be a hotshot as you think. You just have to, like, keep showing up."

Hearing that helped a little, but the day's events had done nothing to reassure me I would make it on the crew. After a single day, I was sore, exhausted, demoralized. The only woman and the weakest link. I didn't think I could feel much worse.

I called Josh in Happy Camp. Our house had already begun to fade as the barracks, the bay, the guys, and the challenges that lay ahead consumed my thoughts. I told Josh about the hike, and he said, "I'm sure you weren't as bad as you think! You're such a strong hiker."

"Babe, I was dead last."

"Well, I'm sure you weren't *that* bad. You trained like crazy all winter! And you know, if you end up hating it, you can always come home."

He sounded wistful when he said the word "home," as if he wished I were there, and for a moment I wished it too. It would be so easy to quit, I thought. Just walk away. Don't suffer even one more day of humiliation. Go back to an easy job where people like you and you feel smart.

The night before, though, I had taped a Post-it Note to the plywood covering the doorway between my room and the kitchen. Knowing I might be tempted to throw in the towel, I had penned a message to myself in all caps, the one and only promise I could make.

JUST DON'T QUIT.

I frowned at the Post-it and sighed.

Okay, fine, I thought. *I'll give it a few more days.*

Chapter 3

Critical 80

On Thursday we lined out for a run. Mist pooled in the river canyon, half obscuring the hills. For two days, I had been spared—endless classroom training, the Pack Test, baseline Covid swabs—but now we gathered in the parking lot in shorts and running shoes, guys squatting and kicking and stretching. The morning felt almost cold as we left the station in a group, jogging comfortably. Moving together was a relief, and I wondered briefly if running was the one activity the crew didn't conduct as an all-out murderously competitive race. Such mercy hardly seemed possible—and it wasn't. As we turned onto Baudelaire Flat Road, Mac yelled, "Alright, let 'em go!"

I mentally added those words to my phrases-of-dread list, along with "On your left" and "Close the gap."

The guys took off as if shot from cannons. Fisher pulled into the lead, his massive legs like oiled pistons. I drove my legs and cranked my arms, but I was a rock anchored in a stream as they pulled around me. I soon found myself at the back of the group, where Wink, radio in hand, ran like a kid in big galloping strides. He fell in beside me, saying, "Come on, b-bud, you got this."

Ahead of us, the line of men strung out. Tall firs filled the widening gaps between the fast runners, the faster runners, and the human lightning bolts.

Three of six rookies were fast: Beryl (immediately known as "Barrel"), a country boy who arrived on day one toting a tin lunch pail; Haines, a tanned and oily gym bro; and long-haired, noodle-limbs Trevan, who had played college volleyball. Three of us were slower. Tall, slightly chunky Keller held his own near the middle of the pack (they'd later dub him "Power Belly"), while Miguel and I fell to the back with a scrawny second year, Hayes, who'd spent his off-season snowboarding, which I knew because Mac taunted him, "Guess skiing all winter doesn't get you in shape, huh?"

Miguel was a short, bearded Mexican man, a father of four, heavy cigarette smoker. Like me, he was in his thirties. Unlike me, he had been hired for his ability to run a chainsaw. He ran duck-footed, wheezing for air. But then, I was gasping too. Somehow, though my watch said I was clocking a sub-eight-minute mile, the main pack was far ahead, almost out of sight around the next bend. *They're running sub-sevens*, I thought. *Dear god, how are they running hilly miles in the sixes?*

Oh yeah. These guys were real athletes.

I couldn't help but resent the edge the dudes had, being bigger, stronger, and younger than me. The average temporary seasonal was twenty-six years old, the average rookie twenty-four. I had a few years on our Captains, Wink and I were about the same age, and the only person born before me was Van, who rarely joined us for running and physical training, aka PT. When they found out, the guys were shocked. *Thirty-eight? I thought you were twenty-five!* Bless my grandfather's youthful Greek genes. But if this were a professional sport, I would've aged out long ago. So I perceived a further disadvantage: female, or small, and *old*.

But that line of thinking was useless. I knew plenty of small female firefighters who were faster than big men, and nobody had begged me to come here. I had pursued this job, even if that choice looked a little crazy now. I was the only one who could make it work.

Urged on by Wink, I pushed myself to pass Hayes on the next straightaway. I passed Miguel, who then passed me with a smile and a shrug. Near the end of the loop, the boys from the front of the pack started running back toward us. *What?* Crew practice, I learned, required the fastest runners to finish, then circle to the back to scoop up the slowest, running with them to the end. Like so many crew traditions, I couldn't tell if this was meant to humiliate or encourage. Maybe both.

As we turned onto the highway, someone said, "Sprint to that sign, GO!"

Startled, I broke into a sprint. I raced the last hundred yards, feet pummeling the pavement, and slapped the road sign that served as a finish line, stumbling into the parking lot. Thankfully, the guys kept walking. Miguel and I exchanged a smile. "Ay de mi, Kelly," he said, and I agreed, "Sí, dios mío." Hayes, the snowboarder, jogged in behind us, limping in knee braces.

Well, I hadn't been *last*. A guy my size they called Bao gave me a pep talk I barely heard. "Try to push, pass the guy in front of you . . . gotta fight for it." My face was hot. I could feel my vision closing in, but I nodded like he was right, so right, gee thank you.

That *was* me fighting for it, I thought. There isn't more fight than that.

Each day, we ran or hiked and PT'ed, sometimes all three. A PT included whatever weight training and calisthenics the guy in charge felt like putting us through. Fisher favored traditional circuits of pull-ups, planks, squats, and lunges, while Mac threw out awkward and surprising moves that tested little-used muscles (bear crawl, hop like a frog, crab walk . . . now *sprint*). Sometimes we'd get a wild card, like thousands of dips or dumbbell squats.

The PT didn't get me down too much. I wasn't great at pull-ups, and it was humiliating when a guy had to hold me around the thighs while I strained for more reps. But after years of yoga, a one-minute plank was easy, and in a two-minute wall sit, sheer will and stubbornness counted.

One afternoon, we lay on our stomachs in a circle on the grass. Mac called out, "Plank!" We popped up. The first person did a push-up, yelling, "*One*," as they pressed back to plank. The push-up pyramid waterfalled around the circle, each of us doing the movement and shouting the number. Waiting for your turn, you held plank, beginning to tremble and sweat. The circle continued, around and around, the push-ups increasing: two, three, four, each male voice shouting "*FIVE!*"—and my voice, oddly high and small. We hit the top and descended (four, three, two, one). At the end, it was a blitz: as many push-ups as you could manage until failure . . . at which point you could collapse face down in the grass.

That day, I kept going. I paused, then squeezed out one more. A bead of sweat threaded the bridge of my nose, dangled at the tip, and dropped into the grass. I hadn't noticed that I was one of the last few people still going with the big-chested, Popeye-armed guys like Ryan, Haines, and Eddie. My push-ups were uglier than theirs, but I didn't stop. I pushed through one more shaky rep, grunting as I wobbled back to plank.

"*Yeah*, Kelly," Mac said, white teeth flashing. My face flushed with pleasure. He wasn't easy to impress.

I had learned something important: Effort meant a lot here. Trying might even be enough.

*   *   *

At the end of the first week, we drove into the forest. Our buggy assignments weren't settled yet, but I was placed in Bravo, or B-mod, for the day. So far, I liked Bravo—several people who had been nice to me were there. Funny Eddie, sarcastic Bao, who looked like a Filipino movie star, and Luke, a bearded man with sad blue eyes, gruff but kind.

A buggy, or ten-person Crew Carrier, featured a cab with an attached rectangular box; picture a cross between a moving truck with windows and a short bus. The driver and navigator sat up front on air-suspension seats; between them lay control panels and radios. A large window rimmed in rubber—the boot—connected the cab to the box, so communication could flow freely. The box had two lines of four seats, and eight firefighters entered and exited through a door at the rear. To either side of the aisle, above the black captain's chairs, were overhead shelves with clip-in mesh covers, and by our armrests, flip-top bins for personal items. An ice chest strapped to the front of the aisle was filled with bottled water and Gatorade. At the back, just inside the door, metal shelving held our line gear stacked two packs deep on either side, contained by mesh netting that buckled closed. The interior didn't smell bad yet, but it would: feet, body odor, food, farts, and smoke. Not fresh, woodsy campfire, but old, acrid, bitter smoke.

The buggy's exterior corresponded to the agency for which a given hotshot crew worked. So ours was a pale, institutional green for the U.S. Forest Service (others were white, for National Park Service, or yellow for Bureau of Land Management, and so on). Our crew's name was proudly emblazoned on each side of the box, above the windows: ROWDY RIVER HOTSHOTS. Utility compartments covered the exterior, with metal doors that swung open to reveal tidy worlds: Squadie's and Captain's bins, supply bin, medical bin, tool bin, saw bin, vehicle bin, etc. Each bin had a designated manager on the crew.

On the inside of the back door, when buggy assignments were settled, we would find a sheet showing our names next to our assigned chores: saw or tool bin; picking up meals in fire camp; water and ice; sweeping; trash; cleaning the windows, and so on. Chores were to be done first thing in the morning—before being asked.

Altogether, our fleet included two buggies, the Superintendent's utility truck (the "Supt truck"), and Charlie, a six-seater pickup, so named because the buggies were A and B, so this third vehicle was C, or Charlie.

Typically, the Squadie drove the buggy while the Captain sat shotgun, though they'd trade off for long trips. Bravo's Captain was Salomon (or "Salmon"), a tall man with a dark beard and prominent, jug-handle ears; he faintly reminded me of my favorite mouse from the animated *Cinderella*, Gus-Gus. Matthew Fisher, the Bravo Squadie, was a mountain of muscle with sandy hair and wire-rim glasses. Tattoos covered his thick arms and most of his torso. As he drove, he bellowed over his shoulder. "This year, I'm done with oysters. It's *sardines*," he announced. "Sardines are so much better, there's like, no fuckin' comparison. They're the perfect food. Think I'm gonna get a sardines tattoo."

It didn't seem to matter whether anyone responded, but Eddie said, "Sounds good, Fish!"

We followed the river canyon, then climbed gravel roads to a ridge called Low Divide, which opened to panoramic views of the undulating hills and, from one switchback, a long view to the Pacific Ocean, glittering beyond a bank of fog.

Eddie was DJ for the drive, and he was playing country, Americana, and bluegrass.

"Change it," Luke grumbled. "I can't handle this sleepy shit."

"I'm in charge! Deal with it," Eddie shot back.

"Is this Sturgill Simpson?" I asked over Keller's shoulder.

"Of course it's Sturgill, Kelly," Eddie said, twisting in his seat to look at me. "Only the best musical artist of all time."

"Maybe, if you've never heard of Townes Van Zandt."

Soon we were comparing a Tyler Childers concert in Amsterdam to Shakey Graves at a dancehall in Luckenbach, Texas. Artists, favorite venues—Eddie was the first person I'd met in a while who shared my taste. He stood out from the others, neither a redneck bro nor a nerd with a forestry degree. He had no tattoos. His ego seemed smaller.

Bao jumped in. "Who do you like the most, Kelly, is it Bruce Springsteen?"

Knowing it was a setup, I admitted that, yeah, I did like the Boss.

Bao, with a catlike grin, said, "What a boomer."

I rolled my eyes, ready to take the age jokes all year. But we were parking, and the smile dried on my face. Every day was a trial. Today's was digging line.

Though I had only dug line once or twice, I understood the principles of fireline construction, an act so simple it hardly seemed like it could work. Three elements must be present for combustion to occur, the so-called "fire triangle": fuel, oxygen, and heat. You can't remove oxygen from earth's atmosphere, but you can try to cool a wildfire by pouring water on it; this is what helicopters do, dropping buckets to dampen a burning edge. Engine crews string a series of connected hoses (a "hose lay") to the fire and spray hundreds of gallons on the flames. This helps, but water alone seldom halts a large fire.

Crews like ours exist primarily to tackle the "fuel" side of the fire triangle by constructing fireline (also known as "hand line," because it's made by hand). We remove the plant material—trees, brush, etc.—making a twenty-to-fifty-foot "cut" of cleared vegetation. Then we dig the grasses, mosses, and roots from the surface, leaving a "line," or a "scrape": at least a two-foot-wide strip of bare mineral soil where nothing organic or combustible remains.

When the fire hits the fuel break—the road-sized swath where we've removed larger plants—it has little left to burn, and it slows to a crawl, smoldering through whatever remains on the surface. When, in the middle of this fuel-free corridor, the fire stumbles into the dirt of the line, it has nothing to consume, and it simply . . . stops at the line's edge. The fire is held inside the line like a careful child's shading inside a box.

Hand line doesn't always work—high winds or a running crown fire (a fire that carries from treetop to treetop, racing aloft through the canopy) can blast over the line and ruin everything. But it works often enough. Fireline was the method early firefighters employed, cutting with axes and digging with shovels and picks, and for all our technology—air tankers streaming pink fire retardant, fleets of bull-dozers plowing dirt highways through the trees, drones dropping incendiary marbles, choppers that launch waterfalls from the sky—we often relied on the simplest method: human beings cutting trees, digging dirt, and when necessary, lighting a backfire between the line and the blaze. Because, more often than not, that's what worked.

Fireline was created in two phases, and crews were organized accordingly. First came the saw teams: those who run chainsaws, or "sawyers," and those who carry away what they've cut, "swampers." Our crew ran three or four saw teams, sequenced by skill and seniority, with First Saw (or "lead saw") as the most coveted position on the crew. Behind the saw teams came the rest us, "the dig," a group of people with various hand tools who chop and scrape the earth until they've made what looks like a meandering dirt trail. But it's *not* a trail, and don't you dare call it that, unless you want to fistfight some hotshots.

We'd evolved slightly beyond axes and shovels. The hand tools we used most were the Pulaski and its juiced-up iteration, the Super-P, plus the Rhino, the Chingadera, and the rake. The Pulaski was an axe-like cutting tool with an adze, or blunt wedge end, for the purpose of breaking up soil and roots. The Super-Pulaski, or Super-P, was a Rowdy River special—we welded custom tools—with an axe side and an expanded scoop-like shovel side, for extra dirt removal capacity. The Rhino, the

Rogue hoe, and the Chingadera (Spanish for "that fuckin' thing") were shovel-like scoops welded perpendicular to long wooden handles, for the primary purpose of scraping away the dirt the Pulaskis loosened and chopped. Occasionally, in rocky terrain, we'd break out a pick mattock to pry boulders from the line.

Last in tool order came a person (usually Winkler) wielding a micro-rake. We raked to remove any lingering debris, leaving a perfectly clean line. This was almost silly—the minute someone walked the line, the rake's perfection was trampled. But a rake finish was a matter of pride for the crew, as quality line construction is a matter of honor for all crews. "We stand by our line," was the common refrain.

I had dug before, and I'd used a falling axe and a splitting maul, but I was by no means experienced or confident with any of these tools.

"Here, Ramsey," Fisher said, handing me a Pulaski.

I gripped the smooth wooden handle and studied the steel working end: the sharp blade and the blunt adze. I ran my finger over the blade, which drew a scratch through the whorls of my fingerprint.

"I sharpened that. You're welcome," Bao said.

I grimaced. This didn't seem like a great tool for me. The Pulaskis went up front and shouldered the brunt of the labor. Did they actually think I was strong enough for that?

The sawyers pulled cord, and the saws fired up, engines sputtering to life. Now the air was loud with four thrumming machines as the sawyers clipped on orange chaps and secured earplugs and sunglasses. I wondered if their reputation for being the most badass came from the work they did or from their style.

It was a foregone conclusion that Luke would be first saw. He'd been running saw for a decade, half of those years on this crew. And the moment he began, I saw that seniority wasn't the reason he took the lead; what he had was a gift.

He began to move, swinging the saw, cutting a swath as he turned. He was an artist. The saw was an extension of his small-waisted, compact body, and his movements were graceful and deadly precise.

This process, what we called "brushing," was its own skill; a young sawyer might bog down in a thicket of Ceanothus (a type of lilac bush), while an experienced cutter knew how to sweep the base of a plant, leveling a bush in one motion. A seasoned swamper knew to draw back the limbs, exposing the stems for his sawyer, arms already wrapped around the body of the plant, carrying it off the second it was cut free. The swamper-sawyer relationship was a delicately timed duet, one in which the swamper's safety relied on mutual, wordless communication. You could rarely be heard over the screaming of the saws.

Luke approached a stand of small timber. In the most basic sense, you fell a tree as follows: cut out a mouth-shaped V in one side of the trunk, facing the direction you want the tree to fall (the "face cut," or "the face," and where you want it to land is the "intended lay"). Then, flip the saw over, walk around the tree, shout the word "Falling" to alert anyone nearby, and make a flat, i.e., parallel to the ground, cut into the opposite side of the trunk (the "back cut"), two inches above the hinge of your face cut. As your back cut comes close to connecting with the hinge, the tree's weight forces the mouth of your face cut to close, and in an ideal world, the tree falls where you intended. If something goes wrong, it falls in the wrong direction and may kill you. Just in case, when you remove the saw, you back or run away from your intended lay.

Luke reached a small tree and looked up, quickly assessing. He put in a face cut in seconds, the chainsaw moving like a hot knife through butter, bap-bap-bap. He took a step around the tree, flipped the saw, zipped in the back cut, stepped back, and paused as the tree tipped and fell just where he'd wanted it to. Then he moved to the bole wood (the stem of the trunk, which now lay on the ground) and zip, zip— removed the limbs and cut the trunk into manageable logs. Without a backward glance, he moved on.

Eddie, Luke's swamper, scurried behind him, hefting and throwing the rounds, gathering a thousand sticks of brush into a bundle and tossing them into the green (the unburned side of the line—the burn side is "the black"). Luke was cutting so fast that Eddie had to operate at a scramble, and even so, he was often left yards behind his sawyer facing mountains of brush, bushes felled in a halo like petals dropped from a daisy. This was called "burying" your swamper.

The other saw teams followed, some of them strong cutters, some less fluid, none of them like Luke; what looked awkward and effortful for them was, in his hands, a ballet. I saw now that you could be a master of physical work, just as you could master domains of the intellect. Suddenly I longed for what he had: the strength and skill to make a masterpiece of my body's labor.

After the saws came the dig. Westbrook, our leader, was a tall red-headed man who looked strong, though I'd heard the guys say he was lazy. He swung his Pulaski and scraped some dirt, just enough to show where the line should be placed, following an imaginary fire's edge. Behind him came BJ, a human tornado. His squat triangle of upper body muscle and previous career as a Marine converged in a wave of swinging and cutting. He moved quickly, raising the tool over his head and bringing it down axe-first to cut a root, then twirling to the adze end and swinging low, kind of like you'd swing a croquet mallet, scraping the dirt each time—hit, hit, hit—to clear the soil. Dirt flew out behind him in great clouds. Two people in, and it already looked like a completed line. Okay. Wow.

"Let's go! Hit and move," BJ called out, urging us to dig faster. Hit and move meant take a swing, step forward, and swing again. Hit, step, swing, step, and so on, the line moving forward in staggered unison.

Third in the line, I tried to imitate BJ, using the Pulaski to chop roots out of the ground, break up the hard earth, and move some dirt out of the way. But I was slow. Half my swings were misses, and my scrapes of dirt were like thimblefuls. From the way Fisher and Benjy watched me, feet set wide, arms folded, I knew I looked nothing like BJ.

They offered tips: "Try lifting the tool all the way over your head"; "No, *all* the way, really swing it!" But from the frowns wrinkling their foreheads, I could see I wasn't getting it right. Welp, another test failed. We climbed into the buggy to head home, and I dropped heavily into my seat. My arms ached from just a couple hours of digging. My back was in knots, hands raw. The job was exhausting, and I wasn't any good at it.

As we bumped along the gravel road, we talked about where people might be assigned for the season. I leaned in to Luke, Eddie, and Bao, and said quietly, "I want to be in Bravo. I hope they put me here."

Luke smiled. "We want you here, too, Kelly."

On that comment alone, I could survive another week.

The first two weeks were called the "Critical 80," meaning eighty hours of intensive training—though common practice required a *month* of physical brutality and information cramming before you saw your first fire.

Week two, week three. Hike, run, PT, dig. Hike, PT, dig, run. A classroom hour, a lecture on a "tragedy fire" (a fire where firefighters were gravely injured or perished). Another hike, a medical drill. A practice shelter deployment—that's when the fire's gonna burn over you and you crawl into this shelter that looks like a tinfoil chrysalis, and it might save you, though usually it does not. First aid and CPR training. Radio training. Strapping each other to a backboard. Not fast enough—try again. Hike, run. PT, dig.

My mind and body were on overload. Every muscle ached. My palms formed thick callouses, and dirt stuck in the creases of my skin and wouldn't wash out. I was always hungry. Left alone for ten minutes, I'd fall asleep sitting up.

All this for $16.33 an hour. For the entry-level firefighters with no previous federal experience, it was $13.32 an hour—hence the joke that we were "paid in sunsets."

After work, we swam where the Middle and North Forks of the Rowdy River converged. A bank of flattish boulders lay at the edge of a deep, clear swimming hole. A popular local spot, there would always be a bunch of kids blasting music or a family with a dog, but we could usually find a place for our group: the barracks boys, me, and the dirtbags who stayed at Grassy Flat in their trucks and campers.

I dove into the water. The cold was needles, knives; and for a split second, you feared you'd never breathe again. Then you'd come up sputtering, drawing a breath as sweet as your first taste of oxygen. I'd been a swimmer, though soundly mediocre. But I loved water, and I lingered, treading and watching the boys talk. I floated on my back, letting my sore muscles go numb. The current sloshed in my ears. The sun lay golden on the green ridge, muted music drifting over the river's surface. It was paradise.

In the classroom one afternoon, we studied the fire outlook for the season. The drought map showed the entire American West in red—one vast, parched, thirsty scarlet blotch. Temperatures were predicted to rise again. And with fuels already looking dry in mid-May, it didn't bode well. The outlook all but called for apocalypse, though I couldn't imagine what was coming. Aside from a column seen at a distance on the Klamath, I hadn't witnessed big fire. I was in for a show.

*   *   *

Almost every culture on earth has a myth about fire: Prometheus stealing fire from the gods; the Cherokee tale of Grandmother Spider; and the African San peoples' IKaggen, who stole fire from the ostrich. Celtic lore features Brigid, deity of flames; and in Polynesian culture, the fire thief is Maui. For Aboriginal Australians, Crocodile took the fire stick.

Wildfire has existed since the arrival of biological life on Earth. With the evolution of the first plants in an oxygen-rich atmosphere, and the advent of lightning raining from the skies, the fire triangle snapped together, and the world has ignited and burned at random for millennia. Fossil charcoal dates the presence of fire back 420 million years.

When early hominins first found fire, they got a life-giver: a warmth by which to live through cold nights, a flame to deter predators. They soon learned to use fire creatively—to hunt by flushing out game, to selectively encourage crops, and to forge metal into knives and tools. But perhaps most importantly, early humans used fire to *cook food*, unlocking nutrients our stomachs could not previously access. As a result, the human brain doubled in size. And those big smart brains are the source of all that followed, from advanced agriculture to the industrial revolution, from the internet to the Tesla coil. Though our memories are short, and we've forgotten, we are a species made powerful by fire. We would be nowhere without it.

Hence the universal story of *stolen* fire, a power that feels like a shortcut, a cheat.

When we gaze into flames, we almost remember. Mesmerized by the light and warmth of a crackling fire, our awe is unmistakable. Respect—and fear. As if seeing our creator.

Late in week two, we passed our readiness review. The officials inspected everything from supplies in the storage bins to a binder of paperwork.

We demonstrated line construction and performed a mock medical drill, then stood in a circle for a lecture about the heroic history of hotshots and our crew. At the end of the day, Van told us proudly that we were officially hotshots now. Soon we'd go available for a fire.

He raised a finger. "Daaaaay . . ."

"Day one!"

At the end of that week, we did a hike the guys called Brokeback Mountain, a narrow stitch of hand line that climbed an exposed ridge above the Rowdy River. "Broke" was a murderous route with sheer vertical pitches, and I felt like a stumbling child but didn't fail as badly as I had on French Hill. Later that afternoon I was assigned to Bravo, where I took the left rear seat across the aisle from Trevan.

I was happy with the module, and excited to fill the storage bin under the armrest with snacks, Band-Aids, headphones, pens—and tampons, of course. In the overhead compartment, I wedged a stack of books between my running shoes and hotel bag. Bao didn't miss a beat in mocking my "library," but I knew he had books in his bin, too.

Two small wins. Yet when I got in my truck to drive home for the weekend, I crumpled. I was beaten down. And while every part of my body hurt, my most fatigued muscle was the one I tensed to hold myself together in front of them. Smile, laugh, stay positive. Don't lose your shit, don't show your fear.

Finally out of sight of the guys, the facade unclenched, and I felt all that I'd held in day after day: the fear of failure that made my stomach burn and heart thud with each new task, the crushing sense that I *was* failing. Then, too, the feeling of physical vulnerability, of my body on display, its difference and weakness an object of unspoken but constant scrutiny. My hips and ass. My breasts, jiggling as I ran. My long hair, its wild curls wrestled into a braid. With every movement, every word, I proved myself to be unlike them. And you had to resemble them to equal them, right? It seemed impossible.

I wept as I followed Grayback Road, climbing to the pass and zig-zagging down into the green valley of Indian Creek. I cried for the full hour and a half I had to myself, the road blurring. I had to get it all out before I got home, because I didn't want Josh to see this.

"They're jerks," he would say, as he had the weekend before. "Just quit!"

But I couldn't give up. If I stayed, there was hope for improvement. I needed to see if I could survive.

That Saturday, I hiked a pack and a chainsaw up Mount Motherfucker, the local crew's hardest training hike, a one-hour grind up a chalky dozer line with little shade and no mercy. Van had said not to train too much on weekends, but the holiday gave us an extra day. There was just one way to get better, and I *had* to.

In week three, for a hike called Middle Hand Line—aka Middle *Hell* Line, I grabbed a chainsaw.

"Kelly! Look at you," someone said as I left the saw room.

I gave a sunny smile, as if this weren't patronizing. Then I watched as man after man grabbed a saw, until the saw shop was empty and men were jerry-rigging fivers of fuel and Dolmars to add weight, until nobody remained carrying only a tool. The average saw weighs twenty-five pounds; the average fiver, forty-plus—so everyone was carrying the seventy pounds I toted . . . or twenty more. *Wow.* They couldn't let a girl appear to outwork them, even on a single hike.

The male ego would've made me laugh, but I had bigger problems. I was sick with fear. My weekend hike had proved I still wasn't fast—or even mid-speed—toting a saw.

But to my (and everyone's) great surprise, I wasn't too bad.

I didn't finish with the front group, but I wasn't in the back. And midway through the climb, on a little recovery stretch, I started passing people. I passed Bao, as I should have because he was carrying the Stihl 660, our heaviest saw. But I passed others too: Hayes and Miguel and BJ. I showed up in red-faced distress a respectable distance behind the front pack. A few guys glanced at me like, *huh*.

At the end of a climb, the guys gave a signature call as they saw each body crest the rise. They loosed the same cry while trying to locate another Rowdy River person in the woods on a fire.

"Give us a hoot," they'd say over the radio, and you'd hear an unmistakable yell echoing through the trees, a drawn-out "whoa" punctuated by a guttural, abrupt "huh." *Whoaaaauuuh-huh!*

You could hear Fisher in the distance as he reached the top first. Then other guys chiming in, *Whoah-huh!* The boys thought it was funny to make me try—"Kelly, come on, give us a hoot!" But when I made an effort to imitate them, it was ridiculous. I tried, deepening my voice to a grunt.

"Yeah," Trevan said. "That was pathetic."

Hiking Broke later that week, Mac called me out. "Kelly, stop drafting off Scotty! I know you can go faster."

Dang it, he was right—I was hiking behind round-faced Scotty, who kept a patient, steady pace. But he was favoring a hurt knee, and Mac could see I had more to give. He shouted again, "Pass him, Kelly! Let's *go*."

I groaned. "On your left," I breathed.

Scotty smiled as I trudged by, brushing sleeves with him. "Yeah, Kelly!"

Then Mac named the next guy ahead of me, twenty yards up the hill, and yelled, "GO. Catch him."

I did. And by the end of week four, I had a strategy for Brokeback. Try not to gap in the first pitch. If you lose the pack there, it'll be hell to make it up. If you do lose them, fight to catch them after the third knob, where the trail briefly flattens. *Run*, you can gain on them. Look to the person in front of you, focus all your energy on catching him. Catch him. Pass him. Find the next guy. Pick them off, one by one, until you've clawed your way forward.

By the end of the month, I had it. I could consistently finish with the pack. And I'd learned that the key wasn't a stronger body, even if all our bodies had gained muscle. The real battle took place in your mind. You'd think, *I can't*, or, *This is all I have.* But you had to tell yourself, *I know you've got more.*

While my "success" wasn't impressive, it was a world away from where I'd started a month earlier. The guys noticed. I even got a fist bump from Fisher.

That weekend, the first we were nationally available for a fire assignment, I stayed in Baudelaire. There'd been a Covid scare in Happy Camp, and Josh had been exposed to the virus. I didn't want to risk going home, having to quarantine, and missing our first assignment.

While Cal Fire and local firefighters may be relegated to their state or county, federal hotshot crews are national resources, meaning they can be pulled where they're most needed—anywhere in the U.S. and beyond; hotshots regularly go to Canada to fight wildfires, and there's the occasional exchange with Australia.

We'd been keeping an eye on the Southwest, where wildfire season peaks in May or June. With activity picking up, we stood a solid chance of going to New Mexico or Arizona. Since crews left the state on a rotation, our crew was unlikely to "come up" to leave California again before the season ended. This could be our one shot to travel and see fire in a different landscape, and a real assignment meant overtime, or "OT," and hazard pay, or "H," our first chance at decent money after a long off-season scraping by on unemployment.

I hadn't worked this hard to sit on the sidelines.

Saturday afternoon, I went to Crescent City with the barracks boys, the camper boys, and Fisher and his girlfriend, Jenny, a former hotshot.

We played frisbee golf in a park near the jetty, damp air rising off the waves at South Beach. We drank beers, and it felt nice to hang with the boys outside of work. Almost like we were friends.

Staying at the station had been a good choice, because Saturday night we got the call. Well, the text. I read it with a racing heart. *Resource order!* it read. *Be at the station at 0600. Going to Arizona.*

Chapter 4

Bush, Hog, and Red Salmon

Arizona, middle of June, somewhere east of Mesa. Air a hundred degrees and smoky. The blacktop simmered; I could feel the heat through my boots. There seemed to be three fires: the earth blistering my feet, the air searing my face and cooking my skin through the Nomex, and the blaze on the landscape. We stood on a closed-down highway that shimmered like water at the horizon. Behind us lay rolling hills covered in sagebrush, sotol, and saguaro cacti. In front of us were the same hills—on fire.

The Bush Fire had ignited the previous day and quickly burned close to thirty-seven thousand acres northeast of Phoenix. Fires used to be named whatever a local authority felt like calling them, which resulted in some spicy titles (Red Bull, Pigs in Shit, Dead Goat—or my faves, the ironic "Warm Fire" and self-deprecating "Not Creative" fire); now, they were named after a nearby town or geographical feature. This incident, rumored to be human-caused, began near the Bush Highway.

We lined up on the road awaiting orders, along with a dozen engines and a handful of other crews. Hazard lights flashed, hose stretched across the highway, and the voice of incident command crackled over many radios at once. Helicopters sliced through the sky, taking turns dropping water on flames we couldn't see from here. I shifted from one aching foot to the other, the weight of my pack bruising my tailbone. A plume of smoke began to boil up from a valley to the east. I said to Hayes, who stood beside me, "Look, my first column!"

"Kelly, that's not a column. That's nothing," he scoffed.

I twisted the end of my braid as I watched the white smoke darken from the center out, ink spilling upward, a chemistry lab in the sky. "How will I know when I see a real column?"

"You'll know."

We had taken two days to drive from California, a blissful road trip, save for my perpetually full bladder and the struggle to find urinary privacy in the barren pullouts where the men stopped for pee breaks. After a brief pre-position in Silver City, New Mexico, we worked a few days on a small fire called Blue River on the San Carlos Reservation in Central Arizona—until the Bush blew up. We'd been pulled here on day six of our roll.

"Line out, we're hiking in," Van called. His eyes gleamed. He'd been dreaming of this moment.

We shuffled into tool order, saw teams followed by the dig. I took my place behind BJ as Fisher pointed to a dirt road ahead of us. "Sounds like we're going up this two-track and lighting. Fire's coming this way pretty fast, so we'll have to move quick."

As he spoke, the wind began to howl in our ears. Benjy looked up sharply, a hunter catching a scent. He grunted at Van, "Gonna get eyes on it," and climbed a cut bank off the shoulder of the highway. When he reached the top, he squared to the wind. With his long dark hair and beard to his belly, he looked like an Indigenous Gandalf, palm resting on the handle of his tool like a staff, barrel chest puffed at the not-yet-column of smoke, as if daring it to a duel.

Van boomed out, "Let's go. Moving!"

We called out "moving" one by one as we filed up the overgrown dirt road. We hadn't had a briefing or even a weather report, and this felt faintly dangerous. *But what do I know?* I thought. Not even enough to decide whether I should be afraid.

"Rowdy River, Division Alpha on Tac," said a man's voice coming out of BJ's radio. Only half of us had radios, so I was forever eavesdropping. "Can I get your location?"

Van informed the man that we were hiking in to help the other crew burn. As he did, Benjy's voice came over our private crew channel, Gray, and said, "Hey Van, fire's pickin' up. It's not lookin' great. We still got time, but I don't love it."

"We've got time," Van countered, speaking to Benjy. "Let's do this. Come on."

"Rowdy River," the Division said on Tac, almost stern. "I'm gonna need you to pull out of there. It's not safe. We'll burn off the highway instead."

"Are you sure? The boys are ready to go. We can burn our way out," Van suggested.

"It's an order, Rowdy River. Come on back to the highway."

A "Division" was both an operational section of a wildfire and shorthand for the person in command of that wedge, the Division Supervisor. Divisions, in turn, were grouped into Branches, who reported to Ops (or Operations), who in turn reported to the Incident Commander (or the IC).

A firefighter could be qualified as an Incident Commander for different tiers of wildfires, starting with the smallest and working up. Mac and Fisher could act as IC-5 for a tiny incident with just a few resources, whereas the Bush Fire, a Type I incident with hundreds of resources and over one thousand firefighters, required a Type I Incident Commander, or an ICT1. Because it took decades to gain the experience to command a beast this complex, there were a limited number of Type I teams in the country.

Once an incident blew up and went Type II or Type I, its management followed a rigid structure. Beneath the IC, in addition to Ops, were departments for Logistics, Planning, and Finance/Administration. The management team occupied a city-sized encampment of air-conditioned white tents—sometimes placed in a vast lot in a remote town, sometimes in a field in the middle of nowhere—its workings complex enough that entry-level firefighters took a mandatory class, ICS-100, "Introduction to the Incident Command System."

The Division, even if he was an ordinary Engine Captain in his regular life, now outranked every leader in that territory and could assign the crews, engines, dozers, aircraft, and other resources as he saw fit, shuffling us like infantry pieces in a game of Risk. On a fire, our Division was essentially Van's boss.

"Copy that, sir," Van said tightly. Then he turned to us and commanded, "RTO!"

Reverse Tool Order: turn on your heel and leave, the back of the line becoming the front. As one, we spun and strode back the way we had come along the rutted dirt road. The guys muttered that this was stupid, we'd been totally safe, but I was relieved. As we quick-stepped, packs shifting and tools bouncing, I thought about my fitness in the preceding month and what a slow runner I'd proven to be, especially in the shelter deployment drills where we had to run in boots. If the fire really came, would I stand a chance?

I had known, abstractly, that this was a dangerous job, but so far it had all been a training exercise. Now I felt the reality of the risk: annihilation hovered nearby, close and tangible, for the first time in my life. Death's menace would become so familiar, though, that like everyone else, I would almost cease to notice his cold breath on my neck.

*   *   *

We rolled into night shift and started burning. I had done a little lighting with my crew on the Klamath, burning piles and helping with prescribed burns. Burning on an active wildfire was different.

People like to call it a backfire, a burnout, a backburn, or sometimes, "blacklining." We just called it burning. This is, in essence, fighting fire with fire. You establish a barrier, be it a hand line, a dozer line,
or an existing road. Sometimes a natural break like a creek or river
can act as a line, too. Inside your line, you deliberately set fire to the
landscape, burning everything between the barrier and the oncoming
wildfire. The idea is that the main fire, deprived of fuel, charges into
this pre-burned forest and simply gutters out. Unlike a line alone, a line
with a well-done burn is tremendously effective.

The danger is that your burn could send embers into the green, creating spot fires outside your line. So any burn show is divided into two
roles: lighters and holders. The lighters put down fire, and the holders
spread out along the length of the line, face the green, and look for fire
where it shouldn't be.

To light, we used drip torches, red canisters holding a mix of gasoline and diesel with a wick on the end of a steel tube, which literally
pours liquid flames onto the ground. When you light with torches, you
have three to five people in a stagger pattern spaced from the edge of
the line out to several hundred feet into the woods.

We also used a launcher, or Veri pistol, essentially a flare gun fired
with blanks. And we used a throwable or "hand toss" flare device called
a "chubbie" (also simply called a "chucker"), a cylindrical canister about
the size of a baseball, full of flammable powder; you lit the fuse and
lobbed it overhand into the brush, where it would ignite like a small fire-
work. All flares burned at four-thousand-degrees Fahrenheit. Once lit,
they'd even burn underwater. These devices shared a purpose: to establish

depth. If you only burned a few feet in from the line, the main fire's momentum could easily blow through your burn. So it was important to get a depth of several hundred feet, more if possible, to establish the largest possible "catcher's mitt" for the oncoming fire.

Our first couple night shifts, I was holding. A long line of us, strung out in fifty-foot spacing, stood in the dark, watching the shadowy green. The person in front called "Movin'," and we each bumped a dozen yards forward, calling "moving" in return, and then the call was passed down the line until: "Holding!" We stopped, standing and staring.

It's boring—or it can be. But if you've never seen a large-scale burn operation before, as I hadn't, it's amazing. The flames twinkled in the darkness. Experienced lighters like Ryan and BJ charged through the brush, leaving dots of fire behind them. The dots spread, merged, and became a carpet of flames on the hillside. Up ahead, I could hear Fisher shout, "Firing," followed by the sound of the pistol and a spray of sparks as the flare arced like a comet and hit home at the top of the hill. Chuckers spiraled through the air and landed in sizzling clouds that burst into flame. It was a symphony, a light show, a medley of bonfires and shooting stars. There is no beauty quite like flame, and no stage that showcases it quite like night. I gaped, awestruck, until someone scolded me, *Eyes on the* green, *Ramsey!*

Burning was often supported by the quad or the utility task vehicle, or UTV. The all-terrain vehicle (ATV, four-wheeler, or "quad") was a four-wheeled rugged motorized bike with handlebars and a seat for a single person, whereas the UTV, sometimes called a "side by side," was more like a souped-up golf cart, its all-terrain capabilities paired with seating for up to four people. Either vehicle could scale a steep dozer line. On a burn, the UTV was handy for shuttling bodies, torches, and fivers of burn mix up and down the line.

While it was clear that a few guys had a monopoly on the coveted "lighter" roles, the overhead tried to give each rookie a chance.

One night, I was Fisher's "fuel mule," carrying a steel box of ammo and scrambling to keep up with his stride, passing him blanks and a handful of flares each time we stopped. He taught me to use the pistol, made sure earplugs were jammed in my ears, and said, "Okay, Ramsey. Go."

I held the gun with two gloved hands and aimed for the hillside above us.

"You gonna shoot that thing, or what?"

"Firing!" I shouted, my voice tiny in the dark canyon. I pulled the trigger, the flare shot into the sky, and I grinned as the bushes exploded.

"That's it; you're a natural," Fisher said. He took the pistol back and charged ahead.

Another night, Benjy pulled me, Miguel, and Barrel aside for a lesson in running drip torch. He sent each of us out for a trial run, the flames on our waiting torches yellow in the dark.

"Kelly, run out there and squiggle some fire in that brush."

"Like, how far out?"

"Fifty, hundred yards." He shrugged.

"What kind of pattern? Like do you want dots, or a strip—"

"Strip ain't gonna work. Just put down some fire and see how she takes."

Burning was the most exciting part of being a hotshot so far. Between our two common tasks, digging line and lighting fires, I'd take the flames. Even if, almost nightly, the end of my braid got singed.

Day eight, back on day shift, we were sent to private property. The fire was heading this way, and the place, Winkler's Ranch, hadn't been suitably prepped, so we'd been asked to cut out brush and put line around the perimeter. Driving there, we laughed, because Wink's full name was Shane Winkler.

"We going to your ranch, old man?" the guys asked.

"Yeah," Wink quipped. "I bet you guys didn't know I was r-rich."

Wink wasn't rich and neither was whoever owned this land, an overgrown scrap of desert with a couple trailers and a modest tract home. In the garden, white flecks of ash speckled the tomato plants. The saws fired up and took off through the brush, swampers tossing bales of cut grass over the property line.

We began to put line in the dry, sandy soil. I was digging behind BJ. Westbrook, while technically our leader, had a habit of wandering off and leaving BJ in charge. This day was no different; West swung his tool for five minutes, muttered something about "scouting ahead," and vanished.

I waited for it.

"Kelly, take more!" BJ barked.

There it is.

"Okay," I breathed, trying to sound cheerful.

I swung harder, trying to move enough of the parched earth that I didn't leave too much digging for the next guy. I was laboring, sweating, digging well—or so I thought.

"Speed up!" BJ called. When I glanced ahead, I saw that I'd fallen half a dozen yards behind him. We were supposed to stay at a spacing of no more than ten feet. Whoopsie.

"Let's go. Hit and move," he said, annoyed.

"I thought you wanted me to take more," I protested when I caught up. "If I take more, I'm slower. If I hit and move, I'm not taking as much. That's how it works."

"I don't need *you* to tell me how it works," BJ snapped. "I've done this for three years. You can drop the attitude."

"The—what? I was just trying to explain—"

"Don't explain, okay? Just move. You're not taking enough, and you're holding up the line."

I looked at the guys digging behind us. Though I'd raced to catch BJ, they remained thirty feet back, moving the same speed. Scotty was in the lead, and he dug deliberately, calmly, with a smile on his face. He was telling a story to Keller, who paused to laugh. Hard to believe that I was the sole person at fault for our lack of speed.

"So I'm going too slowly, but I'm still not doing enough work for you," I said, this time with a hint of what you might call attitude.

"Yep, that's about it. I'm glad we understand each other." He gave me a cruel smile.

My face grew hot. I opened my mouth, ready to tell him I *understood* that he was an *ass*—

"Hey, what's the holdup?" Westbrook popped out of the brush, a few flecks of sawdust caught in his beard. "Saws are way ahead. It's not like this is hard digging."

"Just showing the rookies how it's done," BJ said, long-suffering. I scowled.

"Well hurry up, alright?" Westbrook said. "This is pathetic. I mean, I can't even see the saws."

He bent and swung his tool, and BJ jumped in behind him. The two dug in tandem, swinging fast and launching buckets of dirt. I bent and swung and scrambled to keep up, knowing I took only tiny scoops with every swing of my puny, worthless arms. In my hands, the Pulaski seemed to bounce back from the surface of an unyielding planet.

Each day, after we were done digging, a different man sat beside me and showed me how to sharpen my tool, an act performed with a metal file. Each had a different technique and was convinced that his was the only correct way. When I abandoned Westbrook's method for Bao's, West snatched my Pulaski from my hand. *What are you doing? Did you forget how I showed you?* It was maddening, but I assumed, since I had six dissatisfied teachers, that I was no good at sharpening a tool.

As rookies, we shouldered the brunt of the chores, and I was failing there, too. Westbrook reminded me to take out the buggy trash *before* it was overflowing, and Fisher changed the small rubbish bin from the cab when I forgot it. BJ had pulled me aside to point out that when I wasn't doing trash or my other duty, picking up lunches, I should be helping everyone else with their jobs: ice, bottled waters, helping Keller to sweep, or smearing Windex on the buggy windows. As a rookie, he said, you should *always* be helping. You can't sit around and chat if there's work to be done.

The implication, of course, was that I was lounging around, a chatty schoolgirl. It didn't ring true—I felt like I was constantly scrambling, half jogging across fire camp to keep up with the man beside me, my body canted to offset the weight of something heavy and dripping. But I didn't scramble *enough*? I should be more like Haines, who moved with a square-shouldered swagger that projected how capable he was. Even when I performed the same task as someone like Haines, it seemed less . . . visible to them. I didn't look cool doing it.

I had never felt so useless and dumb. Digging behind him, I stared hatefully at BJ's broad back. *I'm glad we understand each other*, I thought. *Dickhead.*

But it wasn't just him. The criticism rained down from all sides. So the problem was me. The whole thing made me feel like a child, and what was I even doing here, over thirty-five with a master's degree and taking orders from a meathead about how to dig with a stick? I wasn't good enough at *trash*?

But I clamped my mouth shut and kept my head down. My friend Paige, who'd worked on crews for years, had given me some advice about being a woman in this job: "Never let them see you cry. It's blood in the water."

So I slid on a pair of dark sunglasses and trained my eyes on the ground. I stepped and swung, hit and moved. Tears left pale lines in the dirt on my face. I kept digging.

*   *   *

By the end of its spectacular romp through the desert, the Bush Fire had consumed over 193,000 acres. On the last day of our roll in the Southwest, when someone approached me to explain how a Pulaski's blade could be properly sharpened, I lost it. I threw my tool to the ground and stood up, addressing the sweat-covered men in the clearing. "I will be taking no more advice on how to sharpen my tool," I announced. "Seven people have shown me how to do it seven different ways." A snicker or two. "I hear you. Now let me practice on my own. Thank you."

I plopped down in the dirt, grabbing my metal file and hooking the Pulaski handle under my leg for leverage, and went back to work on the edge of the axe.

The boys generally disregarded my announcement, but Mac sidled over, a wicked grin spreading across his face. "Hey Kelly. I'm not sure if you know *my* technique . . ." he began, and I dissolved into laughter.

After Arizona, the season rolled forward like a wave. Everything but fire was obliterated from the world. We went on a fourteen-day roll, had two days of R&R, and by the second night off, the order for the next assignment awaited us. Roll, R&R, roll, repeat. If Josh was home from a fire, I'd see him for a night or two, and we'd collapse on the couch together, comparing fires. Most of the time, though, he was away on his own assignment, and R&R was just me and the dogs. Then back to work.

On a fire called the Flat outside Willow Creek, California, we climbed a hill pitched so steeply we slid backward while crawling up, grasping roots for leverage. As we put in hot line (hand line directly next to the flames), the end of my braid began to burn, though I quickly grabbed a glove and squeezed it out. Hiking down, Miguel lost his footing and sprained his ankle. We carried him off the hill.

I tried to read *Anna Karenina* on slow days, my hands leaving smudges of ash on the pages like a criminal's fingerprints. My callouses ripped off, leaving blistery open wounds on my palms. We all had poison oak, but Haines got it the worst, with red, pus-covered arms and hands that swelled like water balloons. He was sent to the hospital for a shot of cortisone.

Since we'd left the 116-degree Southwest, we slept "like real hotshots"—on the ground. A tarp, sleeping pad, and sleeping bag: that was it. We kept tents in the buggy but almost never used them. On the Flat fire, we slept in the playing fields behind an elementary school; often, we slept in the forest to be closer to the line.

On the Hog, an incident outside Susanville, I watched Eddie scrape a loop of hand line around a stump, and when I asked what he was doing, he pointed to a nest lodged in a hollow in the wood.

"Are there birds in there?"

"Oh yeah. Bunch of little babies." He breathed hard as he finished digging.

Eddie was *saving the baby birds* from the fire, which roared faintly below the road in a dense stand of pine. I paused to consider the man beside me for a moment, marveling, before moving back to my position in the line of firefighters spread out along the highway.

Midway through the roll, at a picnic table after dinner, Mac offered me a Zyn, the tobacco-free nicotine pouches that the non-chewers among us kept tucked in their lips.

"Kelly?" he said, offering the small plastic can.

"Nah." I shook my head.

"Come on," he urged. "One won't kill you."

"It could. You never know."

"It's July, Kelly. It's about time you assimilated."

What a powerful word. I gazed at Mac, the crew's quiet thunder, its soft-spoken authority. His eyes twinkled.

"Fine," I said. "One." I pinched a white pouch and placed it on my tongue.

"Don't *suck* on it!" Eddie laughed.

"Wet it on your tongue, then put it inside your lip," Mac said.

I left the Zyn against my gums for a couple minutes. The world began to spin.

"Whoa! I'm dizzy." I giggled. "I feel drunk!"

The guys roared. *You're ridiculous. Such a lightweight!*

As we climbed into the buggy to get our stuff for bed, though, Eddie started to chant. "One, of, us!"

The others joined in—Bao and Luke, Trevan and Keller. "One, of, us. One Of Us! ONE OF US!"

I laughed, tripping unsteadily out of the buggy, landing hard from the two-foot drop off the back bumper. My heart was being pressed into juice. This was everything I longed to hear from them, but it wasn't true yet, only a joke.

I lay on my sleeping pad staring up at the smoke-blotted stars. The guys coughed nearby where they lay among the trees, and I vowed to make it real. If it took everything I had, I would become one of them.

After the Hog, we fought a few small fires near Lassen National Park: the H8, the H12, and the Cow Head. The last of these was tucked so far up in the armpit where California met Oregon and Nevada that it was hard to tell which part of the black lay in the Golden State and which was Silver State territory.

Fisher sent me to fetch water in a bladder bag from a scummy little pond about a quarter mile outside the black. The surface of the water looked like old urine, and a snake swam away in a writhing letter S as I approached. I made several trips, and every time I slung the heavy, slosh-ing yellow bag onto my shoulders, it knocked my hard hat to the side and snagged the end of my braid—the same plait that had repeatedly caught embers and singed with a smell like death. As I trudged back and forth between the pond and the fire's edge, staggering under seventy pounds of gear and water, my braid got yanked and wrenched until my scalp ached.

That was the final straw: I was over being a long-haired girl. It didn't work for this job.

The next R&R, fresh out of the shower, I stood before our bath-room sink in Happy Camp. My hair draped in a dark, dripping curtain that fell well past my breasts, tickling my lower ribs. "Mermaid hair," as a child once called it. Well, *fuck it.* I grabbed a fistful of wet curls, picked up the scissors, and began to cut.

Ten minutes later, my hair hung in blunt, chin-length waves. Dark piles of chopped locks littered the counter and sink. I shook my head, pleased with the new weightlessness, then smiled in the mirror, uncertain. It looked cute, right? Less feminine, but cute? I was sud-denly scared that I had sacrificed something I could never get back, like Rapunzel losing her powers. Irrationally, I feared that the men would think I was ugly now.

What does it matter? I reminded myself. *You're not here to be hot.*

Back at work, we headed to our first big fire of August, the Red Salmon Complex—a "complex" being several fires that merge or are close enough to be managed by the same team.

My new look caused a stir. *Whoa! Haircut? Damn, Ramsey!* But to my surprise, they loved it. One man even said, careful to avoid a direct comment about *me*, that he thought long hair was overrated and "always found short hair more sexy on women." I could've died gig-gling, if a girlfriend were around.

We slept in a crunchy stretch of woods where a deer woke me each night with indignant snorts, as if we'd trespassed in his home. We put in line and ended at an outcropping, from which I saw my first real column, white and thick and twisting, a tether from the earth to the outer atmosphere. Like an unseen bomb had gone off, a tower of boiling smoke. I was awestruck.

"Oh," I said, and Hayes, who happened to be beside me again, said, "Yeah, Kelly, *that's* a real column."

By day eight, we were mopping up. Mop-up is the finish work you do after the fire has passed through. The flames may be gone, but lots of stuff will hold heat and continue to smolder for weeks or months, if left alone. So crews go in and hack apart burning stumps, dig up smoldering ash pits, and turn over hot earth with hand tools until the dirt is cold and no longer smoking. If you're lucky, an engine will put in a hose lay, so you'll have water to cool it faster. Without water, it's called "dry mopping," which is the worst.

Mop-up was tedious, and I was annoyed until I got grouped with Eddie and Luke, two of my favorites. When we were putting in line I rarely caught sight of them, since the saws were usually ahead.

We had no radio and Westbrook, who did have one, disappeared up the hill above us. Luke began to grumble about West as he dug around in a steaming stump hole, using a Madrone limb to dig because he and Ed had just one hand tool between them. Luke's tool was the saw.

I was digging, too, trying extra hard to show them what a hard worker I was, how diligent. Chink, chink, chink went my Pulaski in the dirt and roots and white ash. The ash pit was hot, and my feet burned. This thing could happen where if you stood in an ash pit for too long, your boots (and feet) would get blisteringly hot, and then they wouldn't cool off for hours. It was painful.

Engine crews had plumbed the line with "trunk," a one-and-a-half-inch hose—usually yellow—that followed the fire's edge. Every one hundred feet, lengths of trunk were joined with a gated Y. "Lateral" sticks of one-inch hose attached to the Ys to allow firefighters to drag water into the black. Sometimes, instead of official "lats," we screwed a reducer onto the Y and used fifty-foot sticks of pencil or P-hose, essentially a three-quarter-inch fabric garden hose. For a day like this, you'd grab the mop-up kit, a green satchel full of reducers, nozzles, and rolled sticks of P-hose.

The water pressure was weak and inconsistent. We'd get to a hot spot or see a snag burning, and just when we needed water, the line went limp.

"God*damn*it," Luke said. "West!" Luke yelled up the hill. We couldn't see anyone. "Westbrook!"

No response.

The three of us shouted together, "*Westbrooooook!*"

Nothing.

"Copy that," Luke said, embittered. "No contact, thirteen twenty."

We'd gotten an English muffin with some ham and cheese in our lunches, and Eddie found a bit of foil, so the boys toasted their sandwiches on a hot spot in the black (an area where the earth still smoldered, warm enough to heat your food). The boys sat eating side by side, long legs outstretched in orange chaps stained darker where the sweat soaked through.

We'd seen worse food. Often, camp caterers would fulfill the requirement to give us five thousand calories a day by fluffing out grade-school-style lunches—sandwich, mealy apple, baby carrots—with candy, rock-hard protein bars, Smucker's Uncrustables, and disgusting nuts nobody wanted (dehydrated garbanzo beans? *Soy* nuts? Even I would not). After breakfast, we tore open the paper lunch bags, and pounds of undesirable crap would sail over my head into the trash can hanging on the buggy's back door. Trades commenced: "Who likes iced animal crackers?" (me). "Who's collecting summer sausages?" (BJ). Universal rage, if the sandwich was roast beef.

Since five thousand calories wasn't even enough to replace what some guys burned in a shift, the frequent failure to provide solid nutrition—on top of the risk of death, the smoke, the injuries, cancer, and PTSD—was a source of great bitterness. As one firefighter wrote on a popular subreddit about Uncrustables: *They don't care if we live or die.*

During lunch, Eddie played a song on his phone, the glitzy sixties ballad "Just My Imagination." He sang loudly, gazing deeply into Luke's eyes, substituting the words of the song for a story about being his swamper.

"*To have a swamp like meee,*" he crooned off-key. "*Is really a dream come truuuue!*"

Luke stared at him, expressionless.

"*Out of all, the temps, in the world . . . no one swamps like meeeeeeee,*" Eddie finished with a sweep of his arm, and Luke cracked the tiniest bit of a smile.

"Yes!" Eddie said. "I got you."

"No you didn't."

"Yes I did. I got you, motherfucker. I made you laugh."

"I'd hardly call that a chuckle."

After lunch, we worked a while longer without seeing or hearing anybody. Then we started yelling.

"Hey! Can anyone hear us down here, anyone? Westbrook!!"

Finally, Westbrook's lanky frame appeared above us. "What," he said irritably, leaning on his tool handle. "What do you guys need?"

"Well," Luke yelled. "There are three of us down here with NO RADIO, and no one with a radio anywhere near us, and NO ONE CAN HEAR US."

"Okay," Westbrook said slowly. "Well, what's the problem?"

"The problem is: What if something happened to us?" Luke shouted. "What if someone got hurt? There's no radio and nobody in fuckin' SHOUTING distance. Don't you see a problem with that?"

"But no one is hurt."

"It doesn't matter! Someone COULD get hurt and then where would we fucking be? S-O-fucking-L, Westbrook!"

"Okay. Well, I'll stay nearby, okay? Jesus."

"THANK you," Luke said. "Wow. Thank you so much. That's really fucking amazing of you. I really appreciate it. You're a goddamn hero."

I looked at Eddie, who gave a little shrug. Torn between feeling sorry for Westbrook and wanting to laugh, I said nothing and trudged uphill toward the next section we needed to work.

At the end of the day, the trail spilled out on the gravel road where we dropped our packs behind the buggy to sharpen tools and refurb. I emptied the trash again, twice that day, but by now I was taking a strange little pleasure in getting the timing right and having an open bag of trash there on the ground at just the moment when everyone emptied the leftover lunch snacks from their packs, when Eddie was refilling Sigg bottles, the aluminum canisters of gas and oil we all carried. It was probably an opportune moment to see if Fisher and Salomon had a full can of trash up front. When you got them right, chores could be like choreography, well-timed and elegant. There was a beauty in trash, I saw that now.

We loaded up sweaty and happy and the buggies wound up the switchbacks of the narrow road. When we reached Drop Point 10, where the blue rooms (porta-potties) and food caches stood, we paused. It was 1900 hours, why were we still sitting there? A rumor ran through the buggy like a current of voltage.

"We're being reassigned."

"Where?"

"I don't know."

"Now? We're leaving now?"

I knew it! The transfer often happened on day eight, with enough time left in the roll for us to be useful elsewhere for nearly a week.

Things were slowing down here; in mid-August, there would be some new emergency that needed us more. Besides, we were over this fire.

I'm not sure why we didn't like the Red Salmon. Fires have personalities; they have feelings to them, the sum of a million little factors like where you sleep, how they feed you, and what you're assigned to do . . . whether your leadership seems dumber than you, whether your work is valuable versus soon undone, rendered useless . . . yeah, all these things make up the disposition of a fire, just like a person, and we did not love the Red Salmon. So while we had no idea where we'd be sent, we were happy to go anywhere else.

We drove downhill and out of the fire to the town of Orleans, where we set up camp near a creek to sleep before traveling. I bedded down near the dampness and trickle of the stream. There was no resistance between the air and my body, between inhalation and my lungs filling. Oh, right. That was the absence of heavy smoke.

A giddy glee coursed through me as I wiped and powdered my feet. It felt like a good novel—where would we go next? What would happen?—only it was real. This was our job.

Some job. I could see how a person might become addicted to this.

Chapter 5

What It Takes

Dad took us to a bar. I was eleven or twelve, so Courtney was seven.

I had matriculated to a middle school where the bathrooms smelled like cigarettes and the girls wore name-brand clothes, training bras, and heavy eyeliner. Well, some of them did. Others were like me, stubbornly clinging to childhood in baggy soccer shorts and pocket tees. Some of them—*ahem*—dragged a cello down the hall for orchestra rehearsals.

That summer I flew to Green Bay, Wisconsin, where my dad and his wife Renee had now produced four children: Courtney, white-blond hair, oldest, and bossy. Steve, a hyperactive five-year-old who enjoyed putting on karate demonstrations. Evan, a shy toddler who walked on his tiptoes; and Madeleine, the baby, a gorgeous imp.

They lived in a long, narrow rented house with octagonal chambers at each end. The kids slept in bunk beds in a single room. My dad's office occupied one of the octagons, and we could hear him in there making work calls and playing country music. We could also smell the smoke that snuck under the door.

One day we staged a "protest" and crawled into the room with wet washcloths over our mouths. We'd plastered his door with handmade signs: *No Smoking! Young Lungs Are Growing!* We coughed dramatically, and I told Courtney to stop, drop, and roll, and Dad roared *Out I said Get OUT.* We ran.

Another day he took me to an empty lot that was for sale. "I'm gonna buy this," he said, "and build a house for the family. For all of us. It'll be your home too." He described this dream house, with bedrooms for all the kids, a hot tub, a playroom. He was a contractor, so why shouldn't it happen?

But I knew it wouldn't. His voice had the sound that adults made when they wanted you to buy an idea they didn't believe themselves. Home was all I wanted, so for both of our sakes, I lied. "That's great, Daddy. I can't wait."

A few days later, Dad took us to the bar. It was afternoon, and the sun shone through the rippled glass cubes that blurred the world outside. "Aren't you cute," the bartender said to my sister and me, and Dad lifted Courtney onto a stool and ordered us Cokes. A beer appeared in front of him that I don't remember him asking for. We were excited about the bowls of Chex Mix and peanuts sitting on the bar.

And a jukebox! Courtney asked for a quarter, and I said, "Me too?" Dad rolled his eyes, but he was smiling. He dug some coins from his jeans pocket, and my song came on first.

A long, long time ago, I can still remember . . .

"This one, huh?" Dad chuckled at the opening line of "American Pie."

By the time the chorus came, Courtney and I had slid off our seats and started to dance.

"Come on, Dad! Sing with us!"

He joined.

That was the summer visit, or maybe it was the year before, that Dad strapped my brother's ear. Evan had an ear that stuck out from his head like the stop sign on the side of a school bus. He was born that way (though he would eventually get surgery to address it). Dad got a strap that tightened down, like a ratchet or a belt, and he secured it to Evan's head so the ear lay flat to his skull. He told him to keep it on overnight, it would grow right if he slept like that. But Evan tore off the strap in his sleep, and Dad seemed furious. "Why won't you listen to me?"

Because he's too little. You're hurting him, I wanted to say.

But was he being harmed? My brother remembers how, several years later, he asked Dad to help him with his ears because he was tired of being bullied about them in school. He recalls our father's assistance as an act of kindness.

At night, in the bunk bed, my brother slept curled in a ball like a little bunny. Face down, he bounced himself to sleep, and I wondered if—even with all these people in the house—if he felt alone. Sleeping, my siblings looked small and doll-like by the faint glow of the stars stuck all over the ceiling. I vowed to protect them.

My sister and I danced, *Them good ole boys was drinkin' whiskey and rye*, and Dad watched and let out his real, throaty laugh, the one that often turned to a raspy cough. He stubbed his cigarette in an ashtray. "You girls," he said. "My, my. You girls are somethin' else."

His attention was the sun itself shining upon Courtney and me as he tilted his beer and the last of it flowed into his smiling mouth. It wasn't late, so he ordered another.

I couldn't help thinking of my dad as I walked through Reno, Nevada, my body slicing through an afternoon so hot it felt like the oxygen had been pressed from the air. My face prickled with sweat. I didn't want to be out here, but I couldn't sleep after working night shift, with the brightness of day fingering the edges of the hotel drapes.

A man stood barefoot in the middle of the street. Two police officers watched him from the curb. "We need you to get out of the road," one of the cops called in a deep voice.

"What are you gonna do, *make* me?" the guy shot back, holding his phone high, recording them.

He wore a filth-grayed shirt several sizes too large. Sun had browned his bony forearms and reddened the tops of his feet. Feeling pressure behind my eyes, sadness trying to hijack my face, I skirted the police and came up short at a corner lined with human bodies.

Many of the unhoused men who leaned on the corner near the food bank had my father's eyes. Oceanic, infinitely sorrowful. I didn't find what I was looking for (a coffee shop), but I found my dad everywhere. I gave up, turning back toward the hotel.

A man from Stockton rode his bicycle beside me and tried to get my phone number and "make plans for later." I politely declined, informing him that one, I had a boyfriend. Two, later I would be busy fighting a fire. "That fire," I said, pointing to the smoke that hung in the afternoon sky like the graphite smear left by a bad eraser. Stunned, the man wished me luck and rode away.

By the time we drove out to the line, darkness had fallen, and the fire was backing downhill through the shadows of trees. Fire in the dark is exquisite; it twinkles and shimmers and moves like a wave crawling over a beach, like molten lava streaming from a volcano. You could hear the familiar tinkling music of a dozer pushing earth.

We were assigned to night shift on a fire called the Loyalton, day-sleeping in a Reno hotel. We'd been pulled here from the Red Salmon on day eight; while the former fire was skunking around wet drainages on the edge of a wilderness, the Loyalton had gobbled thirty thousand acres of the easternmost edge of California, threatened several communities, and produced its own weather system, creating a rare "fire tornado." *It's the firenado, bro!* someone said as the buggy approached the column on the horizon.

When we drove in the first day through a yellow pea soup of smoke, I saw a line of cars and a tractor trailer on somebody's farm, burned to metal skeletons, flames shooting through melted frames, and my heart fell into my belly.

The night following my failed search for coffee, shift ten or eleven, we tried to burn, but the relative humidity (RH) was too high, and the burn went nowhere. So we sat in the dark waiting for daylight.

"I hate cutting," Trevan said. "And I hate digging line, and I *really* hate swamping."

"What do you like?"

"I like when the fire's really ripping, and there's nothing you can do, so you get pulled back and then you just get to watch the fire rip. Sitting and watching it, that's what I like."

Eddie laughed, spat. Trevan gazed over the darkened valley below us.

"You know what else I hate? Baked potatoes."

Trevan's dislike of baked potatoes was well known to me. But the others hadn't heard this routine, so I egged him on. "What's so wrong with a baked potato?"

"What's wrong? What's WRONG? Everything! It has no flavor. It's dry. It's so parched you have to cover it with other shit just to make it edible. You smother it with cheese and bacon bits and sour cream just trying to cover up this lifeless, dehydrated turd that's like chalk in your mouth. It's *bullshit*."

Eddie's big, warm laugh rang out in the darkness.

In these moments I felt so fond of Trevan, but other times I couldn't connect with him at all. Nothing fazed him; nothing appeared to scare or overwhelm him. He wore apathy like a kind of armor. Further, he didn't seem charmed by me, and I seldom liked men who didn't find me attractive or at least strongly likable. Of course, that was *my* problem (one of them).

But in an unavoidable way I did like Trevan, because he sat beside me, day in and day out, and I knew him—the way he drummed his fingers to his music, the tilt of his head, the drape of a skinny forearm over the armrest, the loose, loping way he walked, how he was always clearing his throat—*ahEM*—how he petted the ends of his mustache when he was thinking and twirled his blond hair while he talked, and the "I love you" on the phone to his girlfriend, soft and sincere—I already knew Trevan too well to do anything but love him.

Morning came—cold, bright morning—and soon we sat in the buggy and Trevan pulled the chock from behind the tire and yelled, "All in!" and off we went in a cloud of dust, back toward the hotel and the homeless of Reno sleeping in doorways. Reno, where I would go straight up to my room and pull the blinds tight against the day. I'd wash off the ash and climb into that white bed, so soft, unbelievably soft, and try to fall asleep without wondering where my father was.

Day thirteen, a new moon, we drove out in the dark through a ranch with stubbled grass that was colorless under the black, starless sky. We passed a driveway with a gilt sign that read ARABIAN HORSES, and then we were in the fire scar, where the earth was white, the ash like deep snow.

A burned-over horse trailer stood among the shredded trees. I wondered if the owners felt that this was a personal disaster, or if they would see, as I saw, that these tragedies were happening everywhere at once. Nature wasn't malicious. This was life with fire in California, or—as we joked—the "California Complex," one fire in which the whole state was burning.

Past the trailer, where the black met green, we parked and geared up. Mac soon called and asked for someone to bump a fiver of burn mix up to his squad. "I'll go!" I said quickly.

"Oh ho," Bao teased. "Little Miss Eager Volunteer."

He got on the radio: "Mac, you'll have Kelly coming at ya with that fuel." ("Copy.")

I got some vague directions and moved up the dusty road, my body shuffling behind the funnel of light my headlamp cast. I reached the buggies and grabbed the fiver from the fuel bin. Burn mix was blue in our color-coded system, and the plastic lid was painted blue, so I knew that what sloshed inside was the right proportion of diesel and gasoline, and I could smell that, too, the sharp odor almost an aphrodisiac.

I slid my tool through the fiver handle and slung it over my shoulder. Oh GOD was it heavy—not quite as bad as a couple months before, but it still wasn't easy. The extra forty pounds on the forty-five-pound pack, plus tool, heavy boots—about ninety pounds. The weight pulled on my shoulders and tugged at my waist . . . it was great, just great. I grinned like, *I love this!* which was the new thing I did in front of the guys to show how easygoing and tough I was. Now I did it even when they weren't around.

I took the first dozer line on the right, as instructed. The path snaked up the hill, and I climbed, breathing heavily but moving at a decent clip. In either direction I saw nothing but darkness and a veil of smoke. To my left, however, a chainsaw started up with a faint whine. Good *lord* it was far away. I adjusted the fiver over my shoulder and followed the dozer line, contouring the hill.

The line ended a hundred yards later. Now I was bushwhacking through a series of drainages in the dark: down into a hole, where a creek used to run through the gullet in wetter times, and then up the other side, pulling pitch to a ridge . . . only to find another drainage in front of me.

Great work, girl, I thought. Way to be out in the green in the dark without a radio pulling pitch cross-country when no one knows where you are. *Nice job, genius.*

Huffing up out of the third or fourth of these drainages, I spied a familiar glow ahead: our burn. The orange of the fire lit the sky from beneath like floodlights on a movie set. Smoke billowed up through the flickering light. The sound of the saws grew louder (was it *bap bap baaaaap*, or more like *brum brrrrrrum*, or maybe *whop whop-whop whopppppp?*). Soon I could hear voices, too.

I barreled into the hole, hit the bottom, and began to hoof up the other side. When I glanced up, Benjy stood above me on the ridge, watching me come. Damn, he was a sneaky old goat—always popping out of the green unexpectedly. From below, he had that man-of-the-mountain look again, scraggly hair cascading out of his hard hat, dark eyes failing to conceal amusement.

"Where the fuck're *you* comin' from?"

I laughed. "Oh, you know"—I gasped for breath—"Down there somewhere." I waved a hand toward the valley below us.

"'Bout fuckin' time." Benjy grinned. "How's that fiver feel?"

"FINE," I said. "It feels great."

I covered the last few yards and slung the fiver to the ground. "Easy." I laughed. Sweat plastered my face, chest, and back. I breathed heavily.

Benjy laughed, but he cuffed my shoulder affectionately. "Nice work, dude."

I asked who needed the fiver and loped off to find Mac, secretly beaming.

By the last week of August, we were working a fire called the Cold Springs in northeastern Lassen County, where a valley that had once been a lake gave way to peaks pointed like witches' hats. The fire had burned about sixty-nine thousand acres of the middle of nowhere.

We went direct on a "little piece" of line that became a much bigger chunk than Fisher had thought. It peeled uphill, then hit a ridge and dropped off the other side, where it snaked and fingered and dove into the hole. Not a hot black edge, though, just creeping.

I had finally gotten the custom Nicks boots I'd ordered early in the season. Walnut rough-out leather, fourteen inches—fully to my knee, since I was shorter—and a double-stacked heel. I was thrilled with the beautiful deep-brown leather and how they hugged my feet, how thick knee-high wool socks slid into the footwell, hand and glove. But I'd made a mistake and checked the box "yes, I am a climber," so my boots bore a lineman's patch over the big toe knuckle.

"That's the stupidest thing I've ever seen," Trevan said when he saw the patch. Other guys pointed and cackled every time they glanced at my feet. I laughed with them, but I was embarrassed. My soles cramped and burned as I broke in the stiff new boots.

We returned to the small-town baseball field where the sprinklers came on in a different place each night. "Nobody better be shitting in that field where we're sleeping," Fisher warned as we pulled our PG bags from the overhead bins.

"I shit the other night, on the far side of the fence," Bao said.

"You can't do that! If you're gonna, it had better be an emergency."

"It was an emergency."

You could never tell whether Bao was being serious.

Sleep was a perpetual concern and hard-won achievement. The simple bedroll of tarp, pad, and sleeping bag was necessary, because packing up in the morning was a race—we had five minutes from wake-up to be in the trucks fully dressed, boots laced (the most time-consuming part), and you were forbidden to walk around before wake-up time lest you cut short someone else's rest. The urgency, and my fear of being seen in states of undress, made me so anxious that I always woke ten minutes early to change inside my sleeping bag, where nobody would see my boobs by mistake.

Some people snored (Scotty, Eddie) and some didn't sleep at all (Luke). We all used sleep supplements: melatonin, or "mellies," Benadryl, and true sleeping pills. The "bennies" were almost as profligate as Zyns, cans of Copenhagen, instant coffee packets, caffeine pills, and scoops.

"Who's got bennies?"

"I got bennies, and I got mellies—the threes."

"No six millis?"

"Six, are you crazy?"

"Nah, dude, that's what it takes. Two sixes."

That's what it took. We took what we needed to wake up, stay alert, remain focused on the line. Then we took what we needed to come down again. I popped a melatonin gummy and lay awake for half an hour waiting for it to kick in. We were spread out ten, twenty feet apart in a scatterplot on the field. The tossing and turning fell to grunts and snores, and the stars were faint above the small, smoky town, and at last I slept.

On day six, I picked up the banjo, a round jug that carries a few liters of water, and wished I hadn't. My legs felt like they'd peaked in strength; now they were on the decline. That night, I saw a text from Josh and sent one back, saying I missed him too. Was that true?

Truth be told, I didn't think about him much. I felt guilty about it, but we were so busy, and I was overwhelmed with trying to do a good job sixteen hours a day; as soon as the trying hard ended, I was asleep. So that night I tried on purpose to miss him. I remembered the day he taught me to fly fish. This was no spinner rod, and I could barely cast the stupid thing; I kept tangling my line in blackberry vines on the riverbank. But standing in the thigh-deep water of the Klamath together was a peaceful kind of companionship. I saw Josh there, in waders and a hat, wearing his little-boy grin, the one that was almost too eager, like I was a rare butterfly who might flicker away. Still, it felt warm to remember I had someone who cared for me like that.

On the seventh day we were allowed to leave our tents (tents!) staked in the meadow that sloped down to Lost Lake, even though it had been so windy the previous day the helicopter couldn't fly in the hot buckets. I'd been excited to see what a hot bucket was, what it looked like, but no luck so far. Instead, I got a freeze-dried meal cooked in the white light that poured from the buggy door.

Yet the heat steaming off the pouch was a thrill. We were allowed to sleep until seven, an extreme luxury. A cow lowed on the far side of the lake. You could only just barely smell the wildfire—or maybe that was my nose crammed full of ash and black soot boogers. To be in a tent at all was a lavish indulgence, and I watched a horsefly hovering outside the mesh and thought, *You're not getting in here, fucker.*

First light came orange, then yellow. Day had not yet touched the lake, only the bowl of trees surrounding the glassy water. We hiked into the fire on the south side of the canyon, where we put in line in rock. Rock upon rock, everyone broken from digging boulders. Westbrook bonked his knee and was limping. Fisher hung near the back with me, Miguel, and Wink. He made up a song to "My Humps" about everything on his body that hurt. *"My neck, my back, my chafe and my crack!"* It was comforting to know that even Fisher's body ached; he was human after all.

Barrel dug beside me using a pick mattock. His big-headed rectangular body was strong but awkward. Somehow, he wasn't very good at digging yet. He wedged the pick under a boulder and leaned his full weight on the handle to free it from the dirt.

"What did the man say when the salesman tried to sell him a dishwasher?" he asked.

He waited. Nobody spoke up, so finally Wink uttered a deadpan, *W-what.*

"He said, 'I don't need one. I already have a wife!'"

I wheeled around. "Barrel!"

He wore a big, psychotic grin that told me he'd done this on purpose. Still, I couldn't stop myself.

"I know you're joking, and I know you're doing it to piss me off, but goddamnit—"

"You shouldn't take the lord's name in—"

"Shut the fuck up, Barrel! You shut up. You are not Christianity's best representative."

He giggled again and I said, "Stop it! You cannot make a joke comparing a woman to a dishwasher. You just can't—not in front of me. I know you'll say it's just a joke, but it's offensive. It's not okay. I know I act cool with a lot of stuff, but there's a line. Just don't fucking do it."

"I'm sorry, Kelly," he said, hangdog.

I could tell he wanted to giggle again when I turned my back, but he felt bad, too. He would apologize again later, and I would forgive him.

We put in line for six, seven hours. Then we sat quietly, staring at the sky as a ship (fire for "helicopter") brought bucket after bucket to the upper part of our slope, where trees were torching out of sight. Torching has a kind of unhinged beauty. The tree is engulfed in flame from base to crown in a breath, like someone blowing a candle *on.* Awesome but terrifying. We could hear the trees go up in flames now and then, and we could hear the water sizzle and rain down through the canopy, but it was quiet where we were, and we had tied in our line, so we watched the helicopter appear and hover and drop and turn and labor out of sight like a heavy insistent insect.

September had snuck in almost without my noticing. In fire, they called August "Dirty August" (it had been) and September "Snaptember," because this was the month, they said, when firefighters worn down by months of hard labor and poor sleep started losing their cool. People mentioned it that day, *Ooh, it's Snaptember, boys, look out!* But so far, everything seemed good. I hoped it would stay that way.

Waiting for us at camp were the hot buckets, which in this case meant meals in black takeout containers and convenience store apple pies in little cardboard boxes (sometimes they really were buckets filled with bags of hot slop, I was told). But they were delivered by *helicopter.* I was very excited, yet everyone seemed to take it in stride that a helicopter had delivered us coolers of food in the middle of the wilderness. Keller caught a fish from the lake, and we sat around the campfire as he roasted it in foil. Ed and Bao were talking about something that was made in America, and Ed said, "You know what else is made in America? This body."

"Show them your body, Ed," Bao prodded.

Eddie flexed his biceps, kissed each one, and then punched his own muscles. "That's right. Made in America, baby!"

It was stupid but funny, and we all laughed, but I looked away so I wouldn't be caught looking at Eddie's body.

He'd had a hard day. They moved him off the first saw team, though with good reason: Luke didn't share the saw, so as first swamper, Ed wasn't getting any trigger time. Eddie would join third saw ("turd saw," as the joke went) with Trevan, who didn't mind sharing, and Eddie would gain the skills to become a sawyer in his own right.

"I know they want what's best for me," he'd confided earlier that day. "But it still hurts."

"Of course."

"Luke's my saw partner, you know? We have a relationship. It takes time to build that."

"Honestly, though, I'm excited for you, Eddie. You're gonna run saw so much more. It's a good thing."

He smiled. "Thanks, Kelly. 'Preciate ya."

I said, *Of course, dude*, using "dude" as a friend-zone check, but those eyes. Those stupid, pretty eyes.

That night in my tent I thought again of Eddie's muscles and his sweet, dimpled smile. Then I thought, *Stop*.

I had learned a lesson that day, one I planned not to forget: neither brag nor complain about what you carried. Someone will put you down ("that's rookie stuff, that's what you do" or the sarcastic "yeah, thanks for doing your job") and remind you that you're not special. Because you aren't. Even if you can carry nearly your own weight up and down a mountain.

"Women in our family are pack mules," my mom always said.

I wondered what my mom was doing. It would be late in Virginia; they'd be asleep. I pictured my stepdad, Phil, snoring heavily, and my mom on her side with the old tabby cat, Tess, curled against her shins. I saw the woods around their house and the paths to the pony pasture and the swift waters of the James River pulsing by.

I was so far from home, from the landscapes of my childhood. Sometimes it ached to admit how completely the past had slipped away, traveling so far downstream that the memories themselves felt unreal, bubbles on water.

"We're family now," Van liked to say, about the crew. "We take care of each other."

I looked at the woods and the tents and the lake. The smoke had cleared enough that the stars appeared, little white knives in the smoke-wraithed black. Trevan coughed and Luke sighed and Eddie moaned sadly, the tell that he was beginning to drift off. The water lapped at the shore, indifferent to the battle we waged by day up the hill. It was always a different field, yet it was always the same. I felt comfortable there. It was the closest thing to home I had known in a long, long time.

Chapter 6

Intergalactic

The day before the apocalypse, we slept at the UC Davis Forestry camp, a cluster of wooden buildings all neat and homey under the pines. We couldn't go inside them, mind you, but some guys slept on the porches, some in the gravel lot; I found a divot in the woods down a hill behind the main building, and though it wasn't really flat, it was cupped and covered in leaves, so I felt like a baby bird in a little nest, and that was good enough.

We'd been moved on day nine from the Cold Springs to the North Complex, south of Susanville, which, at just under forty thousand acres and 45 percent containment, had begun giving crews trouble, getting squirrelly, threatening to jump the Feather River. By the end of its tenure, the North would burn over three hundred thousand acres and leave sixteen people dead.

We'd been working the high country above the river, where the fire had slopped over a ridge. The day was a laconic grind. We hiked down the dozer line, and the Plumas's fine dust rose in clouds. We coughed and choked. I closed my eyes and held my breath and sank into the dust up to my knees. We said nothing—complaining didn't help—and soon it was over and we'd reached the line.

There wasn't much heat, just blackened grass and poofs of white ash, and we scraped half-heartedly, mopping up. It was day thirteen of our fifth roll of the season; we were into September now, Labor Day in fact, and motivation wasn't high.

Benjy called for bodies to help the engines distribute hose. We hiked off the hill to the road, where coils of rolled hose lay stacked in the dirt. One by one we turned our tools upside down and threaded the hose rolls onto the tool handles. I looked at what other people had taken—two, three . . . five of them? Oh Christ.

Okay, sure.

I loaded up my Pulaski handle and slung it over my shoulder. I had a banjo (a canteen holding four quarts, or about a gallon of water) already strapped to my pack, and now the rolled hose stacked awkwardly on top of that. I felt like the peddler character from one of my children's books, who stacks fifty hats on his head. I tried not to do the math: pack, forty-five pounds; tool, five or ten pounds; banjo, ten pounds; hose, ten pounds each, times four; total . . . one hundred pounds? I wasn't sure of my own weight, maybe 140 or 150, so what I carried was 70 percent of another me . . . ? *Don't think about it.*

The guys were already climbing the hill, and I scrambled to catch up.

How to describe the feeling of hiking like that? You take a step and ask your leg to straighten and push you upward so you can take another step. It doesn't want to. The hill looks vertical. The leg is tired; it claims to be broken. It's so fucking tired, and it tries to tell you, like a whiny child, *I can't.* The muscles clench and scream. You can't breathe. Or you're breathing too much, you're gasping, but you still can't get enough air. It feels like the hand of a massive, wrathful god is pushing down upon you with all his weight. God wants you to remember every time you've failed and every person you've let down.

Yet this is your job. You've got to get the stuff up the hill; you have no choice. You must carry the god who hates you. And sweet Jesus, try to walk faster because you're already losing the guys.

So you tell your legs, *Yes, you can.* Just take a step, and then another step. Grind it out.

Pushing, gasping, I reached the intersection of the hand line and the dozer line. Benjy was sitting in the black leaning back on one elbow, grinning.

"I'm good," I yelled, and smiled defiantly.

Benjy laughed. "I know you are."

"Huh," I grunted and kept walking.

After a few trips down and back up, the engine people had enough to finish their hose lay, and I headed back to my mop-up spot. On the way, I ran into four women from some engines on a Tahoe strike team. We stopped to talk. They were so pretty, with their braids and nose rings and high, sweet voices. Why was I obsessed with them?

As they spoke, I realized with a jolt that I hadn't laid eyes upon a woman for the entire assignment—in thirteen days. Thirteen days of men. Thirteen days of bro jokes and farts and putting each other down. Thirteen days of hard hiking and digging and period-bleeding through my underwear and being crushed under the ass of a patriarchal deity, all with no women to tell about it. So of course these were angels from a promised land of milk and honey.

I envied their togetherness. One engine had three women; another, two. They seemed to have some reverence about me being a hotshot—as if this were something hard to attain, admirable, a little out of reach. And while I demurred that if I could do it, anyone could, there was a pulse in my ego's craven little heart, which I always picture as baby-sized Voldemort when he finally gets back into physical form and is essentially a wrinkled fetus.

I liked being seen as special. Good god did it feel good. To these women, I wasn't the smallest and weakest just struggling to get by. I was a *badass*. "Keep it up, girl!" they said, and by the time we said goodbye, I was floating.

It's dangerous, on a hotshot crew, to spend even a moment thinking you're special. The god of fire (what did we call him? Big Ernie) would be delighted to smite you off that pedestal. As I'd soon find out.

Shift ended, and we shuffled through the black to meet on the dozer line. Benjy, who as far as I could tell had been sitting on his ass listening to the radio and chewing tobacco all day, took the lead on hiking us out.

We began to climb a steep stretch of dozer line, the same one we'd come down, with the two feet of powder dirt. So now we had to climb *uphill* while sliding downhill in the loose dirt and sucking in clouds of dust. No big deal, really, except that Benjy thought day thirteen would be a fine time to power hike out of the hole.

A power hike is when somebody takes a regular hike that should be done at a nice slow pace—usually, the end of day departure from the line—at an unnecessarily fast pace. "Power" because it takes strength and endurance to move at that speed, sure, but mostly because it's a power *play*. It's a flex. A power hike is almost always led by a man who's been sitting all day while the crew has been working. So *he* has plenty of energy, while everyone else is gassed. He knows this is unequal and unfair, but he doesn't appear to care. Actually, that's the point. He seems to get a kick out of breaking everyone off.

Benjy picked up the pace, and I tried to hang. But bit by bit, I started to fall a few steps behind the guy in front of me. We were a short squad at this point and jumbled out of regular tool order. A day of hiking the banjo plus the hose rolls up and down the hill had caught up with me. My leg muscles were done, sapped, weak and wobbly as a baby deer. I had nothing to give. I slowed down, and to my total surprise, rather than slow down with me, someone passed me.

What? It wasn't a training hike. This wasn't *June*, for fuck's sake. This was September, the end of a hard roll.

BJ passed me. Then Keller. As Wink began to shuffle by me as well, I lost it. This was too much. Months of trying as hard as I could and offering to carry every heavy thing they needed, and still—*still*—I was the slowest one. I was the weak link, and they wouldn't miss a chance to remind me.

"Go ahead," I yelled at some poor guy climbing the hill. "Pass me! Show me how fucking slow I am. Like it's a fucking PT hike. Go *ahead!*"

I burst into hot, noisy tears. They hiked by me, avoiding eye contact.

Soon Salomon was behind me, though, and he touched my shoulder. "Hey Kelly," he said gently. "Stop for a second."

I stepped aside as Salomon said, "Take a break, okay? Take a breath. What's going on?"

"I'm so tired!" I burst out. "I've been carrying this banjo for days, carrying this banjo up and down and up and down, and nobody ever drinks any of the extra water, and my legs are just so tired. And then Benjy hikes super fast, and I can't go that fast today. I can't."

"Hey," Salomon said. "It's okay. We're leaving the line; it isn't important. You don't have to be fast right now."

"But I'm tired of being last. I'm tired of being the worst one. I hate that I'm so bad at this, when I'm trying—all I want is to be good, and I'm terrible at everything."

I fell into incoherent sobs, and Salomon awkwardly patted my back. Then he told me what we were gonna do. We were gonna hike up the hill together, side by side, as slowly as I needed.

"It doesn't matter," he said. "Hiking out doesn't matter. You did the work all day, and that's what counts."

"Okay." I sniffled and started to move up the hill.

As we climbed, he said, "You *are* doing a good job, Kelly. We see how hard you're trying. People see that you always volunteer. Don't think we don't notice that."

I nodded, sniffling and wiping my face. I was sure that if I spoke, I would start to cry again, and we were nearing the top of the hill. I wanted no sign of weakness when we got to the buggies. But I saw Salomon as he must have been outside of work: a sweet dad to those million little kids he had. He was younger than me, I always forgot. I wondered at how a man, almost any man, could somehow make me feel like a child. But in this case, I was grateful to be fathered.

"Thanks, Salmon," I whispered, as I peeled off behind the buggy.

The trucks stood just off the dozer line next to the black, a wasteland of skeletal burned manzanita. I slung my pack down in the dirt and started to refurb, pulling out my lunch and my bladder to refill the water. Now everyone was looking at me, sidelong or out of the corner of an eye. I refused to make eye contact. But Westbrook came over.

"Hey," he intoned. "Are you alright?"

I tried to say yes, but my eyes leaked.

West wrapped his long, freckled arms around me.

"Don't look at me or I'll cry," I whispered. "It's fine. I'm just tired."

Westbrook's blue eyes softened. "It's okay," he said. "We're all tired. That hike was bullshit; don't even worry about it."

He said a few more encouraging words and left me to sharpen my tool in peace. But our friendship had changed. He could be—I saw it now—*kind*.

Finally, my pack was set up and tucked in its shelf and clipped in, and my tool was sharpened and returned to BJ, the tool manager. I climbed into the buggy and sat staring out the window, relieved to be hidden in a back seat where no one could look at me. The guys clambered in one by one. Nobody said anything about what had happened.

Eddie reached his seat, two in front of mine, and when I looked up, he was gazing at me over the empty seat between us, smiling. It was a smile of sympathy and solidarity, a smile that said, *You're okay, we care about you, that was dumb, you're fine.* He kept up the grin until finally I smiled back. Then he gave one last dimple and turned around. Fucking *Eddie.* The smile lingered on my face as—"All in!"—we bumped out into the road.

When we got close to Quincy, I texted Josh a short version of the day. *Hose packs, Captain power hiked us out of the hole, got broke off and had a meltdown. Humiliating.*

Fuck those guys, he wrote back. *What a bunch of assholes.*

No, I wanted to say. That's not it. Actually, people were nice today. Sometimes it's worse when they're nice because then you know you're really pathetic, that they pity you. But they're trying, and I love these guys, don't you get it?

It seemed like too much effort to explain it to Josh. I felt (whether this was fair or not) that while he worked in fire, he wouldn't understand. Not the crew, not how it felt to be me on the crew. And certainly not the way in a single day I could feel physically drained and like a superhero and then like a piece of burning gutter trash, a "rat of lowly origins," as my friend Emily says. And yet, by the end of it all, I felt oddly loved and encouraged and buoyed up by the guys. They were, to my great surprise, supportive.

And Josh wouldn't understand how being this tired made you fragile, prone to outbursts and sudden shifts of mood, how you couldn't trust any emotion because it might be fatigue in disguise. Had he ever dug line for this many days on end? Had he ever been, I wondered, this tired?

I didn't bother trying to explain. And by the next day it was forgotten, because half of California was on fire.

*   *   *

Long ago—pre-contact, and pre-humanity—California burned all the time. The *world* burned ceaselessly (with a few wet exceptions, like the UK). Flames trawled the understory and sprinted over grasslands unchecked. Watching the earth from space 100 million years ago, you'd have seen pools of smoke swaddling the planet.

Fire returned to places like California in predictable intervals, so a given canyon might burn every ten to twenty years. Regular fire was beneficial, preventing overgrowth, providing browse for animals, and renewing the soil. Late-fall smoke cooled streams and assisted salmon migration. Some species learned to survive fire, while others evolved to *require* it.

California, home to both the tallest and the oldest tree in the world, is the most biodiverse state in the country, supporting 25 percent of the biological diversity in the continental U.S.—and the lion's share of our nation's wildfire. This may not be a coincidence. Scientists suggest that pyrodiversity (the diversity in frequency, scale, season, and type of fire) leads to greater biodiversity of plant species.

The Indigenous people of California were (and still are) expert fire keepers. Native burning mimicked and augmented natural fire, keeping the land parklike and open. Across the range of tribes and linguistic groups in the Golden State—one hundred languages sounded here, as of 1542—the use of "good" fire was almost universal.

Colonizers who approached California from the ocean gasped, seeing smoke columns up and down the coast. Early Spanish explorers, blown away by the fiery-orange poppy bloom and the frequent sight of flames, called the California coast "the Land of Fire."

The day after Labor Day, we woke to the wind. It threw dirt on our tarps and whipped hair into my mouth as I zipped my bag. I pulled on a beanie to block the cold. Great gusts shuddered the trees, stripped the napkins from our hands at breakfast, and slammed the buggy door with a bang. A mass of air pushed against the vehicles as we swayed down the mountain, or what felt like a mountain, back into Quincy and out the other side and up the winding dirt roads to the forested ridge, far above the Feather River, to our piece of the fire.

The morning was sunny, which should have been a warning. Sun means the inversion has lifted—a temperature inversion happens when warm air "caps" cooler air, trapping smoke in the valley overnight, dampening fire activity. Once the temperature rises, the fire awakens.

We stood in a circle to brief. Wind whipped Trevan's pale curls across his face. Luke squinted into the sun. Hayes spat. Benjy spat. Keller spat, standing self-consciously hunched down from the full height of his frame, one thumb tucked in a pocket. I stood on a little knob of Manzanita root, bobbing up and down. The sun slanted through the trees. The pines bent in the wind.

"The East Wind Event they've been talking about arrives today," Van said. He had gone to morning briefing with all the other superintendents, where they'd learned about the weather situation. "As you can see, it's already here."

"Event," somebody scoffed.

"Ooh, a big event."

"Come on, guys," Van said, with a sharp sideways look. "This is serious."

Red flag warnings stretched from California to Washington State. The wind was historic, a once-in-a-hundred-year phenomenon. Incident management teams along the West Coast were on edge. They would have increased staffing, but there was nobody to add; everyone was already committed, and short-staffed at that.

"You really need to be heads-up today," Van said.

"Lotta trees could come down in the black," Salmon added.

"What's the worst that could happen?" Eddie quipped, with a sly smile.

"Are you serious? Why you gotta fucking say that?" said Luke.

There was some precedent that when Eddie uttered that phrase, everything went to shit.

"Stop it, Ed!"

"Yeah, shut the—"

"You guys are too superstitious. I'm not God, you know." Eddie grinned.

"Oh, we *know*, ya turd."

Van told us the mission for the day, which was mop-up. On day fourteen, we would take it. A nice boring shift, if Eddie was wrong, and we hoped he was.

We broke the circle, trudging through deep dirt to the buggies. I could feel the wind inside my yellow, and I shuddered.

"Come on, load up," Fisher called, and fired the engine. I collected my hairbrush and stuck a boot on the bumper and pulled myself up, and the back door of the buggy clanged shut, a lid closing. "All in!" Trevan yelled, and we were wheels rolling toward the black.

We hiked in on the same dirt-powder line. Cloud of dust, choke, cough. "Let's not take banjos or dolies today," Fisher had said before we left, and I felt a hot wave of shame. He didn't say so, but I knew this was because of my meltdown. I had complained, and now they were lightening everyone's load. The guys probably knew that.

But maybe they didn't mind. Westbrook was silent, Luke oddly pale. Hiking in, BJ looked wobbly and winced.

"You okay?"

"I'm hurting," he said softly. "I'm just trying to get through this."

I muttered, "Sorry, dude, that sucks," and I *was* sorry—I felt a surge of pity for BJ with a plate in his ankle, the titanium that held him together since he'd broken several bones in a dubious "PT" on crew time (other guys still grumbled about how he'd ruined the tradition of Friday ultimate frisbee). I knew his foot throbbed with every step, and I was remorseful for resenting him. He was just trying to survive. We all were.

We reached the black and spread out along the line. Everything here was holding, and we were set up with a hose lay and engines pumping water from either end. We moved as a group, finding hot spots and digging as the wind picked up.

The wind howled and roared, bending the trees. Big old conifers creaked and popped. Some were burned out at the bottom, some were cat-faced (with a burned hole or hollow, like a cave), some crispy carbon sticks all the way up. It didn't feel safe.

Boom! A massive tree fell, somewhere out of sight. The big ones sounded like bombs. The ground shuddered, meaning it hadn't landed far away. Luke cursed under his breath. Westbrook stopped, scanning the black above us. Bao looked up too, and said, "Thanks a lot, Ed."

"Yeah, Ed! Look what you did," Luke grumbled.

Eddie laughed and said, "Come on!"

Boom! Another tree. Everyone's head was on a swivel. "Head on a swivel" was a shorthand phrase of Van's, but that's also what it looked like: a tree fell, and our heads snapped around, our expressions asking *where* and *how close.*

Boom!

"That was too close. Too fuckin' close." Luke looked unnerved.

A crew got on the radio and said they were pulling out. Too many snags comin' down, the crew boss said. "The wind's too high, and we don't feel safe to continue." They said they were hiking out. Division said he copied.

"You think we'll leave too?" I asked.

"Oh, hell no."

"No way. Hotshots gotta be the last ones to leave."

"Don't worry, Rowdy River'll do it!"

"Perfect time to get after it."

"Find the boys an outlet. We're gettin' plugged *in.*"

Bitter sarcasm was our only resort. The eerie wind stirred the stump holes and swirled embers into the air. Where we were, the wind threatened to coerce a dead fire back to life. But elsewhere, where we couldn't see, the risk was much worse.

Salomon, who was posted on the ridge as lookout, came on the radio. "Hey, uh, this thing is making a decent run. It's starting to put up a pretty good column."

Van confirmed that he was seeing the same thing from wherever he was hiding out. We kept digging. Then Air Attack came on the radio.

For whatever reason, most Air Attacks sound alike. I don't know if it's the quality of the radios in their planes or just the type of guy who's chosen for the job (always a guy, surely there must be a female Air Attack somewhere, but I'd never heard one). Maybe it's the way they're trained to speak. Their voices have a jauntiness and efficiency that can make even the worst of circumstances sound like a classic movie.

"This is making a big push," Air Attack said. "The fire has jumped the Feather River drainage and is making a big run to the south. It's moving fast. I'm seeing—I'm seeing a campground and some structures here, in front of the fire, and you need to send people out there to evacuate anyone in this thing's path. Tell everyone to get out of the way. It's—it's not stopping."

My skin prickled. We couldn't see any of it—the column, the fire pushed by these winds, jumping the river and racing toward a campground—but even I had been doing this long enough that I could picture the flames, and the urgency in Air Attack's voice made my blood run cold.

He came on again to say that this wasn't the only fire seeing explosive growth. "I've flown everything from here to Redding," he said. "And I hate to tell ya, but it's just columns everywhere. All of California is columns, far as you can see. Intergalactic columns."

We burst out laughing. "Intergalactic?"

"Did he really say that?"

We'd never forget it—it was a joke for the ages. We'd later get to a fire that was putting up a column and someone would intone, *Intergalactic*, with a wink, and people would laugh, and I would feel a chill. Because that is how a single column looks, like a rope from earth to space, and to imagine them spread over the breadth of this nation-sized state was to picture . . . the apocalypse. Alien invasion. Armageddon. With one word, Air Attack had conjured a vision of the end times. And he wasn't wrong.

We kept working our way down the line, mopping up. Bao lethargically churned his tool through a stump hole. Eddie sang a country song under his breath. Luke looked miserable and very pale. Was he unwell?

Opening my pack to grab a snack, I saw I'd missed a call from Jossie, the friend in Happy Camp who was watching our animals. She'd never called me before. Was something wrong with one of the dogs? I asked Westbrook to use my phone (on the line, except during designated breaks, your phone should be out of sight, and you needed permission to make a personal call). Sure, he said.

"Hey Jossie," I said when she answered. "Everything okay?"

"I'm at your house," she said in a rushed voice. "I have the dogs. Is there anything you want me to grab?"

Huh? I was so confused, the best response I could summon was, "What?"

"There's a fire in Happy Camp. I thought you knew."

"What? No, I didn't know."

Ice. As if someone had poured a bucket of it over my head. Cold water flowing over my body and entering my veins.

"Yeah. It's right outside town, they're evacuating everyone. I've been trying to get Josh on the phone, but he isn't answering."

"Oh yeah, he's on a fire too. He probably doesn't have service."

"Okay. Well, so I have to leave, and I've got my dogs. I'm guessing you want me to take yours?"

"Yes," I said. "Please."

"I tried to get the cat, but he ran away."

"That's okay. Cats are smart. Tommy will hide." My voice caught in my throat. Poor Tommy, the scrappy stray I'd bribed into our home.

"What about Sam?"

Fucking Sam. There was no loading a large goat into Jossie's small SUV. "Um. Why don't you let him free in the yard, so he can escape? I guess."

Much as I loved to hate Sam, the idea of abandoning him to flames turned my stomach. I remembered his brother, Alex, who'd fallen victim to a mountain lion attack the previous fall. We buried him near the blackberry bushes above the river. The body fell heavy and crooked into the hole.

Poor old Sam.

"Okay, I'll do that. Is there anything else you want from the house? Any important papers or anything?"

My mind reeled. What did I want? I thought about photographs from my childhood, pictures of my grandparents, of my dad with a guitar, old birthday cards and love letters and the programs for plays I'd been in as a teenager, early terrible poems . . . my life, or the hard-copy record that it had ever happened. I saw it catching fire, curling at the edges, turning to soft gray ash, rising in flakes on the wind. I looked around me, at the black—the nuked remains of trees—and I saw our home like this, our trees, our yard a field of ash. Ours, and everyone else's. Oh god.

My throat was closing. The trees around us, columns of carbon, creaked in the howling wind.

"No, just the dogs." It was almost a whisper. "Please take the dogs."

Chapter 7

Their Girl

The sky had gone orange. The atmosphere hung low, bloody and dark, as if someone had steeped the sky in an amber tea, the smoke like cloudy billows of just-poured cream. We were all taking videos, because it was insane that morning could look like the middle of the night.

We'd left the North Complex, headed home. Miles upon miles spooled out under the buggies' tires, wildfires in every direction. Everywhere we turned, roads were closed. We had to reroute because I-5 was shut down: a fire near Ashland, where my friends lived. Cold prickled my neck. We took a back road, a two-lane highway between orchards, their gnarled limbs menacing under the heavy sky.

Happy Camp wasn't the only tragedy in California. A headline about the North Complex read: "Tiny California Town Leveled By 'Massive Wall Of Fire'; 10 Dead, 16 Missing, Trapped Fire Crew Barely Escapes Blaze." The North had grown explosively, barreling southwest and consuming the town of Berry Creek, leaving only three houses out of twelve hundred standing. Meanwhile, in the western Sierra Nevada, almost four hundred campers were trapped when the Creek Fire blew up; the Army National Guard rescued them in Black Hawk helicopters.

By October, Governor Newsom would request a federal disaster declaration for six major wildfires in the state.

The windstorm had also fueled five simultaneous megafires in Oregon, damaging four thousand homes, schools, and stores, killing several people, placing 10 percent of Oregon residents under an evacuation order, and incinerating more of the Oregon Cascades than had burned in the previous thirty-six years combined. The Almeda fire leveled, among many other structures, my friend's mother's Polish restaurant in Talent.

In Washington, the towns of Malden and Pine City were mostly destroyed. The Cold Springs Canyon fire grew from 10,000 to 175,000 acres overnight, an insane rate of spread. The Pearl Hill fire jumped an almost unheard-of nine hundred feet to cross the Columbia River. Smoke blanketed British Columbia and the Western U.S. and, funneling into the atmosphere, drifted and spread to cover the continent. Air quality advisories were issued as far east as New York. College students hid in their dorms in Berkeley; older people sheltered from the dangerous particulates outside. We were a nation huddled, terrified. The smothering smoke implicated each one of us for our part in making a hotter world, enabling such a catastrophe.

This was a disaster. There was no other word.

News drifted back from Salomon and Fisher as updates and rumors blinked onto my phone over an image of my favorite swimming hole back home. *Home.* The Slater fire had blitzed north through Happy Camp and crossed over Grayback. It had jumped Indian Creek east to west, then the wind had shifted and it had jumped back again. The fire had gone everywhere at once and made a one-hundred-thousand-acre run up Indian Creek and over the ridge into Oregon. That ridge, where an undivided stand of Brewer spruce grew. *Had* grown? The canyon where so many homes . . . had been.

Chris and Tara's house was gone. Jason's. Gavin and Melissa's place in tribal housing. Jossie and Elvis's trailer, and, actually, the whole Indian

Creek trailer park. Ken's Cabins, where I had almost rented a home last winter, gone. Serena's parents' place, a rickety hand-built house reached only by a half-mile hike, perched on the edge of a bluff above the South Fork of the creek. Gone. Three quarters of the Meadows neighborhood. Every structure on Doolittle Creek.

Jason, who was an LEO (Law Enforcement Officer—like a Forest Service cop) and could get past the closures, posted a video from the Meadows. The houses had collapsed, like fire had kicked their legs out.

The air felt oddly cool under the inversion, and I sat as still as possible, trying to keep the knot centered in my throat. I had to think. The Slater was headed for Baudelaire; they were evacuating the town, even the Forest Service compound and the barracks. On the other side of the crest, the fire was moving west, toward my house. Home evacuated, station evacuated. I had nowhere safe to go and couldn't get Josh on the phone. For all I knew, our house was gone.

On we rode, now nearing Redding. Eddie looked back and I tried to hide my tear-streaked face, but he gave me a smile of great sympathy, and I thought, *Eddie, you are the best of them.* I desperately needed kindness, and the others were afraid to look, as if fear and sorrow might be contagious. I knew they were just uncomfortable with big feelings, their own and anyone else's, but when they turned away—the men with whom I'd spent nearly all my time for the past four months—I felt abandoned.

Back at the station, I rushed through chores, grabbed a few critical items from the barracks, and threw my PG bag in the back of my truck, hitting the road almost before the words "day one" had ceased to sound. I had finally heard from Josh that our house was okay, and I headed that way.

It grew dark as I drove the winding road through the Redwoods. On the ridge, huge grass meadows covered the rolling land that spilled into darkness on either side, the eponymous Gold Hills of the long way around, to the coast and inland again up the Klamath River. The pavement ended, and I was fishtailing around a gravel curve. Smoke obscured the stars. The night was black and the road narrow, and I was so tired. It seemed to go on forever.

At last the road spiraled down from the ridge into a Douglas fir forest and spat me out in the outskirts of Weitchpec, a town that was itself an outskirt to the middle of nowhere, and the road turned to pavement again and hit the highway, where I headed for Somes Bar, where Jossie had the dogs.

Finding her mother's trailer, we stood in the dark as I awkwardly struggled to string words together. "I'm so sorry," I said, meaning sorry that her home was gone, a pile of melted metal and ash.

"Me too." She shrugged.

I hugged her tight, loaded the dogs into the bed of my truck, and told white lies to talk my way through the roadblock, headed for Happy Camp. I drove into the smoke, which grew so thick near town that I almost missed our driveway. But there it was: driveway, gates, woodshed, house, fruit trees, garden—all intact. Josh had told me our home was standing, but I still felt a visceral relief at the sight.

Sprinklers were set to soak the roof, their little *tic-tic-tic* sounds perforating the thick, smoky quiet. The dogs spilled out of the truck and dashed through the yard, butts wiggling and tails whipping, sniffing every bush. I saw a familiar orange glow in the distance, and I realized with a sickening lurch that it was the fire lighting the sky.

Inside, I absently flipped a light switch, and nothing happened. Then I remembered: the fire had burned up power lines. The whole town was without electricity for the foreseeable future. I tapped the flashlight icon on my phone and tiptoed down the hall. The puppy bounded ahead of me.

When I pushed open the bedroom door, Valentine leapt onto the bed as my flashlight beam fell on Josh like a spotlight. He was deep asleep—had been, at least, following a thirty-six-hour shift where he'd fought to save our friends' homes. When the puppy and the light hit him, he bolted upright, white-faced and disoriented.

"Who is it?" he said in a frightened voice. He reached for the shotgun holstered to his side of the bed.

"It's me, babe," I said.

"Oh my god. Sorry. I was asleep."

I went to him, and we embraced, and he murmured, "I'm so glad you're here," and I said, "I'm so glad you're okay," and we held each other. It felt good, safe, like everything would be okay if we just had each other. I told myself this was my person, and we'd be fine. I remembered the summer-themed party we'd thrown the winter before, "Juneuary," when we heated the house into the 90s with Madrone logs so everyone could wear Hawaiian shirts and sundresses. I reminded myself that this man's favorite movie was *Homeward Bound*, a children's film about pets finding their way back to their family.

He quickly fell asleep again. I lay staring at the ceiling, the walls, thinking, *Will they hold?* Though the incident map showed a flaming edge a quarter mile from our house, if the fire did move in this direction (which Josh insisted was very unlikely), it wouldn't come quickly, now that the wind had died.

Still, I lay awake with an uneasy feeling. After weeks of being gone in the woods, the person who lay beside me felt like a stranger. Our disoriented reunion lingered in my mind, turning over in a lumpy, unpleasant way, like a wet towel in a dryer. He'd been frightened of me, as if I were an intruder. And his scared face looked ghostly—in the moment before I recognized him, he was a ghoul. For a split second, we were strangers. I couldn't forget it.

I spent two lonely days in Happy Camp, where the town was filled with smoke and grief. Josh left before dawn each day to fight the fire, returning after I was asleep with the smell of char on his skin. Without the bubbler to oxygenate their water, our fish died and floated, one by one, to the top of the tank.

That Friday, I made the four-hour trek along the coast back to work. They were calling the catastrophe the Labor Day Firestorm, a name almost too cute for a freakwind that had wiped hundreds of communities off the map. Smoke rose from the burning houses, from the forests engulfed in flame, and it spread across America, an ever-expanding mushroom cloud. It covered the country like an oil spill.

We woke in a field and dressed and laced our boots. It was quiet in the buggy, and a little cold—mid-September, but already the mornings were sharp with the chill of fall. Sniffles and coughs lit up the silence like sudden sparks. Luke slouched low in his seat with his face deep in the hood of his sweatshirt, a bat in a cave. BJ coughed and lay his head on his armrest. Keller was slouched to the side, a limp asparagus person. When I asked if he was sick, he nodded mutely, eyes miserable.

They couldn't smell, a couple of them had said. So we knew what it was. And I was baffled, I was astounded, that nobody was saying anything, but especially not Van, who'd been adamant about disinfecting and taking temperatures and, *Tell me if you're sick, tell me right away.*

Now they were sick as hell, they COULD NOT SMELL, and no one said a word, except to joke about "the buggy crud," the cold or flu that hit most crews this time of year. No temperature checks anymore, either. I kept opening my mouth to say something, then closing it. I knew that if we called this what it was—*Covid*—we'd be sent home and nobody would make any money. These men had children. They had mortgages, car payments, babies on the way. Their lives were at stake, and mine, too. To miss even one roll would be financially devastating. Federal firefighting was a broken institution that only paid us a living wage when we earned overtime and hazard pay. We hadn't created the system; we just had to survive it.

We drove to town. We were assigned to the Slater fire, the blaze that had taken Happy Camp, which now sat at 137,000 acres, 10 percent containment. Because the fire spanned two states, its management was divided between two Type I teams, with "Northern Rockies Team 2" taking the Oregon side, while Team 10 kept the California portion, where Josh was assigned.

I was a shell of myself, though I wasn't alone. Those who were sick were tired, but those who were tired were tired, and at a certain point it was hard to tell which was which. We'd been running for months now, fire after fire, poor sleep in a field, sleepless night after night in the woods, mouthful after mouthful of smoke—swallowing it, hiking on. Cutting the tree, digging the line, lighting the edge—again and again and again. Fatigue is an illness, too, one that scrambles your mind.

At the store in Cave Junction, where helium balloons floated on tethers above a display of cut flowers, almost everyone got a can of Bang, the energy drink. A disgusting, cloying syrup, but I got one, too, and gulped it down like medicine. Fisher had stolen Grizzly Long Cut (loose tobacco with a wintergreen flavor) from Miguel. Fish glissading the slope from Zyn to true tobacco was a sign that he, too, was feeling it.

We went to the line, but Keller stayed in the buggy. When he tried to get up to come with us, Fisher said, "Hell no, sit down. You look like the goddamn crypt keeper."

By midday, I stood giggling in the dozer line with Miguel as Trevan and Fish ambled toward us, dripping fire in the yellow grasses off the edge of the dozer push. It was a mellow lighting job, the burn creeping gently uphill through the field like a glowing orange wave. Gentle fire, one of my favorite types, appears to melt grass. Like a welding torch making metal weep, gentle fire reddens, curls, and vanishes plants into feathery ash.

"What are you turds so happy about?" Fish shouted.

"No te preocupes!" I yelled back.

"Yeah, none of your negocios," Miguel called.

"Copy," Fish said sarcastically. "You think you're better than me with your fancy foreign languages."

But he was with Trevan, so he was happy. He loved that Trevan was cruel to him, like he'd really dig in. "You disgusting hog," Trevan was saying. "Look at you. Spit just dribbling off your chin, you brainless cretin."

Fish giggled delightedly and punched it right back to him: "Look at yourself, Trevor." Trevor was what we called him to get under his skin. "You weak, skinny, long-haired, hashtag van life, wanderlust, hippie piece of shit."

Both of them smiling huge, every insulting syllable an expression of love.

Keller slept all day in the buggy, a feverish lump, and when we came back covered in dirt, he felt awful and apologized for missing work, and we consoled him, *Same old shit, Keller. You'll see it tomorrow.*

Day five, we stood in the smoke, a full white-out. I coughed, eyes stinging. We couldn't wear masks because the job was too physical; without air flow, you'd go tits up in a heartbeat ("Going T.U.," as we called it). And while the contact lenses I wore created a thin barrier against the acrid air, they weren't enough. Because my hands were always filthy, I rarely removed the contacts—didn't want an eye infection—so they were pasted to my eyeballs. Once, when I'd worn my glasses for night shift, the guys passed them around, trying them on like drunk goggles, laughing at the coke-bottle thickness of the lenses. *Dude, you're blind as fuck!*

Now we were smoke-blind. I couldn't see Fisher ten feet away from me. I wiped at the tears and snot with one sleeve, smearing ash over my face.

"Yummy down on that!" Fisher howled, coughing. "Best day of your life! Best it's ever gonna get!" and he burst into his goofy laugh, *heeyoo hoo hoo!*

Day six or seven, I stood next to Eddie in the line of holders and confessed to him that, since the fire in Happy Camp, I wasn't sure my heart was in this. I felt guilty that I hadn't been home to help when the fire came. And I was up and down—loving the job one second, hating it the next.

"It always feels that way," Eddie said. "That's just fire. You love it, you hate it. You feel everything about it. That never changes."

At the end of that day, loaded in the buggy, Salomon announced that we'd be going back to Baudelaire for the night. This division was close enough to our station that it made just as much sense to go home as to camp at the lake.

"We figure you guys could use a shower," Salomon said. "Like those of you with poison oak, seriously, take a shower."

I wasn't sure if this was pointed at me, but I appreciated it. I was fine with stewing in my own filth for two weeks, but the poison oak rash I'd been battling and scratching open for days would benefit from soap. So we were wheels rolling west on the 199, following our name-sake river, going home.

Close to town, a handmade sign in somebody's yard read, FIRE-FIGHTERS OUR HERO'S THANK YOU.

Misspelling of heroes aside, that was sweet. We backed up in front of the crew bay. It felt so good to be back in the place where we trained and lived and had all our things. The engine folks across the lot waved and said, "Welcome home!"

We piled out and grabbed our hotel bags. In the bay, Wink passed out mail that had come in for us in our absence. Some people—me, Trevan—pulled our yellows out of the trucks so we could wash off the poison oak. Hayes came over to me in the parking lot and held up a picture on his phone.

"Check this out. My mom's preschool class made drawings of us."

The drawings were made with crayons on paper plates. The kids had colored a bunch of "boy" firefighters in boots and greens and suspenders. They were obviously male: beards, mustaches, short hair. But the kids—almost every one of them—had also drawn a singular female firefighter, so indicated by a long braid and, in some cases, longer eyelashes (totally ridiculous, my eyelashes are almost invisible, but whatever). It was the braid I had worn at the start of the season.

"That's you!" Hayes said, pointing.

I swallowed hard, pushing down the knot in my throat. "Oh my god, it is."

"I told my mom we had a girl this year. I sent her the crew pic from Arizona."

"Dude, that is so cute. Thanks for showing me."

"Yeah, dude. Hell yeah." He gave me a fist bump and walked off.

It was more than cute. My eyes began to sting, and I turned my back to the buggies to pull it together. Come on, Kelly. No crying. Not again.

I wiped my eyes, straightened my shoulders, and sucked in a deep breath. When I turned, the men were framed by the open garage doors. Nineteen guys moved in and out of the bay, a hive of energy and noisy strength. They carried saws and boxes, sharpened tools, talked shit and laughed and punched each other. They ate and spat. They were the same people they'd been on the first day one, or maybe not. I wasn't quite the same person, though I couldn't tell just who I was becoming. Now, though, they weren't strangers. I knew them, and I loved them. My nineteen men.

And I—for better or worse—was their girl.

Chapter 8

Badlands

My childhood ended in a coffee shop in Appleton, Wisconsin. I was seventeen.

A few years before, on the cusp of high school, something miraculous had happened: I became . . . pretty? At least that was how people started treating me, which was confusing to a kid who'd always been semi-chubby and fully uncool. A growth spurt transformed my awkward body overnight, and suitors and boyfriends appeared. My social circle shifted, too, until my friends were not dorks but a middle-tier, smart, socially accepted group.

Junior year, I stopped eating. Lunch was a plain bagel and diet iced tea from the cafeteria, and my mom's dinners of chicken breast and steamed broccoli didn't make up for the calories skipped. My limbs winnowed, ribs articulated. I was pleased.

That summer, on my annual visit to the family in Wisconsin, I ran daily. The roads outside Neenah, where my dad and Renee lived, were long country highways through fields of soybeans and corn. I put Bruce Springsteen's *Darkness on the Edge of Town* into a Sony Discman, popped on headphones, and went racing down those straight empty roads under a bright, endless blue sky. The land was so flat that it felt like you could go forever and never hit anything to slow you down.

In the evenings, home from long days at the job site, Dad sat in his office, a glassed-in sun porch off the lower floor of the split-level house. He smoked cigarette after cigarette as an exhaust fan drew the smoke out the window into the darkened three acres, drifting over the chicken coops and apple trees. On his desk sat a tumbler and a bottle of Kessler whiskey. He drank from the glass, listened to Emmylou or Willie or Waylon, refilled the glass.

As he often took his dinner in the office, you had to go sit on the stool facing his desk if you wanted to hang out with him. Madeleine, a girly first grader who loved to parade the house in borrowed heels, padded down each night to fill him in on her latest, or—more likely—to listen. If you went to see our father, you were mainly there as a listener, audience to my dad's main character.

"I come from nothin'," one of his standard stories began. "Nobody never gave me anything, and I had to figure it out myself. But I did. I got a job workin' construction and I worked my way up, and look at me now. Got my own company, taking care of all these children. Good lord, children everywhere, and have you seen how they eat . . ."

I knew the one about how his dad was an S.O.B. who left the family, how they were "dirt poor" in Louisville. I knew the one about the commune, and I really knew the one about my mom, who wouldn't stop trying to control him with to-do lists. Though I knew he had cheated on her, and he liked to retroactively cast his exes as domineering, that list story resonated a little.

When he turned his attention upon me at last, it was a spotlight, moonglow on water.

"Kelly," he said. "You got it all. You're smart, beautiful, you're gonna go to college. College! Can you even imagine that, a child of mine going to college? You've got everything ahead of you. Every morning should be the happiest day of your life, like a bunch of baby bunnies just burstin' up out of a hole."

I nodded, never sure of the best response. Not for the first time, I was confused by the paradox of my dad's benevolent neglect. He loved his kids, of that there could be no doubt; he was gentle, admiring, and seemed to accept us as we were. When you came to see him, his face lit up. Yet he couldn't seem to spend much of his time looking in our direction.

Bunnies were a nice metaphor. I had it all, apparently, yet I woke up most days weak and hungry, and when I asked my mom for clothes from American Eagle and the Gap, she said, "Kelly, we've got ninety dollars in the bank and the electric bill is more than that. Don't ask me again, okay?" We weren't poor; we were basically middle class. But all I wanted was to be preppy or rich, cooler, different than I was. My life, like my body, wasn't good enough.

The yellow lamplight shone like gold on my father's soft brown hair. His face was so handsome, his forlorn blue eyes misty with nostalgia. I loved his lean, strong hands—capable of building anything, yet graceful and expressive. He was intelligent, and under different circumstances might have done something wonderful. He was a gorgeous tragic character who'd peeked at the script; it was like he knew the plot and couldn't contain his grief about the ending.

As I came and went through the garage—running, taking the family minivan to drive Madeleine to the mall, dropping Courtney at a friend's house—I passed the recycling bin, where the bottles of Kessler piled up. One day, I stopped and frowned. In the bin lay an empty bottle corresponding to every day of my visit.

One afternoon, Renee took me on a girls' date. She was a notoriously skilled secondhand shopper who could spot a name brand from across the St. Vincent de Paul thrift store. We found some clothes that might help me look more like everyone else, and she took me for a cappuccino at a cafe in downtown Appleton. Seated at a wooden table by the front windows, I finally broached the subject.

"Renee, does Dad . . . does he drink a lot? I noticed the Kessler's and he's just— So is that, like, a phase, or . . ."

She took my hands across the table. Her eyes filled with tears, and I'm grateful that she didn't even try to lie. If I was old enough to see it for myself, it was time. Her children were all too young, and I imagine she hoped they didn't notice or understand; she must have felt so alone with the truth.

"No, honey. It's not a phase. That's what he does."

"Since when?"

"I don't know. It's hard to say, you know, it's been getting worse. But maybe ten years now?"

Ten years. Since I was the size of Madeleine. Since Courtney was a baby. Most of the time that I could remember knowing my father, this had been happening, and I hadn't seen. How could I have known? My mom never drank—well, maybe a single beer at the beach during summer vacation. The same bottle of Maker's Mark had sat in our cupboard collecting dust for years. I didn't know what alcohol *was* or how it affected a person until my friends started drinking.

Now I thought back to every evening conversation with my dad, and I saw that a lot of what I'd considered his "personality"—long stories, slurred speech, getting suddenly emotional, passing out . . . this wasn't just *who he was.* He was drunk. Looking back, I could hardly recall a time I'd seen my father sober.

"We have to do something," I said. "Don't we?"

"Yes. No. I mean, what do we do?" Renee said. She ran a hand through the long blond hair I'd always admired.

"We ask him to stop," I said firmly.

"I've tried. You can try, honey, but don't get your hopes up. He says there isn't a problem."

"Oh."

She wiped a tear from my cheek and said, "Oh, sweetie." I blew my nose on a napkin. We sat in silence with the truth between us, a grave responsibility. I could do something about it, or not. It was a heavy question, one I was bound to carry like a load upon my back for many years to come: How do I save my father's life?

I would never be a child again.

I ran. The sun was high over the farms and fields. Springsteen's voice cried, *Lights out tonight, trouble in the heartland. Got a head-on collision smashin' in my guts, man.*

The planted rows and the stupid cotton clouds in the ever-blue sky blurred as I sped over the flat roads. I ran until chills covered my body, until my skin was stippled with goose bumps and I thought I might vomit, until I was empty.

I vowed to save him, save this family. But I had no idea how.

Chapter 9

Snaptember

The problem with the Slater fire was that it never seemed to end. And we were wet.

By late September, they'd moved us to Division JJ (Juliet Juliet), which lay in steep, rocky country north of O'Brien, Oregon. After a daily hour-long drive along bumpy gravel roads, we shuffled down a dozer line, peeled off a peninsular ridge and dropped into a deep hole that we had to climb out of at the end of each day. It began to rain.

We were wet and our gear was wet and our feet slipped in the mud and the muddy ash. Rain soaked through our clothes, which didn't dry overnight, and we put them on, clammy and shivering, the next morning. Barrel came down with a bona fide case of trench foot, the skin of his soles gone spongy white, peppered with rotten black holes. He showed us, baring his teeth in a savage, almost-proud grin, and we groaned, *Dude, get some new socks! That's nasty.* Like everyone else, I had taken to powdering my feet with Gold Bond morning and night. Still my skin sloughed off in soft, flaky sheets.

The fire was out, extinguished by heavy September rains, but we had to walk every inch of its meandering edge—not just walk it, but cut the brush from the perimeter and put our hands in the wet ash to confirm that, yes, every last millimeter of this fire is cold. We coughed, wiped snot. We were tired of each other and of this job.

On the morning of day fourteen, when we'd usually go home, Van told us the extension he'd requested had been granted; we'd stay on this fire for three more days. We'd forgotten we even agreed to this plan, and nobody was pleased. Fisher's face darkened like a summer storm, and BJ muttered, *Oh no, it's gonna be one of* those *Fisher days.*

Day fifteen, we plugged in and went direct in the mud. Four crews worked together: us, a veterans crew, and two crews from the contracting company Grayback. We'd all claimed segments of a deep, fingery slopover off the back side of the ridge.

Bao and I paired with Trevan and Eddie—saw team cutting out the edge, diggers "cold-trailing" with hands in the ash. Down and down we went into the steep dark drainage, boots slipping. At noon, the Division came on the radio, calling all resources on Juliet Juliet.

"Yeah, change of plans," he said. "I've been thinking about it, and I'd like all of you to come out of there, make your way up to the road. We're gonna move you over and have you prep to burn on Golf Golf."

"Juliet Juliet, Rowdy River. Just confirming: All four crews?" Van asked, not quite keeping the incredulity out of his voice.

"A-firm," Division said.

You could hear Luke's wail from a hundred yards away. "FUUUUUUUUUUUCK!"

Burning on Golf Golf meant two things. One, everything we'd spent half a grueling day doing was about to become pointless, because a burn off the road above us would incorporate all this ground, creating a new fire perimeter. Two, we'd need to immediately hike out of this hole, a hateful climb that we'd imagined completing gradually while working our way up the far side of the slopover. Now, it was a PT hike in the mud.

"Fucking stupid," Trevan said, shouldering his saw and turning to start the climb. "This is *bullshit*." A silent, sullen Eddie followed him, Dolmar on his shoulder, hollow eyes on the ground. Most of the time, Eddie was our class clown, laughter trailing him like proverbial clouds of glory. But his disposition could turn on a dime, and his feelings were easily bruised. The guys sometimes called him, to his face, "Emotional Ed." Being teased about his sensitivity, of course, never improved his mood.

Today, though, we were all angry.

"This guy's an idiot."

"Who changes the whole plan in the middle of the day?"

"We don't need to burn *shit*. This fire's dead!"

We hiked uphill to join Fisher, Luke, and Keller, where we waited for the others. When we were all gathered on a bench between steeply pitched slopes, someone started it.

"Yooooo hoo hoo!" Hayes said, in an exaggerated version of Fisher's laugh.

"Heeyoo *hoo*," Trevan jumped in.

Fish himself: "Heeeyeeeeuw hoo hoo HOO."

Soon we were all making noise, a ragged chorus of hysterical fake laughter. It was the best response to the inanity of the day's events, to our wasted efforts, to our absolute lack of control over decisions that could break our bodies and spirits, to the way we risked our lives for low pay and didn't see our families for half a year, to how we ached and were sick and exhausted, and for what? Someone chimed in with the Rowdy River hoot, "Woahhh-huh!" We jumped on that bandwagon, holding the *oh* of the "whoa" in an extended note, our voices blending into a lingering, howling wail of pent-up frustration. Twenty voices, as loud as we could scream, echoed off the steep canyon walls: the sound of powerlessness and rage.

Benjy's voice crackled over the radio. "Uh, what's goin' on down there?"

Fisher had to pull himself together before he keyed up the mic. "Nothing, Benjy," he coughed. "Boys are just blowin' off some steam."

"Copy," Benjy said, thick with sarcasm.

Must have been lonely at the top. It had become obvious to me by now that we "scrotes"—the poor, dirty, lower-class laborers—had the most fun. You thought you wanted to get out of that hole and sit in a truck, running the show from behind a radio, making that good (or better, anyway) money. But when you got there, I imagined, you were one step removed from the fraternity of shared suffering. Our suffering, as much as the humor by which we survived it, formed the bond that yoked us together for life.

Soon it was Sunday, day sixteen. The next day, seventeen, would be our last on the Slater. We descended a wide, sloping ridge through the black. Though the fire had backed down this draw, it had backed *hot*— the manzanita was crisped, each bush a charred sea anemone. Some of the trees remained green on top, but the smaller ones had fried to crumbly charcoal fingers. We threaded the burned landscape, technicolor characters moving through a black and white world.

That night, Luke and BJ were drinking. From my room in the barracks, I could hear them in the living room talking football and sore feet. The familiar sound of their voices was comforting. Then their tone shifted, taking on the bitterness of gossip. My ears perked up.

"Yeah, dude," Luke was saying. "I've never heard even one percent of this amount of bitching about overhead before. Not in six years."

"That's cause the overhead sucks. They're just, like, not even here," BJ said.

"Yeah. Salmon's checked out. You can tell he's done. I don't know what's going on with Benjy."

They continued, and I started to wish I couldn't hear them.

"Did you see Trevan and Ed today?" BJ said. "They were cutting somewhere that was, like, not even part of the black, and when we tried to tell them, they got all pissy."

Luke uttered a grunt, maybe assent. My heart began to thud. I didn't like BJ talking trash—that, and I'd witnessed the exchange in question, and I thought he was in the wrong. Who was he, anyway, the crew's judge and jury?

"What about that shit Kelly pulled with the flagging?" BJ said. We used flagging—rolls of non-sticky plastic tape that came in all kinds of colors, but mostly bright pink—to mark everything from proposed hand line to a hazard tree or the site of a yellowjacket hive.

"What was that? I wasn't there."

"She put a piece of flagging on like, a stick. In the ground. You could barely see it. It was so stupid."

"That's weird," Luke said, noncommittal.

"I don't know what she was doing. Like, nobody's gonna see that. So fuckin' dumb."

Now my heart was thundering in my chest. My face flushed. For a few minutes, I lay paralyzed with rage, trying to convince myself to ignore it and go to sleep. *He's not worth it, Kelly. Let it go.*

I couldn't do it. I peeled off the covers and threw open the door.

Luke had gone. BJ and Hayes sat on the couch against the far wall, watching TV. I hadn't even known Hayes was in the room—he'd remained silent. They glanced at me as I strode to the bathroom, shutting the door firmly. I peed, and as I washed my trembling hands, my face in the mirror looked pinched and pale.

Leaving the bathroom, I stopped short in front of the couch.

"Hey, I could hear you," I said, staring down BJ. "My room's right there."

"So?" He shrugged. He was out of it, eyelids droopy. Drunk.

"You're just talkin' shit on everybody, huh?" I said. "On the overhead, on Trevan and Eddie. On me. How do you think it feels to hear that?"

I don't know what I expected—contrition? An apology? I should have remembered who I was talking to.

"If Trevan and Ed knew what they were doing, I wouldn't have to talk shit. It's not *my* fault they suck," he drawled.

Hayes's face reddened. He was pinned to his seat, frozen, as if he wanted to flee but couldn't risk drawing attention to himself. He gazed intently at the stained carpet.

"They don't suck!" I said hotly. "Those are my friends."

"The crew sucks this year. It was so much better last year," BJ slurred.

It was hard not to take this personally, not to read between what seemed like very thin lines. What had changed between last year and this? There was a woman here now, for one.

"Dude, your *attitude* sucks," I said. "This is my first year on the crew, but there are a lot of great people here. And yeah, maybe I hung the flagging the wrong way. Sorry. But I was out there working hard. I'm trying."

He scoffed, head lolling to the side a little.

"Everybody's worn out right now, but they're trying," I said. "When you get down on everyone, it doesn't help."

"Yeah, well it doesn't help *me* when you can't do your fucking job," he snarled.

Enough. We didn't need to be friends.

"Go fuck yourself, BJ. You're such an asshole."

It wasn't the eloquent speech I might have summoned under better circumstances, and I capped it off with a childish exit. I stormed from the room, slamming my door behind me. The tears were there, waiting just behind my face. I threw myself on the bed and let them come.

Now I knew the truth. All the work I'd done was worthless. It hadn't proven anything. They hadn't *seen* me, and they still didn't think I could do this job. If they didn't think so by now, they never would. No matter how hard I tried, they would dismiss me as weak and incompetent. No matter how much weight I carried or how fiercely I dug line or how positive I stayed, no matter how kind or helpful, all I'd ever be to them was some stupid girl.

On the last day of the roll, I helped wash the buggies and stood with lips pressed, arms crossed, as the guys yelled, "Day one!" When the circle broke up, I was halfway to my truck. I'd never been so ready to go home.

The familiar road climbed into the forest. I passed the pullout where Keller had slept in the buggy early in the assignment. That cold morning seemed like years ago now. I came around a switchback and gasped.

The route I knew so well, which had been a dappled, shadowed, deep green forest, was gone. Every tree—not just one here or there, *every* tree—was burned to a blackened silhouette. Some retained their needles, but the fire racing through had flash fried them brown, all limbs pointing the way the flames had gone. Many were black sticks, black poles, black shapes without a hint of a leaf. The earth was gray, an endless realm of ash. Nothing had survived.

I pulled up alongside a Park Service law enforcement SUV. Luckily, they weren't from around here, and I still wore boots and greens, still smelled like fire. I flashed my Red Card and a tired smile, and he let me through the roadblock without question.

I drove slowly, both because this was a fire scar with snags—standing dead trees—on both sides, and because I was in shock. Just as it had been on the Oregon side of the Siskiyou Crest, so it was on the

California side—worse, in fact. Everything was torched. A moonscape. Mile upon mile upon mile of charred trees in a colorless world.

When I neared a familiar bend, I looked up, straining to see if any of them had survived: the Brewers or weeping spruce. Even a few, I thought, even one or two might be able to re-seed the species, an already-rare strand that had been in decline for the last thousand years . . . but no. The weeping spruce stand was obliterated, and I only knew the spot because even carbonized to bones, the Brewers' branches held their shape, the iconic shrug.

By the time I reached the overlook where the picnic table had stood, my hands were shaking. I pulled off, parked, and almost fell out of the truck. One hand instinctively flew to cover my mouth. No more picnic table, just a few hunks of charcoal. Beyond that, spread over rolling hills and in folded valleys for dozens of miles to the distant peaks of the Red Buttes Wilderness, there had been a rich green forest. Now, it was a valley of black. Everything, hundreds of thousands of acres of gorgeous ancient trees, Douglas firs, rare Western Red Cedar and ponderosa and sugar pine, white fir, red fir, and the sparkling turquoise forks of Indian Creek and all the riotous green brush that had clustered there, the ermine-carpeted slopes rising to Slater Butte—gone. Torched. The fire had raced up this canyon at sixty miles per hour, I knew that. But I'd never seen anything like it. The mass incineration of an ecosystem.

Standing in this spot two years earlier, Jeff had said to us, "Welcome to your office. Sucks, doesn't it?"

My office had burned down. But it had become, in those years, so much more than an office. It was my home. I stood at the overlook and wept, harsh chills coursing over my skin. The destruction was real now, seeing it up close, and I knew in my gut with certainty: half of the town may have remained standing, but Happy Camp would never be the same.

Driving into the valley, following the artery of Indian Creek, I passed dozens of burned homes. They never looked like you'd expect, like the soft mound of ashes left in a fireplace. Instead, the buildings collapsed on themselves, charred but not obliterated, remnants of pipe and frame poking from the rubble. A stove stood in a pile of blackened slabs; a flame-scarred washing machine lay tipped on its side, and a brick fireplace stood guard over a chaotic mound of char. Tears blurred my vision. Where I knew a neighborhood had once stood, there lay nothing but piles of wreckage. These were my *friends'* homes. My stomach turned sour.

I stopped in the Kingfisher market, where a lady was ranting to two contract firefighters in the dog food aisle.

"We've lost everything," she said. "And the Forest Service doesn't care."

My mouth opened behind my mask (thank god I wasn't wearing the new one with the FS logo). I wanted to say, *Yes we do* and *How dare you*, but I stopped myself. You couldn't make people understand. There was no way to make her see the twenty-four-hour shifts, the Hail Mary burns around houses, and how we ached for what we couldn't save. What we gave of ourselves, trying to help people like her. The Forest Service didn't care?

I am a shell of a person, I wanted to scream. *Because of how much I care.*

Yeah, no good. I grabbed some snacks and left.

At home, the dogs ran to the gate, and I almost wept again, I was so happy to see them. "Babies!" I cried and let them jump all over me, rubbing each behind the ears.

Josh wasn't home yet. I was relieved; I needed a minute. Between the fire and the burned houses, the roll we'd just been on, and the fight with BJ, I was a wreck. I hauled my PG bag into the house and dropped it on the floor. Then, pulling off my greens and crew shirt and leaving them on the laundry room floor, I found shorts and a T-shirt, grabbed a White Claw, and went to sit in an Adirondack chair overlooking the river.

The dogs crowded around me, jostling to be closest. I cracked the seltzer and let the cold bubbly liquid caress my throat. I gazed across the river at Titus Ridge, which hadn't burned—not ever, that I could see. It was the gorgeous, untouched green that all of Indian Creek had been. But it was thick, too—overgrown. And instead of thinking how grateful I was for the forest that remained, I thought, *How long? How long before this burns, too?*

My phone rang, startling me from morbid reverie. It was Fisher. "Hey dude."

"Hey!" he yelled, clearly a bit tuned up, as he usually was within the first hour of R&R. "Are you okay?"

"Yeah, I'm alright. Just got home."

"Hayes told me about what happened last night with BJ. What he said to you."

"Oh. Uh, yeah." I wasn't sure what to say.

"Listen. From what I'm hearing, he was totally out of line."

"Yeah. It was . . . not that nice."

"Don't you listen to that bullshit, Ramsey. You hear me? You're doing *great*. You're a hard worker. I see it, Salomon sees it, everybody sees it. You're always grinding, always carrying that heavy shit. You're my fuckin' pack mule, Ramsey. Anybody who doesn't see that is a moron. Okay?"

"Okay. Sorry. Sorry I'm crying."

"Oh, that's okay. Jenny cries all the time; I'm used to it."

"Thanks, Fish," I whispered.

"I just want you to know I've got your back. So does Hayes." Hayes gave a whoop of confirmation in the background. "Don't you worry about this for one minute."

I thanked him again, and he said "Later" and was gone, off to get tanked and ride skateboards down dark suburban streets. I sat staring at the smoke-filled sky, at the ridge, at our yard and the river and the green quiet that lay beyond the wreckage of fire. It was as if the world slowly rotated and dropped into a slot.

That night before getting in the shower, I stood naked before the bathroom mirror and took an inventory. Dirt and ash stiffened my hair and made it sticky to the touch. Black gunk lined my ears, tarlike boogers clogged my nose, and dirt (or ash, or both) filled in the wrinkles beside my eyes, my smile lines, the hollow of my neck.

The skin just in front of my armpits was raw and chafed from the repetitive motion of swinging a tool. A sharp line marked the place where the rolled sleeves of my yellow ended; beyond that, my forearms were sun-browned and fire-blackened. Beneath a crust of charcoal, my palms and fingers bore thick callouses, a rough yellow husk. My fingernails were outlined in black, ditto my fingerprints. Most of my hand was etched with onyx lines, a topographical map.

My breasts, waist, and stomach, which never saw the light of day under a liner tank and my thick yellow Nomex, looked pale—and thin. How much weight had I lost? It looked like fifteen, twenty pounds. My arms were roped and lean, my belly a hollow panel. Almost invisible beneath an overgrown mound of pubic hair was my vagina, a mostly forgotten entity that occasionally plagued me with blood, yeast infections, or mysterious smelly discharges. Another line denoted the end of my boy shorts and the beginning of dirt and black that covered my legs like filthy stockings. My legs, however . . . wow. I flexed my quads and turned from side to side, admiring.

My feet looked as if they'd been tortured for information: blistered and callused and shedding skin in layers like white lace. The toenails were filthy, ash-rimmed, maybe yellowing . . . was that a fungus? I'd worry about it later.

Everything hurt: temples throbbed, arms were stiff and aching, rib-cage scarred from poison oak I'd scratched 'til I drew pus and blood, back in knots, legs bruised and sore, feet that whined and twinged and sometimes went entirely numb.

When I stepped into the water, days of filth would slide off me in sheets and rivulets of black, filling the shower with an inky pool, gray water spiraling the drain for long minutes before it ran clear. It was always a shock to think that all of that had been *on* me, and it made me wonder what had accrued inside my lungs, my veins.

I was a mess. I was a machine. I had the thighs of a champion racehorse.

I'd never been more proud.

Three days later, we were back in Baudelaire. Though October had arrived, megafires continued to burn across California. The resource order was coming, and we even suspected the fire, but dispatch hadn't sent the official order, so we had a couple hours to kill. The morning dawned clear and cool, golden light bathing the ridge above town. The nice thing about late season was that you could PT *alone*. No more races, no grueling circuits. I tied my running shoes quickly, hoping nobody would try to join me.

"Take a radio," Mac called as I trotted away, and I held up my phone.

Alone, I could put on a favorite playlist, keep my own pace, tune out. I ran, taking Baudelaire Flat Road over the bridge. I turned onto a dirt lane past a power plant where, just before the Forks, a trail branched off, climbing a hill and following a bluff above the North Fork of the Rowdy River. The trail emerged in a quiet neighborhood with a Little

Free Library on one corner, a cul-de-sac where old hippies tended their gardens and hung their prayer flags. The street dead-ended in another trail, which crossed a creek and pummeled into a wild, roadless area.

I jogged the trail to the confluence of the creek and the river, rock-hopping boulders to the water. There I knelt, splashing my face. The river was cold, so clear you could see straight to the bottom, and that blue-green color for which no adequate word exists—tropical blue, aquamarine? The shall-we-say turquoise water rippled in a light wind. Cliffs rose on either side, their sheer faces stippled with scrappy, wind-warped trees. This was my favorite place in the forest, and I let out a sigh of relief, water dripping from my chin.

R&R had passed quickly, and I was grateful, because things had been a little strained. Each time I went home after a fire, Josh felt more and more like a stranger. The first night, I was shy and awkward kissing him, like, *Wait, who are you again?* His lips felt foreign on mine, which were chapped and chafed from weeks of sun and fire. He ran a thumb over the calluses on my palms, and I had an impulse to pull my hands away. *Those are mine.*

So much time had passed. The fifteen, or in this case eighteen, days apart felt expansive, glacial. Even when I tried to tell the stories, there was too much; I could never convey what the experience *felt* like. The disconnection was probably more than a little bit my fault, since I hardly talked to him while I was gone—but then again, he didn't talk to me much, either; didn't ask for more. Our lives diverged for two or three weeks at a time, and in just two days we were supposed to patch them together again? I was too tired for that kind of work.

By the second day, the discomfort faded, and we lay in the bathtub together laughing over stupid stuff the Division had done—both of our Divisions, on opposite flanks of the same fire. I began to remember Josh, to warm to his sudden laugh and eager way of telling a story. That's right: I liked him. I had just . . . forgotten him, a little.

He played me a video of the engagement ring he was having made. The jeweler's hand turned it under a light, and the stone sparkled.

"Don't show me that! It's supposed to be a surprise."

"I just want to make sure you like it," he protested.

"I love it."

The ring was gorgeous, but the gesture was like Josh himself: sincere and so sweet, but a little bit lacking in . . . subtlety? The element of surprise?

There wasn't a lot of magic, but we were two nice people who could raise children together. That was fine, right?

I ran back to the station, legs moving under me automatically. By the end of the season, an eight-minute mile was no big deal, my new easy pace. That's no speed record for "real" runners, but for me it was a sign of significant improvement. I was, like, almost a really fit person now.

As I jogged back into the parking lot, headed to the engine building to change, I saw a group of men bullshitting outside the bay, including BJ. I knew I had to make peace with him. Problem was, I didn't want to. I still believed that he was at fault, and *he* should extend the olive branch to *me*. But I doubted he would, and we had to work together for two more weeks. So I prepared myself to swallow my pride.

When I came out of the bathroom, everyone was in motion, carrying cases of water and MREs, moving tools, piling things into the trucks, and cinching down ratchet straps.

"Tenemos el orden?" I asked Miguel.

"Sí claro," he said. "Vámonos, otra vez."

Here we go. Again.

We had the resource order. We were headed to the August Complex, the biggest wildfire in California history. A merger of thirty-eight individual fires ignited by lightning in the Mendocino National Forest, it now pushed toward the Trinity Alps in the north (inland of Eureka on the Humboldt Coast) while ranging south of the Yuki Wilderness, over a hundred miles away. The blaze had already taken a firefighter's life—vehicle accident—in September.

The talk of the internet was that the August Complex would hit a million acres within the week. On the map, the behemoth blob—fatter at the ends, narrower in the middle, like a badly rendered barbell—was broken into halves, then zones, some managed by federal teams, some by Cal Fire. Driving from one side to the other could take upward of five hours. Assigned to the fire were 65 hand crews, 353 engines, and 31 helicopters, for a total of over four thousand firefighters—close to 20 percent of the national wildland fire workforce.

It felt like destiny. We were always going to end up on that fire, a blaze that had been burning for almost two months, waiting patiently to draw us into its ever-expanding orbit. This was our final assignment of the season—one last roll on the craziest incident the Golden State had ever seen.

The arrival of California's first gigafire was the end of an era and the beginning of the unknown. There now seemed to be no limit to the scale of catastrophe the West might endure.

When a bad fire happens, it's natural to assign blame. This is especially true when the source of ignition is, say, fireworks from a gender reveal party or sparks from a careless campfire. To be sure, people (and, ahem, utility companies) should be held accountable for negligence. But the causes of our worst fires go much deeper.

In the nineteenth century, Europeans began to settle the Western United States, displacing Indigenous people. And while Mediterranean Europe—Spain, Greece, Portugal—saw regular fire, these colonists largely hailed from Northern Europe, a wet, foggy place with no naturally-occurring wildfire.

So when the settlers saw Indigenous people burning the land, they were horrorstruck—first, because they didn't understand fire, and second, because they assumed Native people burned out of "savagery" rather than a sophisticated system of land management. So, as they continued the continental conquest begun in the 1600s, the settlers murdered and drove out many western tribes, covered the land with cattle, and ended the practice of burning on purpose.

"Like most peoples, those of temperate Europe took themselves and their landscape as normative," historian Stephen J. Pyne writes in *The Pyrocene*. "Unlike most peoples, temperate Europeans were in a position to influence fire's history across the globe."

With the cessation of good fire, brush and forests thickened.

Then, following the Great Fire of 1910, which burned three million acres in Idaho and Montana, the federal government set out to eradicate wildfire through "full suppression"—a policy designed not only to protect citizens and property but to benefit the logging industry. Blazes were to be extinguished by any means necessary, and they created the "10 a.m. rule," which stipulated that new starts ignited one day should be put out by ten o'clock the next morning.

So fire was made the enemy for over a hundred years. As a consequence, U.S. forests became unnaturally overgrown. Meanwhile, the population exploded, pushing housing close to the woods and driving up global temperatures.

Cut to today. Dense forests are primed to burn hotter and faster than ever before. We live close to the trees, in homes built of flammable materials. We've screwed ourselves. As Pyne puts it, "The more we try to remove fire from places that have coevolved with it, the more violently fire will return."

Though nature has no intention here, no malice, it's sometimes hard not to believe what a firefighter told me as we gazed at a badly scorched forest. He shrugged, accepting the loss completely. "Nature bats last."

To get the engine going, Fisher had to turn the key and jam on the gas while somebody lay under the buggy and banged the starter with a hammer. Fisher floored it, Bao's boots stuck out from under the cab, and *Clang! Clang!*—the buggy sputtered to life. We cheered, hit the interstate, and headed south.

After dark, we pulled into the lot of a Super 8 near Red Bluff, California. My period had begun on the drive; I'd felt the spontaneous gush into my underwear, knowing they'd be soaked with blood and praying it didn't seep through my pants, where it would remain as a smelly brown crust for the duration of the assignment. Perfect. I'd woken at 0430 that morning to drive to the station. A headache gripped my temples.

Still, as we pulled our hotel bags out of the overhead bins and people hopped out, gathering on a triangle of grass to wait for key cards, I saw that BJ and I were the last two in the aisle of the buggy.

"Hey BJ," I said, and he turned, apprehensive. "I want to apologize."

His body softened. "That wasn't a good scene the other night," I went on. "I know it was late, and we were both over that roll and super tired. But I shouldn't have said what I said. I'm sorry."

"Me too," he said quickly. "I don't want to be that guy who's angry all the time."

Surprised, I said, "I don't think you're that guy."

He smiled, almost shyly.

"Can we put this behind us?" I asked.

"Yeah. Definitely."

He gave me a smile I remembered from first meeting him, when I thought he was a sweet angel with perfect teeth. He looked young, all of a sudden, and for a moment I saw into him, knowing some of his past: a boy who'd been caught between worlds, who'd lost his mother too soon. He had every reason to be angry.

How many times would I have to learn? Your nemeses are never villains. They're just people—aching to be loved, trying to prove they're good enough, hoping to make up for something that was broken long ago.

He bothered me, then, because we were so much alike.

Chapter 10

The Green Eyebrow

The orchards flew by in the half-dark of dawn, fruit stands and pumpkin patches denoting an autumn that hadn't arrived. California remained stifling, shrouded in smoke. We knew only two seasons now: "fire" and "off."

I asked to pee and heard Salomon grumbling, probably that it hadn't even been two hours yet and if we stopped this often we'd never get to the damn fire. But my tampon was leaking, I couldn't afford to be polite. Fish pulled over and I scrambled down a grassy embankment, squatting behind a scroungy bush and hoping the guys wouldn't peer over the road's edge. While I emptied my bladder, blood dripped between my boots. As my friend Emily would say, "Le sigh."

At last, we entered the fire. You could tell we'd arrived by the flagged entrances to forest roads, white signs with drop point numbers written in Sharpie, the engines and water tenders staged at every pullout . . . and the thick, yellowish smoke. The black appeared on our left.

Cows stood on the crisp, burned-over grass. I was wondering how these innocuous, lost-looking creatures had survived when the fire raced through here. And where would they find food and water? Even the streams were clogged with ash and blocked by burned and fallen trees.

"One hoof in the black," Luke joked, a play on the firefighting safety rule to keep "one foot in the black" at all times. The reference book we kept in our pockets, the IRPG, featured the "10's and 18's" on its back cover: the 10 Standard Firefighting Orders and the 18 Watch Out Situations. All firefighters were meant to have them memorized, and we mostly did.

"It would be*hoove* you to get some eyes on it," Eddie quipped.

"Jesus," Luke groaned.

"Oh, so you can make a pun and I can't?"

"That's right."

"I heard," Fisher said, "that there were piles of animal bodies in the roads on this fire, right after it came through. Cows, dogs, deer, everything. Just piles of 'em."

"Stop," I said.

"I'm just saying what happened."

"Please don't."

We arrived at a drop point where we were told to wait while Van got some intel. A few of the boys filed down the aisle and stood outside to piss and spit and talk.

"Apple core," Trevan said.

Here's how the game went: when you finished eating an apple, you said, "Apple core." Then, it was a race to see who could say "Baltimore" first. Whoever did, earned the right to name the target.

"Buh—"

"Baltimore!" I managed to be first, which never happened.

"Who's your best friend?" Trevan asked.

My eyes roved through the buggy, deciding who I most wanted to see hit with a wet, sticky object. Depending on the thrower's arm, the impact could hurt. I saw him standing outside, leaning against the truck giggling with Scotty. Oblivious.

"Eddie."

At this point, the person with the apple core throws it at whoever you've named. Trevan launched it out the back door, hard. The apple beaned Eddie in the side of the head, and he stumbled sideways, gripping his skull.

"Ouch! Damn," he cried. "What the fuck, Trevan!"

"Not my fault, I'm just the messenger." Trevan shrugged.

Ed leaned into the buggy and looked around, scanning our faces suspiciously. Then he gave me a smile.

"Was it you, Kelly? Am I your best friend?"

"No," I lied. He tilted his head and gave me a knowing look. "Okay, yeah."

"Load up!" Salomon commanded, and we were off.

On October 6, day four, the August reached "gigafire" status: 1,004,373 acres. The fire's size now exceeded that of the state of Rhode Island. We moved to Division Bravo, where we began to burn midmorning and went full throttle for fifteen hours, 'til after one a.m.

Benjy was burn boss, I lit off the road's edge, and Wink and BJ were lighting interior. I could see Wink on the cutbank above me, then tripping along twenty feet deep in the trees, and I kept well behind him.

Our burn got hot, with the trademark howl of a dozen trees torching at once. I saw a chipmunk run back into the flames and yelled, *No, not that way!* Tears gathered in the corners of my eyes, and Benjy said, "You can't cry for every squirrel, Kelly," and I said, "It was a chipmunk."

BJ was in deeper, speeding through four-foot reprod—that's "reproduction," a stand of trees planted by Forest Service silviculture teams to replace harvested timber, notable for its uniform height and spacing in neat rows, like a Christmas tree farm. "Pines in Lines," as people sometimes joked, reflected the FS's place within the Department of Agriculture. Forest management had "harvest" baked in from the start: it's an agricultural model, for better or worse.

Say what you will (what *I* would) about him, but BJ was great at burning, perhaps because he gave zero fucks and never hesitated to put down plenty of fire. I gave all the fucks, overthought everything, wept for woodland creatures. Story of my life.

For hours, we were blessed with favorable winds. Even with so much torching, the smoke lifted and pulled away from us, into the burn and toward the main fire. We burned for miles with everything pulling in like it should.

We shifted lighters, and darkness fell as Bao and I dripped fire in parallel lines, working our way toward Benjy. Just as we tied into Benjy's group, however, the wind flopped. Bao and I turned to see the smoke bending back over the road. Embers flowed over the green, raining orange sparks exactly where we didn't want them.

"That's not good," Bao said.

"Nope."

"You know what to do," Benjy told us.

We did. We turned and headed into the smoke, peeling off into the green. We began to grid the unburned forest, looking for spot fires. Haines joined us. The darkness made walking a little perilous, but heavy night was helpful, because a spot would show up as an obvious flicker in the shadows. We spread out and crossed the green until we hit a dirt road, then turned to make another pass. I glanced to my left and caught the tiniest glimmer of orange.

"Hey guys. Is that a spot?"

Bao called for bodies on the radio as Haines and I began to scrape and throw dirt on the small fire, putting in a scratch line around it. This could've been bad: an ember had lodged in a dry stump, which had taken fire and grown to a ten-by-ten blaze within minutes—could've started a whole new fire.

Soon a few engine folks and more of our people showed up to help. We handed the operation over and returned to gridding.

"Good eye," Haines said, giving me a nod as we set off into the woods. I blushed.

Half an hour later, I found another spot fire. And an hour after that, as Bao and I strolled through an area between two segments of the burn, what Van had to my great amusement been calling "the green eyebrow," I found a third one.

Bao called in an engine to help us with the second spot, and while he served as ad-hoc commander of the mini-incident, I lined out a couple engine folks and led them in digging around it. I watched them swing their tools, taking very little dirt (not their fault—they were from some desert town and hardly ever put in hand line, whereas we had spent months doing this). I realized, with something like pride, that I could dig now.

I'd looked just like them in May, I was sure. But now, after months of digging, hundreds of hours of swinging a tool, I finally moved more like the seasoned hotshots I'd been emulating, swinging savagely, dirt flying. I sliced roots clean through in a single swing.

Hot damn. I had improved.

I stood on the edge of the green eyebrow waiting for Bao. The column remained bent over the road, but the particles, cooler now, lifted high into the atmosphere. Smoke flowed across the dark sky like a river winding through the stars. Bao returned, stood beside me, and looked up.

"Looks like a river," he said.

"Right?"

We stood quietly, watching the sky. I could hear an engine nearby, pumping water to one of the spot fires. Farther away, the main fire continued to torch with a faint roar. But where we stood, the night was almost peaceful.

I glanced at Bao's straight-nosed, handsome profile. He was often a bit lazy, always joking and fucking with everyone, but I'd seen a new side of him that night. He'd been sure and decisive. He was smart, experienced, capable—all qualities he took great pains to conceal. I wondered why.

"Nice work tonight, Boomer," he said.

"You too, Bao."

By the time we returned to our sleep spot, it was almost two in the morning, and I really, *really* needed to shit; I'd been holding it in for hours. But we were sleeping in an open field, and there was nowhere to go—no tree cover, nary a bush, no blue rooms nearby. At this moment, I would almost have welcomed the dreaded "blue kiss," the disaster of pooping in a freshly cleaned porta-potty and having the biocide liquid splash back on your undercarriage. But no luck. I would have to wait until morning.

Oh well. I spread out my tarp, blew up my Therm-A-Rest, and shook out my sleeping bag, peeling off boots and greens and tugging on long underwear. When I went to clean myself up with baby wipes, I found a little smudge of something in my undies. Yep. At some point in the course of the evening, I had low-key shit my pants.

That was about right. The minute you started to feel good, to think you might be getting competent at this whole hotshot thing, you found poop in your drawers.

Too tired to care, I gave my crack a couple good swipes with a wet wipe and pulled on clean underwear. I lay back, watching the wide black sky, eyes growing heavy.

Just before I lost consciousness, I wondered what my younger self would think of the person I had become, this filthy pirate bedding down in a field. I wasn't sure she'd care about how fast I could climb a hill, but I thought she'd be glad to see that I made it to California—that in some of the ways that mattered, I had finally gotten free.

My twenties were hell. The new burdens of becoming an adult were hard enough, but at the same time, my family collapsed, and fallout from the implosion blackened everything in sight.

Or was *I* the implosion?

My dad was drinking, sure, more and more. But he was far away in the Midwest. Back home, my mom fell in love, had a rough breakup, and sank into a depression, which I noted with concern at Christmas. But out of sight, out of mind. I had my own life at college to worry about.

In Virginia, I found poetry and art and the weirdos who made both, defying the preppy culture of the Southern college, which referred to itself pretentiously as the University. I collected typewriters, went to indie rock shows in basement clubs. My friends and I drank coffee milkshakes at the Blue Moon Diner, snuck into an apple orchard in the mountains, explored the steam tunnels beneath campus.

In the spring of my first year, I met William in a poetry workshop. He was handsome, played rugby, and minored in Esperanto, which seemed exotic. After an evening I'm sure he considered a one-night stand, I fastened myself to him like a barnacle. He was perfect. It was meant to be. I had *manifested* him. My "love" for this boy I barely knew was so intense, it hollowed my belly. A place in my chest that I mistook for my heart felt wet and heavy. I called him more often than any reasonable person should.

William, who had the sense to spot a psychopath, backpedaled and gently dropped me.

You're amazing, but—

There's nothing wrong with you, but . . .

I don't blame him. There *was* something wrong with me, an aching wound that howled with need. William was only the first in a series of men I chased in a now-all-too-obvious effort to replace my absent, slowly disintegrating father. If the most important man in my life wouldn't look at me, then I'd damn well make sure the rest of them would.

There was the Texan in the ten-gallon hat to whom I gave blow jobs in the bathroom at parties. The math major in the hippie fraternity (famous for removing my tampon with his teeth for some sloshy period sex). The actor with Billy Joel eyes, and the poet who was great at eating me out. The dropout from Chapel Hill who moved into my dorm room and spent his days gulping Carlo Rossi and listening to Brian Eno records. The bartender. The painter.

This tangle of conquests and fucking and falling in love happened so fast, my friends lost track of who I was with, and I lost count of how many morning-after pills the pharmacist slid into my sweaty hands.

Most of them were alcoholics, pot heads, or both. Still, it was fun, if a little dark. I loved sex, and if being a slut hadn't been wildly taboo at the time, I would've openly reveled in it. Secretly, I did. I liked the thrill of attracting almost whoever I wanted, and men themselves were an endless fascination. I loved their largeness, deep voices, scratchy chins. I liked learning their secrets and fears, knowing them better than anyone, being the *closest*, like a creature burrowed under their skin. I was a connoisseur, a collector. I tasted and watched and memorized men like other people studied wine, particle physics, or great books. I studied literature, too. But romance received the greater share of my attention.

"Getting" men to love me was an addiction, the ultimate high. In a life where I had often felt helpless, the magnetism I cultivated seemed like a kind of power. Yet it never occurred to me that men's interest wasn't something I *made* happen, a trick. I never once thought they might have loved me for who I was.

Chapter 11

One of Us

Day ten on the August Complex, I was reading Donald Miller's *A Million Miles in a Thousand Years* as the buggy lurched over the broken road. "I think life is staggering," Miller wrote. "And we're just used to it."

Miller was right about regular workaday life, I supposed. But not about fire. It was staggering—every single instant—and it never let you forget. Every day I had my mind blown. Every day I could have wept.

Hearing that Beckwourth Hotshots were coming to the fire, I had talked to my friend Paige on the phone the night before, seeing if we would cross paths. It was deeply comforting to hear that we shared the same mixture of feelings—something like "victorious" and "broken"— as we each neared the end of our rookie year. I thought about the time I'd seen her on the Hog fire, and we had hugged ferociously, no need for words. *You're not alone out here.*

I jumped out the back—"Hopping out!"—and directed the buggy into a wide spot by a shingled vault toilet, quaint as a cabin in the shire. Up here, the trees were enormous, and they bent softly in a gentle wind. The thin air was cool, almost sharp, and laced with birdsong. The peaceful, shaded, old growth feeling of high elevation.

The other guys weren't back from their scouting mission. As we waited, I opened up a book called *The Klamath Knot*, widely considered the Bible of NorCal ecological history and geology. A map in the front showed the region: the mountains of Southern Oregon and the Rogue River; the Klamath; Mount Shasta and the Trinity River and the Coast, the Coast Range; Mount Lassen; and near the bottom, the very spot where we sat, indicated by a few squiggles and the words "Yolla Bolly Mountains."

We had been all over that map this summer. I could remember fires in every part of this region, and that felt pretty exciting. I had never known a place like I now knew this one—not its highways and highlights, but its secret corners and wild outposts and remote trailheads, parts of the woods that in some cases no human being had seen in years.

The guys emerged from the trailhead drenched in sweat. They had hiked ten miles all up and down the wilderness scouting a proposed assignment that probably wouldn't happen. Eddie, tired to the point of despondency, muttered that his knees hurt. We tossed them Gatorades and hit the road.

On day eleven, after breakfast, I approached Fisher.

"Hey," I said. "If there's something to do, like some scouting or whatever, can you take me? I wanna hike."

"Sure, Ramsey. But there might not be anything."

"Yeah, but if there is."

"Okay. Sure." He looked faintly amused.

We had driven into the black and parked at the intersection of three forest roads. Fisher and Salomon went to conference with Van, and I hopped out to pee. I had to walk a long way because everything was so burned—every tree a charred matchstick, every thicket of brush stripped to limbs—I had no cover to squat, so I walked around a couple bends out of sight.

When I got back, Fisher was putting his line gear on the UTV. Behind the buggy, Trevan was gearing up.

"What's happening?" I asked Trevan.

"Me and Fish are gonna go on a hike."

"Are you serious?" I stepped into the road and shouted to Fisher across the wide gravel bench, "HEY! So I VOLUNTEER to come with you, and you pick someone ELSE?"

"You weren't HERE!" he yelled back.

"I had to pee, fuck you! I VOLUNTEERED!"

I was kind of kidding, but mostly dead serious. Fisher looked stunned. I barely recognized myself. Somehow, I had gone from a polite, pretty, "nice" girl to this: an unfiltered, aggressive creature, ready to scrap and fight and curse people out to get where I wanted to go.

"You're like, a dude now," Benjy had said a couple days earlier. *No, no way*, I'd thought, laughing. Now I wondered.

I was sulking in my seat when Fisher popped his head in the buggy door.

"Well, Ramsey, what are you waiting for? Gear up."

"Yes!" I said, hurrying to grab my pack. "Thank you!"

Of course, as soon as we started hiking, I regretted everything.

We had to go way down into the drainage, then out again. Downhill, up again. Scurry up a vertical slope. Climb hand-and-toe across a rock face. Every time we climbed, I fell behind, and Fisher hollered, "Ramsey, come on!"

I cursed myself, cursed my companions for being tall (six foot three or four, in Fisher's case), and cursed the world for being made of hills. Still, it was better than sitting in the buggy watching the back of Keller's neck, the way he tugged the pale hair at the base of his cap to make it curl upward. So I supposed I had gotten what I wanted: we went hiking.

On day thirteen, we left the line at 1800 hours for a new camp. The sun was beginning to set over valleys full of intermittent smokes. We drove past understory fire that looked peaceful and romantic in the golden light of the gloaming. I was listening to Neil Young's "Heart of Gold" on headphones.

The muted light felt like fall. I looked around the buggy. Trevan drummed his armrest. Eddie ran a hand through his dark, greasy hair, which was starting to get long. Luke was listening to a podcast and staring out the window while BJ rapped under his breath. Keller was sleeping, Bao eating. My fondness for them was a sudden flare, that last blinding wink the sun gives off before it drops below the horizon.

I want to live, I want to give. I've been a miner for a heart of gold.

We arrived at the so-called spike camp, a satellite fire camp serving a remote flank of the fire, and while it lacked command tents, we saw catering, showers, dumpsters, and a fuel tender. Barrel and I hopped out to empty the trash for the last time—one from Alpha, one from Bravo. The bags we carried through the lot represented the culmination of a summer spent in constant concern for trash. We'd never be rookies again. We drew our arms back and sent the bags flying high, sailing into the dumpster and landing with a gentle whoosh. We bumped fists.

"Trash done been taken," Barrel said.

"Heck yeah, it has."

We slept in a meadow near a dry creek. I lay under the stars and thought, *This is our last night out here.* My eyes welled up—with grief, with gratitude, and with another feeling that was hard to pin down, one that arose from the knowledge that I was not the same person who'd shown up at the station in May. I tried to hold my eyes open a little longer, to drink in the warm night air and the winking stars.

Endings have always been hard for me.

*   *   *

As the end of college approached, I didn't know what to do. Get a big-girl job, move to a big city? The problem was, I liked my small-town life as it was; I didn't feel ready to move on.

So a few months after graduation, to everyone's (and most of all my) great surprise, I got married. It was so dumb; I did it, unconsciously, half to dodge my mom and drive a wedge in a relationship that had always felt too close, half to avoid moving to Brooklyn with my best friends because I was scared, and half to appease my boyfriend, Matthew, who kept saying, *If you really love me, prove it.* Yes, there were three halves to the ill-considered decision to wed. That's how unbalanced it was.

I married him spontaneously on a weekday afternoon in the Sheriff's office. Then we stood on the courthouse steps in the sun, and I thought, *Whoopsie.*

Shortly after that, my dad left my stepmom. He and Renee had gone out to dinner—steak, red wine—and when they got home, he turned to her and said, "I'm leaving."

"Are you going to get cigarettes?" Renee asked.

He didn't answer. He grabbed a pair of underwear from a drawer. Then he took her by the shoulders, moved her aside, and left the house. Renee assumed he had gone to the gas station for cigs—until he never came back.

After eighteen years of marriage, my dad left her with a mortgage and four teenagers because he'd found another woman, some "trashy skank" (my sister's words) named Tiffany—though Renee didn't learn any of that for weeks.

My stepmom called to say her life was over. She sounded disoriented, and I heard that she had followed my dad down a rural Wisconsin road and sprawled on the hood of his truck, attempting to stop him with the body that had birthed and nursed four children and slept with him and watched him drink for so many, many years.

Please don't do this, she begged, and he said, *Get off my fucking truck.*

But no—that "dirt road" scene never happened. That was a story my dad told when he called to announce that he was finally free; years later, I would find out that he had made it up. He cast Renee in the role previously played by my mother: a nag, a ball and chain, a woman who had tried to possess him, body and spirit. *Nobody owns me!* It didn't sound like Renee, a woman I knew to be tolerant and easygoing.

Still, I told my dad I was happy for him, thinking it was better for the family to be rid of him. I was mistaken. Never having had a paternal presence, I didn't understand how the departure of even a half-hearted father would affect my siblings. Madeleine, who was barely thirteen, would feel it most of all.

My marriage was shaky from the start. I hardly blame Matthew, even if he was jealous, prone to anger, and frequently stoned—I was one foot out the door, a girl who never meant to wed before thirty, if at all. He sensed that I was poised to flee, which only deepened his suspicion, bordering on conviction, that I was unfaithful.

We fought like cats. I was angry, too; one time I got so mad I kicked the bathroom door and the hollow, cheap plywood caved in, the crater lasting evidence of how *I* was hot-tempered and out of line, not him. The longer I stayed with him, the more violent my heart became.

Finally, we made the last-ditch effort of desperate couples everywhere: we planned a trip. We had managed to save about ten thousand dollars, so we put our stuff in storage and took off across the country in the '90s Volvo station wagon my dad had paid for—that era was booming for contractors, tax evasion helped his bottom line, and he was giving all the other kids guilt-money, so I'd decided I might as well cash in too. Dad was always generous, sometimes to a fault; when he had money, he'd give it away like it was going out of style. He always seemed baffled later, when the accounts came up empty.

Though the road trip was three months long, my memories are scant: Camping in the Badlands of North Dakota, where a herd of two hundred bison passed through the campground. Lying curled in the fetal position in a hotel bathtub in Reno, Nevada, my whole pelvis on fire with a urinary tract infection that had crept into my kidneys. Feeling out of place at a Hollywood party with Matthew's sister, a Hollywood person. Seeing my family in Wisconsin—weeks with them, both as we headed west and when we came back again.

In hindsight, I was trying to be there for my siblings in a moment of loss. I had the old impulse to protect them, though by now it was far too late. I had sworn to save this family, but instead I'd avoided them.

My dad had bought himself a lake house. It was beautiful and unfinished, as the homes of contractors always are. A wall of sliding glass doors led to the porch, which overlooked Lake Butte de Morts, eight thousand acres of shallow fresh water between Oshkosh and Winneconne, Wisconsin. Though he'd been there a while, there was little in the house, as if he'd just moved in. A bed, a lamp. Through the glass, the blue water sparkled. On the deck, several tomato plants grew in tangles in terra cotta pots. My dad on his own: A gardener?

"Lemme show ya what I'm doin' upstairs," he said. "Watch your heads."

The second story was stripped down to base flooring and studs. Light poured through the spaces between the two-by-fours, the barest suggestion of future walls. The lake lay like a blue ocean beyond the windows.

"I'm gonna make this into a bedroom for Tiffany's son, Joey," my dad said.

My face went red, and my stomach twisted. Though I was out of college now, a married woman (which sounded so weird, as I felt neither truly married nor anything more than a girl), I resented this little boy as hotly as if I were eight years old. Not even *related to us*, and he gets a floor to himself, in a *lake house*? *Fuck you, Joey.*

We left before my father started his fourth drink. "We'll see you tomorrow for dinner, Daddy."

"Okay, sweet daughter of mine." He grinned, leaning through the cloud of smoke to kiss my cheek.

Back at Renee's house, my sister had become a marijuana dealer. We waited in her SUV at a gas station as she passed a baggie to a stranger.

"Can you not do this while we're in the car?" I asked. Weed was still illegal and highly criminalized in Wisconsin.

"You need to take it easy," Matthew said. "You're gonna get yourself arrested."

"Your husband's a dick," Courtney said.

He could be a dick, but he wasn't wrong. She was arrested within the year.

While Courtney had her new "career," my brother Steve responded to the divorce (as he did to anything difficult) with anger, most of which he redirected into winning power lifting competitions. He wasn't around much, either, and when he and Courtney were home, they stayed in the garage with friends, drinking or getting high.

There was no one to stop them. Renee was in mourning, eyes vacant, blond hair brittle and unkempt. And she was trying to support the family—on her own, suddenly—and finish graduate school for nursing while working part-time at the free clinic. Her children's need swirled around the eye of her exhaustion and grief.

This left Evan and Madeleine, at fourteen and thirteen, largely to their own devices. I took Mad to the mall while Matthew shot hoops with my brother. Evan and I ate big bowls of cereal late at night, our quiet unison crunching a desperate kind of intimacy.

One night, Matthew and I took Evan to meet Dad at Nakashima. The longtime Ramsey favorite was a hibachi grill, one of those places where they cook the food in front of you on a stainless griddle and perform acrobatic tricks with your shrimp. The low-slung brick building sat just off the highway.

"Hey Bob!" the bar regulars chorused as we followed my dad inside. The place was dark, like walking into a cave.

"He-ey, fellas," my dad said in his Louisville drawl. "This is my daughter and son-in-law. And this is my son."

He was already drunk. But his pride was evident in the way he said *son*. Evan, who'd just started high school, took after our dad in looks and athletic talent. Tall and lanky, he was making a name for himself as a running back.

"Why didn't you tell me," Dad asked, as we watched men in cartoonish chef's hats toss our shrimp into the air. "Why didn't you tell me about football?"

Evan squirmed on the low seat, his childlike face half in shadow. "I haven't seen you," he said softly.

"Well, why don't you ever call me?"

"Why don't you ever call *me*?" my brother shot back. It was the question I'd been asking all my life. He covered his face with his hands.

"Oh, Evan," our father said. "Don't cry. I'm sorry; I didn't mean that."

I put my arm around my brother, blinking back tears.

"I'm sorry," Dad said again, helplessly, reaching out to muss Evan's thick blond hair. "Please don't cry."

I remembered another night in another restaurant a decade earlier, when the cheese from Evan's pizza had burned Madeleine's arm, and Dad growled, "You little *shit*," before storming through the doors and peeling out of the parking lot. I remembered baby Evan sleeping in a ball, like a rabbit. I wanted to tell him, *This is not your fault*. I wanted to believe that myself.

By the end of dinner, my dad was so drunk he could barely stand. He weaved into the parking lot, the three of us following nervously. We couldn't talk him out of driving, not even Matthew, who wasn't scared of him. I watched him start his truck, a knot of fear and guilt in my throat.

"This is bad, Kelly," Matthew said.

"Don't you think I fucking know that?" My voice was hateful, a strangled cry of pain.

The next day, when we went to my dad's house on the lake, he was already drunk again and so grateful to see me that he burst into tears. He clung to my shoulders, thanking and confusing me. "I'm sorry," he cried into my neck. "I'm so sorry."

What the fuck? Matthew's eyes asked.

I shrugged. *I don't know.*

His tears were quiet. It was like holding a child. He felt thin and fragile, as if he might break in two.

"It's okay," I said. "Shh. It's alright, Daddy. It'll be okay." Helpless to fix things for him, and frightened because I could see he was headed down a path of no return, I repeated what my mom had always told me as a child. Those placating words of comfort. Those lies.

On day fourteen, the *final* day fourteen, we drove home along the 299, which offered a partial tour of the season's fires: the Hog, the Flat, the Red Salmon. I tried to imagine ten years from now, or twenty. Benjy, with his uncanny, nearly photographic memory, carried a mental map of the past two decades' fires. We'd be hiking somewhere, and he'd say, "Oh, this is where the old such-and-such happened in '07. Hung it up on that ridge."

As the forests and their burn scars raced by beyond the buggy windows, I tried to sort my mixed-up feelings. In moments, I had wanted so badly for this to end. Yet now that we were leaving, I didn't want to go.

"Fire never betrayed me. Fire never let me down. She's the love of my goddamn life." Benjy told me that once.

Eddie wasn't with us. He'd been drafted to Charlie to share driving duties with Scotty, and when he wasn't in the buggy, things felt a little less warm. I was listening to a Tyler Childers song from a playlist he'd made me, and I texted him. "Obsessed with 'Lady May.'"

"Right? The best."

Childers was from Kentucky. The voice and accent of anyone from home was like hearing my father on the other end of the line. *Now I ain't the toughest hickory that your axe has ever felled*, Childers sang. *But I'm a hickory just as well.*

Man, I thought. My dad would love this song.

He gave me a guitar when I was in college, one of few objects he'd ever gifted me, a Sigma by Martin with a honey-colored body and a warm tone. It had been his guitar, so it felt large inside my arms. He'd hung a homemade luggage tag on the case handle, a laminated business card for his latest contracting company, Charter Project Management. On the back he had written in Sharpie, in his characteristic caps, "KELLY GEE-TAR."

I pictured my dad at his desk with his glass of whiskey, lit cigarette in his hand. He would tilt his head back and close his eyes and let the music pour into him. I couldn't count the times I had caught him in this state, as Lucinda Williams' or Waylon Jennings' voice filled the room while he sat frozen in a rapture of pure attention. In those moments, I could see that he wasn't alone, wasn't hurting. The music made him whole again. It could not save his life, but for a moment, it saved his soul.

My first real year in fire had been a doozy, not just for me but my beloved California: 4.2 million acres burned in what the media called the "fire siege," the worst season the state had endured in over a hundred years. Fifteen thousand lightning strikes in a single August weekend. The state's first gigafire. Thirty-one people killed (three of them firefighters). One hundred and twelve million metric tons of carbon dioxide released by our burning forests. A virus with symptoms exacerbated by smoke. And for our crew, one thousand hours of overtime in under five months.

We pulled everything out of the buggies, swept, hosed them out, scrubbed them down, sprayed and buffed the windows, detailed the cabs. We dumped the contents of our line gear onto the bay floor and returned the government property to Wink, who checked it off on our sign-out sheets. When pressed for some detail—Do you need this weather kit organized like before?—he gave a shrug and my favorite of Winkisms, "I ain't care."

A blurry photograph of Wink running past a lake was tacked to a cork board in the corner of the room. Someone had written across it: "This is Shane. He ain't care."

We carried everything from the buggy and Supt truck and Charlie into the bay, organized it, and stowed it away. We washed and dried our sleeping bags before tucking them in the loft. Our line gear got blasted with the air hose, washed down, and hung up in the sun. Every chainsaw received a deep clean, its parts extracted and prodded with Q-tips; every tool was sharpened, the handles sanded and soaked in linseed oil.

During lunch in the barracks, Luke found me in the kitchen.

"Kelly, I'm sorry," he said.

"For what?"

"For that stuff with BJ, for talking shit. I never meant—"

"Oh, dude! No worries. I know you didn't mean anything by it."

"No! I just—I'm so sorry for that, because you're a badass."

"I'm not." I laughed, self-conscious.

"No, you are. You're a badass! You are such a tough chick. You fuckin' killed it this year, and you knowhat?" He said it as one word, and it occurred to me that he might have had a drink or two. "You're a part of this crew now." He rested one big, calloused hand on my shoulder. "You're a hotshot."

I blinked away tears. He wrapped his arms around me.

"Thank you," I whispered, hugging him back.

Later that day we had a barbecue and awards ceremony, notable only for Ryan throwing a small fit when Hayes, and not himself, won Hotshot of the Year. But the rest of us quickly forgot. We were ready for the party.

Most of the crew, particularly the temps, would be going to a bar in town called Port O' Pints. This was "our" bar, in the sense that they knew us and had hosted several crew parties; they even had a crew photo from several years back hanging in a frame on the wall. So it was time to approximate the dress code: overalls and a Hawaiian shirt. A bunch of us got rooms at a cheap motel a few blocks away so we wouldn't have to drive.

The bar was one-story, dark, maritime-themed. They gave us the back room to ourselves and said we could go mask-free in our "bubble" back there, as long as we masked up to buy drinks from the bar. We started off quietly, with a few beers and some snacks. But within an hour or two, somebody fired up a karaoke machine, and we gave impassioned performances to a supportive crowd of ourselves. Then the dancing started.

The dance floor grew more and more frenzied, and soon the boys had stripped off their shirts. Then we were in a conga line. Finally, we stood pressed in a tight circle with our arms around each other's shoulders, swaying side to side. "Sweeeeeet Caroline," we sang, or rather, shouted. "Dum, dum, DUM."

"Good times never felt so good! (So good! SO GOOD!!)"

They never did feel so good. I loved these dumb shirtless boys. We shouted in each other's faces, *I love you, man!* And *You too, dude, I love you so fucking much!* Then the sweaty circle of bodies began to slip on spilled beer, threatening to topple. I ducked out.

I closed my tab and slipped out the front door, a heavy wooden slab with a porthole in the middle. I wasn't sure if I wanted some air or if I might walk back to the motel; I was satisfied with the evening. Eddie was standing outside.

"You trying to Irish Goodbye?" I asked.

"Thinkin' about it."

"It's crossing that line from fun to sloppy."

"It always does." He smiled.

We stood side by side on the concrete in the cone of a weak yellow streetlight. Our drunk friends stumbled out the door, then back in, asking, *You seen Barrel?* Through the window, a shirtless Fisher had instigated a dance-off with bare-chested Haines, whose muscles glistened with sweat.

"Hey Eddie."

"Yeah, go," he said, answering like you would over the radio, which made me smile.

"I just wanted to say. If things were different—" I paused, not knowing how to say it or even whether I should. "I mean, if I weren't with someone, I probably would've made a move on you this summer."

He looked surprised.

"You had to know that."

"Yeah, I had a feeling." He smiled. "Well, if you had made that move, I wouldn't have stopped you."

We smiled at our feet. The road was empty, lit by the fluorescence of the gas station across the way. Trevan's girlfriend, Erin, half-opened the door, then turned back, saying, "Alex, are you coming?"

For half a second I was thrilled. The feeling was mutual. Eddie was so comfortable, so easy to be with, so fun. What if . . . ?

But my heart sank. *Josh*. There was Josh—and the pets, the house, the ring. It would be a royal mess to leave, and I had promised myself I'd be a person who stayed. Eddie was too young anyway; it'd never work.

I looked at him sadly. "Well." I shrugged.

"Well," he agreed with a rueful little smile.

"Friends?"

"Friends."

We hugged for a split second longer than we should've. His body was warm and strong; it felt so good, I wanted to stay. But we broke apart and said goodnight. I walked back to the hotel with Haines, Trevan, and a hilariously drunk Erin, who tackled Haines, clinging to his back. "Not again!" he was yelling. "No!" One time she'd given him such an extreme wedgie, she ripped his underwear in half. I liked her.

As I learned only later, it was obvious to everyone else long before it became clear to me: I loved Eddie. He'd been my favorite person from the moment I pulled into the station and saw him standing beside his camper. *I'm Eddie! People call me Eddie A.*

Well, it was never gonna happen.

I cried myself to sleep.

The next morning, most of the Rowdy River Hotshots showed up for the final day of work hungover as dogs. We skulked around the bay, pale rats scrounging for Gatorades. We swept the polished concrete floor one more time, half-heartedly disinfected tables. Mostly, we sat around, waiting our turn to be called to the office.

"You're up," Keller said, and I padded down the long hallway to sit across from Salomon and Fisher.

"Well, obviously, great job this year," Salmon began.

Was it obvious?

He went on to say that I'd been a hard worker (Fish chimed in, "Pack mule!"), that I'd had the most positive attitude, always smiling, and that—best of all—"Everyone likes you. You're a great addition to the crew."

"We'd love to have you back next year."

My headache vanished. Without knowing, I'd been holding my breath for six months. Though they'd dropped breadcrumbs of approval, you never knew if you'd done well until they asked you back. And they *had*. I beamed, shaking their hands.

Outside, evals complete, Van called us all in for one last gaggle. We stood in a circle, twenty people in green pants and tall boots and shirts with identical logos. Chew spit fell on the ground with a gentle patter. I looked at these men, people I now knew so well, they felt like siblings. I knew their faces by heart, saw them in my dreams, knew their voices and fears and stories and jokes. I would remember them for the rest of my life.

Since childhood I'd been looking for a family. Here, against all odds, I had found one.

Van was giving a speech about what a good, hard season it had been—the busiest season yet, with the most hours in overtime this crew had ever seen. He told us we'd done a great job, he was proud to lead us, and he hoped we'd have a fun and restful winter. Then—pausing, smiling—he raised a finger in the air.

"Daaaaay . . ."

"DAY ONE!"

We shouted the words—so loud they echoed off the pavement and the closed doors of the engine bay, and I imagined our voices reaching the Rowdy River itself. This time, we didn't just disperse; we lingered, hugging and clapping each other on the back. I wished Keller safe travels back to the Midwest, told Hayes I might see him in Bend. Fish said we should meet up, me and "my guy" and him and Jenny. Miguel and I exchanged words in Spanish. Benjy gave me a hug and said gruffly, "Ya done good. You're a dude now!" Wink grinned shyly. "Buh-bye, bud."

That seemed to be the end of it. But when I started my truck, the tire pressure light flickered on. Dammit. I drove to the crew bay, where there was an air hose, and Eddie sidled out the open door in flip-flops and shorts, chewing. "What's goin' on? Can't leave us, can ya?"

Bao was right behind him, grin full of mischief. "She can't get enough."

I laughed and protested, "I've got a low tire."

"That's what they all say."

They helped me blow up the tire, and I screwed the cap on the air nozzle and thanked them. We hugged again—Bao, then Eddie— and I thought, *Of course it would be these two at the end.* Eddie and I exchanged sad little smiles. Then I hopped in the truck, waved, and pulled away. Going home had never felt so much like leaving home.

A story's gotta end somewhere. For me, it ended with driving over a mountain.

Or so I believed.

PART II

Season Two

Work is its own cure. You have to
like it better than being loved.

—MARGE PIERCY

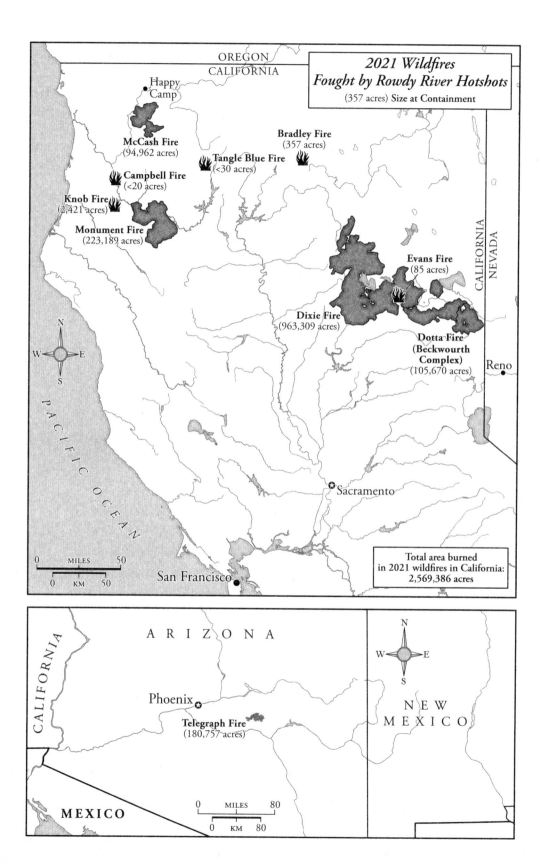

2021 Wildfires
Fought by Rowdy River Hotshots
(357 acres) Size at Containment

OREGON
CALIFORNIA

Happy Camp

McCash Fire
(94,962 acres)

Bradley Fire
(357 acres)

Tangle Blue Fire
(<30 acres)

Campbell Fire
(<20 acres)

Knob Fire
(2,421 acres)

Monument Fire
(223,189 acres)

Evans Fire
(85 acres)

Dixie Fire
(963,309 acres)

Dotta Fire
(Beckwourth
Complex)
(105,670 acres)

CALIFORNIA
NEVADA

Reno

N
W E
S

PACIFIC OCEAN

0 MILES 50
0 KM 50

Sacramento

Total area burned
in 2021 wildfires in California:
2,569,386 acres

San Francisco

ARIZONA

CALIFORNIA

Phoenix

Telegraph Fire
(180,757 acres)

N
W E
S

NEW
MEXICO

MEXICO

0 MILES 80
0 KM 80

ROWDY RIVER HOTSHOTS

2021 Roster

Superintendent ("Supt"): Samuel "Van" Van Allen

Alpha (A-mod)
Captain: Benjamin "Benjy" Rose
Squad Boss ("Squadie"): Andrew "Mac" Macaluso
Senior ("Lead"): Scotty Castaldi
Senior ("Lead"): Shane "Wink" Winkler

Temporary Seasonal Employees ("Temps"):
Edward "Eddie A." Ahacic, 5th year
Mason Jones, 5th year (returning after 1-year absence)
Blake Haines, 2nd year
Beryl "Barrel" MacCrum, 2nd year
Miguel Rosario, 2nd year
Addison Campbell, rookie
Ender Cahill, rookie
Brandon Bellomo, rookie

Bravo (B-mod)
Detailed Captain: Jesse Hale
Squad Boss ("Squadie"): Matthew "Fish" Fisher
Senior ("Lead"): Ishmael "Bao" Bayabao (on detail in Idaho)

Temps:
Luke Dawson, 7th year
Eli "BJ" Jones, 4th year
Alexander Trevan, 2nd year
Shaun Keller, 2nd year
Kelly Ramsey, 2nd year
Aiden ("Shaggy") Orzech, rookie
Max Englefield, rookie

Chapter 12

Fire Dreams

The storm came early to the Klamath mountains, filling the quiet valley where Happy Camp lay like a sleeping child. Snow arrived with a massive, muffled silence, each flake erasing the one before. It lay heavy on the pines and crusted the blackberry bushes on the banks of the river, which rushed through an all-white channel, churning and flinty, black water the only color in the world.

The dogs jumped from the porch, bounding through the drifts. I pulled a beanie over my ears and trudged to the woodshed, taking hold of the splitting maul's frosty handle. Finally, after more than a year, I'd gotten the hang of this.

I placed a wood round on the hardwood stump, lifted the maul, and swung it down, sliding my top hand to meet my left so the full weight of the tool dropped, heavy with gravity, into the meat of the wood, its wedged tip aimed at a crack that crossed the rings of the tree nearly from birth to death. I hit true, and with a snap, the round split in two, the halves falling to either side of the stump.

I bent to grab one, stood it on end, and swung again—crack, split—until I had a half dozen logs. This was fir, softwood, best for starting fires. Next, I split a round of hardwood Madrone for slow, hot-burning fuel. Last, I split kindling. This process, which Josh could complete in ten or fifteen minutes, took me nearly half an hour. My hands had gone numb, and snot frosted my upper lip. I swabbed my face with a sleeve.

Sam was yelling from his pen. *Mehhh!* he called, his whine cutting through the falling snow. "Shut *up*," I groaned pointlessly. He wouldn't quiet until fed or set free.

I shouldered the canvas satchel of wood and stomped back to the house. The animals streamed inside around my legs, tracking melting crystals across the floor. My face reddened in the sudden warmth. I knelt at the woodstove, made a kindling teepee, and built my fire. Heat began to roll out the stove's open door, searing my skin.

Suddenly, I was back in the desert outside Loyalton, California. We were digging quickly in easy dirt Luke called "cherry," BJ and Bao and I swinging our tools, flinging sand. The sun hung low on the horizon beyond rolling hills of desert chaparral. The fire was small, maybe two-foot lengths at the leading edge, but wind bent the flames toward our bodies. My face grew hot.

"Hee-yoo! This is it, boys and girls," Fisher hooted. "Best day of your lives. Best it's ever gonna get!"

Was it? I wondered, a lump in my throat.

"Hey." Josh's hand on my shoulder. I flinched. Back in the snow, back home—not August, but November. "You okay?"

I attempted a smile. He was bleary-eyed, mussed hair sticking up like the feathers on a freshly hatched bird. He was short and stocky, strong but thick, and he so often wore a hat that I was always surprised to see him bareheaded. He looked ten years older that morning, frown lines etched like the number eleven between his eyes. I could see why some of the temps on his crew called him "The Hawk" behind his back. It wasn't just the eyes, dark and sharp as a peregrine falcon's, but an inner severity, the sense that, for him, life was a deadly serious endeavor. Right was right, and rules were rules.

"Yeah," I said, shoving another log into the stove and latching the door. "Just, you know. Fire." I shrugged.

"You really miss it, huh?"

"Sometimes."

We'd had this conversation too often since I came home. He said I was a zombie, that I didn't seem like myself. True, I admitted. Life felt hollow after fire, as if my purpose had fallen away. And hadn't it? I'd been a firefighter, tasked with protecting trees and homes and stray dogs and human lives, busy sixteen to twenty-four hours a day with the urgent work of saving. Now I was a girl in a house, in sweatpants. It made you wonder if you were anyone at all.

I had a recurring nightmare that we got a resource order, but the buggy left without me. I stood weeping in the parking lot, crying, *But I was here on time! I swear.* In other dreams, we hiked through endless forests of burning firs; some nights, we dug a never-ending hand line. These weren't nightmares. I woke in the sweat of desire.

I didn't mention the dreams, but I admitted to Josh that I missed the crew. Everything felt strange without the guys. It was phantom limb syndrome—in a world where I'd once had twenty sets of limbs.

"So you hate being home with me," Josh snapped. "That's what you're saying."

"No," I protested. "That's not it. Come on, babe. I love being here with you, but I also miss them. I can feel both ways at once."

"Yeah, I don't think so. I don't get it."

Clearly.

Missing them was an insult to him. But wasn't it normal, to miss people you'd been with nonstop for six months? Josh said he guessed so, which meant no. Now I worried that as he stood above me, he was thinking again what he'd said the week before about the men on my crew, the sound a bitter accusation. *You like them more than me.*

I didn't want to go there again. Defending myself was exhausting, and I wasn't sure he was wrong. How could one man compete with nineteen personalities, the fun of working in the woods, the terrible days we had endured together, and how that bonded us for what felt like the rest of our lives?

"You hungry?" I asked brightly.

"Sure."

The power was out, so I fried bacon and eggs in a cast-iron skillet on the woodstove. We ate quietly, then walked the dogs up a snow-covered forest road, our feet leaving fresh prints in the untouched powder. Snow clung to the firs that covered the slopes around Benjamin Creek. We trudged up the hill, each breath a cloud.

Josh got a call to help tow a stranded vehicle. He was forever getting these calls because he had a huge, lifted diesel pickup. To my friends I joked that he drove a "monster truck."

"I'm sorry," he said with an anxious-excited buzz. I imagined it felt good to be needed so often. "I have to go help. I won't be long."

"It's okay." I kissed him goodbye. It was almost annoying that Josh felt compelled to save the world even on his days off, but on the other hand, I didn't get as much alone time as I would've liked. He bounded down the hill, and I continued up, legs working, air cold in my throat. Sometimes, when he left, I felt like I was under a new sky.

Around that time, I got an invitation. Fisher and Jenny were getting married in December, a small wedding in Washington State with Scotty and Eddie as groomsmen. Fish had talked about it all through the late season: where he was getting his suit, how *everyone* should get a suit from Men's Warehouse, there was literally *no* better place to buy suits.

One afternoon near the end of November, he sent me a text. *Ramsey!* he said. *We're having my bachelor party next weekend in Crescent. You gotta come, you're one of the boys now. Hope to see you there, dude!*

My chest constricted. *One of us.*

That night, Josh and I lay in the tub. As a permanent employee he worked through the winter, and after long, cold days of pile burning in the rain, he'd climb into the oversized jacuzzi tub, lighting candles and filling it with bubble bath. The tub was big enough that while I preferred my own bath, sometimes we'd hop in together and soak, talking through the steam. It was a ritual of soothing intimacy, more comforting than sexy. Like the other trappings of our domestic life, the house and raised-bed gardens and the chairs overlooking the river, I loved how it looked. I loved it like someone watching it onscreen.

He told me how annoying people had been at work, how as usual they had heaped extra responsibility upon him because he was the only one who would get it done (or the only *sucker*, I thought). Then I reported that there wasn't much to say about my day. I had tried to write some, taken the dogs for a hike. The usual.

"Oh, but I did get a nice text," I added. "Fisher invited me to his bachelor party. Isn't that sweet?"

"Bachelor party?" Josh's face darkened. "And you want to go?"

I hesitated, a queasy feeling settling in my stomach. "I mean, yeah. It's Fisher. All my buddies from the crew."

"You mean it's all guys."

"I don't know. There could be women, too. But yeah, mostly crew guys."

"So you're telling me you want to go to a party with a bunch of men, where you'll be the only woman. And you don't think that's weird?"

"Maybe if they were strangers. But I just spent six months with these guys. They're like . . . my brothers."

"But you'd be drinking and partying. That's different."

"I've been drinking with them before! What do you think we did on the way home from assignments?"

"That's totally different."

"How?"

"A bachelor party is a big wild party, with strippers or whatever. It's a night for getting wasted."

"I doubt this is a stripper scene. I think it's just a handful of people having some beers."

He shrugged, face cold. "Still."

"Are you saying you don't trust me?"

"I'm saying I don't trust *them*."

"You think they're gonna make a pass at me?"

"Absolutely."

"They would *never*. But you don't trust me to say no? I have, like, no agency in this?" I stood up, water sloshing over the edge of the tub. The heat had left me lightheaded.

"I don't trust them. And it's weird that you even want to go!" His eyes narrowed. "It's not *normal*."

"How is wanting to hang out with my friends from work not normal?"

"When your friends are a bunch of guys, and you're the only girl."

I stepped out of the tub and wrapped a towel around my body. "If they were a bunch of random guys, sure. But they're my *crew*. I'm sure if we asked some other people, like my friends, they would tell you that it's normal."

"And I'm sure if we asked some of my friends, they'd say it was weird. Gavin would never let Melissa go to a bachelor party."

"*Let* her? Like she needs his *permission*?" I started to leave, then turned back. "And of course Gavin would say that. If you had a friend who wasn't a small-town redneck, you might hear something different."

Now Josh stood, the water sloshing violently. "Gavin isn't a fucking redneck!"

"He is! Everyone you know is a redneck."

"You can't seriously be thinking of going!"

"I'm not your ex-wife, Josh!"

A low blow—Josh's previous wife was rumored to have maybe cheated on him while he was in the Coast Guard.

"I never said you were like her."

"You basically did. This is insane."

"I'm not the crazy one. You tell me you're going to party with dudes and expect me to act like that's normal."

"It doesn't look like I'm going, does it?" My voice cracked. "I was so excited. So happy to be included. Don't you get it? I worked all year to fit in with these guys, and now they want me there. I was so happy."

I stumbled from the room, crying, leaving him lobstered and naked in knee-deep water. He was objectively a handsome man, but he looked ugly then, with his stocky, muscle-bound limbs and barrel belly, clumps of wet dark hair above a resentful face. I lay on the bed and wept. He was steely and sullen, his silence like thunderclouds filling the house.

Later, we made up, but he never said it was okay if I went to the party, so I told Fisher the weather was too dicey to make it through the mountains.

Between the day in the snow, the fight in the bath, and other unpleasant conversations, I realized that Josh would never feel good about me fighting fire—i.e., spending all my time with other men. Maybe he had never been okay with it to begin with, but my postseason malaise seemed to confirm his suspicion that I'd replaced him.

So I told Josh I wouldn't go back. No more crew, no more hotshot. I had done it, been successful. I could be done.

"Are you sure?"

"Yeah, I think it's too much, you know? If I'm this fucked up after one season, I shouldn't do it again."

He was so relieved. I was glad to appease him and have an end to the fighting. For several weeks, things were peaceful. I made dinner, split wood, baked cookies. When he came home from work, everything was as he liked it: clean, warm, dogs fed, a meal ready or in progress. It wasn't so much that he demanded everything be in order. Instead, it was the irritation and heavy sighing with which he made the fire or stared at the fridge that told me what I had to do to keep him happy. At night, we cuddled on the couch, cozily bingeing shows.

But my sleep betrayed me. All my dreams were of flames and smoke columns, of digging line and riding in the buggy, of hiking through thick trees. I wanted the crew, wanted fire.

I'd told Josh I wouldn't go back. But I hated him for it.

A week after New Year's Day, I crested the last rise and reached for a familiar stump, panting. Below me, Happy Camp winked like a jewel. Beyond town, the forest was gone. Four months after the Slater fire, the sight remained a shock: the mountains pale, like someone had bled the color out, and stippled with the gray masts of dead trees.

The Indian Creek canyon was changing quickly as fire cleanup efforts accelerated. Giant log decks piled up in the pullouts along Grayback Road, massive equipment crawled over the scorched hills, and men with chainsaws, hard hats, and reflective vests swarmed the wreckage, cutting trees, repairing power lines, directing traffic. Men, I say, because one seldom saw women disassembling the ghost forest.

One by one, the burned houses disappeared, their rubble carted away. Only a rectangle of discolored earth remained to indicate a house had been there at all. The absence of the ruins bothered me more than the fallen walls, blackened ovens, and twisted metal, because removing the wreckage was like archiving the evidence of an unsolved crime. How would the world remember what happened here?

The people of Happy Camp would certainly never forget.

I touched the stump, carbonized by a long-ago fire, and stopped the timer on my watch: 39:25, not bad, though not great. Breathing heavily, sweat trickling down my face, I called the dogs, who nudged in to lap water from a collapsible bowl.

Gazing across town, I wiped my face but didn't drop the pack I had hauled up the hand line—the Knob, a training hike, when I'd only meant to do a casual hoof up the much easier trail. The New Year had arrived, and something in me had called out for this, saying, *It's time*. Now, perversely, that same part of me asked for more. First series of grueling pitches accomplished, I eyed a stretch of dozer line that stitched the saddle to the ridge above.

"What do you think, dogs? Should we go for it?"

Mouse wagged her tail and took off, fur flashing between bushes. Chief followed her at a lazy lope, while Valentine waited by my side, dark eyes shining up at me.

"Yeah, why not. Let's go!"

Valentine galloped ahead. I crossed the saddle at a stride and reached the toe of the slope, where the earth pushed upward in a broken, rocky channel. I breathed out and dug in, beginning to climb.

This was natural now. In many ways, it felt like the only thing I knew. I climbed and descended the other side, then turned and climbed back up, back down. My legs and lungs complained, but in the usual ways. Only an hour later, on the knee-wrenching descent down the west face of the ridge, as the sweat grew clammy under my shirt, did I think to ask myself, *Darlin', what are you doing here?*

I was doing a PT hike. Not just the regular hike but the extended version, a torture I'd invented for those days when you craved extra work.

And I was hiking it, what, for fun? No, not exactly. I was doing it because I couldn't *not* do it. Because I didn't want to stop. *Because I wasn't done.*

There was the truth. I wasn't done with fire.

It took me a week to summon the courage to tell Josh. He wasn't happy, and I felt a pang of guilt. What looked to me like abandonment fears seemed understandable; I recall a mention that his mother, drinking heavily, had left eight-year-old Josh alone for days in their trailer. My heart ached for him. But I wasn't his mother, and we were adults now.

He managed to say that I should work where I wanted, and he promised to be supportive.

Good, I thought. *Some dude's mommy issues aren't gonna keep me from the work I love.*

Because that's what it felt like: a romance, a love affair with work. Like falling for someone used to feel, back when I believed in "the one." Now fire was the one—or I was. I'd fallen in love with the person I became, fighting fire. I loved her physical strength, her dirty skin and two-week-old clothes that had hardened to a crust, how she'd say what she wanted, yell "fuck you" across a parking lot. She was not the careful, compliant girl I had been for most of my life, half-starved to stay thin. She was bigger than that. I had to go back and see who she'd become.

Seasonal firefighters are laid off each winter (they collect unemployment through the off-season) but retain a teaspoon of job security in what's called "automatic rehire rights," meaning you can be hired into the same position without reapplying.

When Salomon called a few weeks later to ask if I'd take the rehire, the answer was easy. *I'll be there.*

"Start training."

"I already am."

*   *   *

As January melted into February, I set aside everything but training. This year, I wouldn't be the new girl who scraped by, the pleasant rookie they'd benevolently assist. This year, I would become a solid crew member. An asset.

I had proven that a woman could survive this work; now I would show she could excel.

Up we went, me and the dogs. I did the usual PT hikes, the Knob and Mount Motherfucker, but I added a chainsaw, a bladder bag, or a pile of disc-shaped iron weights dropped into the musty gut of my pack. Saw over my shoulder, pack dragging against my ass, I put one foot in front of the other, slowly climbing hills that wanted to murder me. Heart rate at max, open-mouthed and gasping, sweat bleeding through my clothes, I climbed. I was used to this, a suffering so familiar it was almost a comfort.

The fire scar was everywhere. With the exception of the Knob, on the south side of the river, every route I took lay in the Slater's swath of devastation. So I climbed through scorched brush, over barren earth. Where there had been shade, the sun bore down upon a stripped land, all the green forest nuked into a landscape resembling the surface of the moon. *You'll get used to it*, I thought, but I never did.

There was a trail, however, that followed the East Fork of Indian Creek. It was burned, and I was held up by downed trees and sudden gaping stump holes. But I saw something surprising.

In the seam between the sooty stumps and the ashen earth, new trees were growing. The hardwood saplings, some kind of elm or maple, were already a foot tall—less than six months after the fire had obliterated this drainage. "Stump sprouts," a forester friend told me. Clusters of ferns and nascent bundles of brush erupted, too, creating green pathways under the black canopy.

The earth was regenerating faster than I'd thought possible. Mother Nature didn't wait for an environmental assessment, permit, strategic plan. She was on it; the seeds of new pines, in fact, released from their cones just after the fire passed through. The forest wouldn't grow back the same, but it wouldn't stop growing.

One weekend at the end of March, Josh and I took the dogs for a short hike. I was confused; we usually spent weekends mired in chores, working on the property, or cutting firewood. I often resented the tasks, especially if Josh used them as a chance to "teach" me how to do something I hadn't asked to learn.

But Josh suggested a hike on a Sunday. I tried to beg out of it, tired and sore from the week's training ("sore" was an understatement, I could barely walk), but he insisted.

"Come on," he said. "It's a beautiful day. Just a short one!"

I gave in, and we drove out to the trail to my favorite swimming hole. We followed the path through a burn scar overlooking a beautiful creek, and as we rounded the final turn before the deep pools of a slot canyon, the trail widened, following an old roadbed. Josh took my hand.

That was weird. We'd never held hands while hiking (who does? It's awkward), but I figured he was trying, and I appreciated the effort. As we reached the bridge over the creek, I saw something strange. At the far end of the bridge stood a small table, two chairs, and a picnic basket. Red roses on the table. *Oh no*, I thought. *We're interrupting someone's date. We should leave.*

But when I turned to Josh, I saw that he was trembling, wearing the fragile smile of a terrified man. *Oh. SHIT.* This wasn't my first rodeo. He was about to propose.

I squeezed his hand to comfort him, but I wasn't breathing either. We reached the end of the bridge, and Josh dropped his backpack and pulled out a box. He opened it, and the ring winked in the cold spring sunlight. It was gorgeous, the raw diamond milky and irregular in the best way. Josh dropped to one knee.

"Kelly," he began, voice and hands shaking. "You're the love of my life. I can't think of anything better than spending the rest of my days with you."

He said some other stuff that I didn't register. I had floated up out of myself and was sitting on a branch with a bird whose call echoed across the canyon, looking down on us.

"Will you marry me?"

Through a curtain of numbness I said yes.

Beaming, Josh clambered down to the creek. The temp from his crew who'd hiked all this stuff out had rigged up a bottle of champagne, kept cold in the water and marked with pink fire flagging. It was too perfect—so us, so cute, so *fire*. He'd nailed it.

But a muffled paralysis had settled over me, woolly and thick, a stillness through which a small voice whispered, *Are you sure?* The very words the sheriff had uttered when I stood before her at twenty-two, about to marry a man I barely knew.

Shivering a little as I took my seat, I pulled myself together. *Yes, you're sure. This is what you wanted.* Josh had to be, if not "the one," then at least the general type I'd been looking for. All the boxes checked: man with a house, steady income, and no addictions; rescues dogs and runs into burning buildings; looks at me like I'm treasure; wants babies. Check, check. The line between practicality and desperation, for many women my age, thinned to a wisp of smoke.

We drank champagne beside the roaring creek and talked about the wedding. Maybe next fall, we agreed, when fire season was over. Then we gathered the furniture, strapped it to our backs, and hiked out.

I was happy. Or at least, I said I was.

That Tuesday, Addison came to hike.

Addison Campbell was a friend of a friend; we'd met at a concert with a group of women two years earlier. After crossing paths on the August Complex, she'd expressed interest in hotshotting, and I had encouraged her to apply to Rowdy River. They said she was the most qualified candidate they'd had for a rookie spot in ages—six years' experience in fire, first saw on a respected helicopter crew in Idaho? They picked her up in a heartbeat.

I was beyond stoked that another woman would be joining us, especially one who seemed more skilled than me. *That* would show them what girls could do. And finally, I wouldn't be alone.

We hiked Mount Motherfucker. As we climbed the steep hill, between gasps, we talked about the coming season, about being a woman in this field, about how fire itself excited us. I barely knew her, but Addison (never "Addy," I learned) seemed cool. She was four inches taller than me, rail-thin but muscular, with black hair cut short, pixie-like, and shaved up the back. She had a sleeve tattoo covering one arm, and a degree of wokeness that marked her as a younger millennial. At twenty-six, she was more than a decade my junior.

Yet I noted a toughness in Addison that in moments made me feel like the younger one. My voice was high and sweet, almost childlike, my persona malleable and soft; I tended to shape-shift to please the nearest authority. Addison spoke with a rich contralto, what you might call a strong or even masculine voice, and had a way of making assertions as if she herself were the chairperson, the decider. It felt like she didn't need to impress anyone, and I envied that.

But as we trudged upward, she pulled ahead of me, and I frowned. Sure, I didn't love being beat on a hike, but I was used to it. What I noticed, as she gained ground and began to lengthen the distance between us, was the difference in what we carried.

I was hoofing a full pack loaded with forty-five pounds of crap (and I knew it was forty-five pounds because I'd weighed it). I also carried a twenty-five-pound chainsaw. The power head, actively dripping bar oil on my shirt, rested on my shoulder blade, and my right arm hung over the bar. The seventy pounds slowed my progress to a shuffle, every step a punishment.

Addison, by contrast, wore one of those tiny backpacks made to accommodate only a water reservoir, in which she carried perhaps two liters. Plus one of Josh's saws. So she was hoofing . . . maybe thirty, thirty-five pounds?

"Nice job," I said when we reached the top and sat down for a water break. "Um, I just wanted to say, it might be a good idea to do some hikes with heavy weight. I don't know what you usually do—"

"I mean sometimes I hike more. But yeah, maybe I'm not going heavy enough. I'm just doing what I'd do to get ready for Pine Creek," she said breezily, referencing her previous crew. "Like at this point, after six years, I know what to do."

"Totally. I'm sure you do." I frowned. How could I argue with that?

"You're thinking it's not Pine Creek, aren't you?" she asked shrewdly.

I laughed. "I mean, I have no idea how tough your crew was. But I thought Crew Two was hard, and then I went to Rowdy River. And the hikes . . . I mean, these guys are *fast*. And the hills are worse than what we just did. Like hand over foot climbing on boulders. It's hell."

Addison nodded, frowning.

"I don't mean to scare you. But yeah . . . I'd just hike as much weight as you can up the steepest hills you can find."

"Okay, I'll try that." She smiled. "Thanks, Kelly."

"Sure thing. You've got this. And I'm here anytime, if you need anything."

We shared a smile, then hauled ourselves to our feet for the descent. I liked this role: older sister figure, seasoned hotshot, supportive coach. I was excited for Addison and equally happy for me, benefactor and champion of women.

What an idiot.

Chapter 13

Tribe

The mountains where I'm from, the eroded ranges of Appalachia and the Blue Ridge, are old and gentle, breasts and hips of time-softened land nudging the eastern sky. The mountains of the West, by contrast, are knuckles and fists; they punch the atmosphere. As I drove the two-lane highway that May, I took in the defiant peaks, feeling—not for the first time—that I had finally found my country. A wild, unruly place. A land of fire.

Pulling into the station was like coming home. The river, the green ridges, the tidy compound. I owned this place—or, no, that was wrong. It owned me. My eyes welled, and I thought, *C'mon, girl, it's just a workplace.* But I knew that wasn't true.

Parking on a careless diagonal by the open bay door, I sauntered in. My style for spring was brown Carhartt overalls, the rugged Chelsea boots—Blundstones—I'd worn three winters now, a striped long sleeve, and a beanie. I called this look "Country Where's Waldo," and I felt confident in the androgynous trappings, as if a conflicted set of identities—preppy, outdoorswoman, nerd—harmonized in this ensemble. More simply: I felt like myself.

The bay was empty. I found my cubby, where my PG bag was just as I'd left it, pre-stocked with a pair of greens that fit me well and a musty sleeping pad that smelled of old smoke. I buried my nose in it, inhaling the promise of summer.

"Hey!" Haines's curly head popped out of the saw room.

"Oh, hey dude!"

"Welcome back," he said, coming over to hug me. He was so tan and muscular this year, it was almost obscene; he looked like an inflated action figure or a Thanksgiving turkey someone had injected with extra broth.

"I'm so happy to be back," I said.

"Yeah, I was losing my mind waiting for the season to start."

"Same." I smiled, because Haines seemed incapable of moping in sweatpants. "You doing the truck thing again?"

"Yeah. You?"

I nodded. We had too many temps for the government housing, and sleeping in my truck—cozy inside the camper top I'd bought for three hundred dollars from a retired mechanic—seemed preferable to paying four hundred a month to stay in a rodent-infested glorified frat house. Especially when I already paid half of Josh's mortgage back home.

"Trevan went to town," Haines said. "Ed's around here somewhere."

"Cool," I said, as if Eddie's whereabouts were none of my concern. Haines returned to the saw room, and I heard the recognizable voices of three comedians arguing on a true crime podcast.

I unloaded my bags, rearranged my cubby, and changed into yoga pants, carrying my mat to the gym. I couldn't remember the code and stood there trying numbers on the keypad. 1357? Not it. 1492? Nope.

The door swung open.

"The fuck're *you* doing?" Eddie in gym shorts, a Rowdy River tank, and a sun-bleached crew hat. His dark hair had grown to his shoulders. His arms shone with sweat.

"Trying to get in this gym, muhfucker," I shot back.

"Hi, Kelly." He grinned. As always, the inside of his warm, strong arms was like a pile of down comforters, a place where you could burrito yourself in covers on a rainy day, safe from the world.

"You forgot the code, didn't you?" he said into my hair.

"Every time."

"It's almost like you don't want to work out."

He went back to his mat, and I unrolled mine nearby, grabbing a foam roller from the corner. Eddie congratulated me on my engagement, and I glanced nervously at the ring on my hand, aware that it could not come to work with me this summer. You couldn't swing a tool wearing a band of gold, couldn't say whether flame or impact would destroy it first; married men wore silicone ring replacements on the line. Somehow, removing the diamond felt scary, like there'd be little left to tether me to Josh.

"Who's the girl on your Insta?" I teased.

"Okay, *Mom.* That's Alexis."

"Girlfriend?"

"Yeah, I guess so. It's new."

"She looked cute."

"She's hot." He shrugged, as if he weren't sure that that mattered.

Something was different about him this year. I'd always thought of Eddie as a goofy kind of cute, but now, with his preseason bulk of muscles and the '70s heartthrob long hair/mustache combo, he looked . . . hot, actually. I was astonished by the thought.

Telling myself that jealousy was not only unwarranted but unfair, I tucked the foam roller under my hip. Ed sat in a butterfly stretch, holding his feet. "I'm scared," he said.

"About Alexis?"

"No. I mean, sure. But I'm scared about this year. Did you hear they made me first saw?"

I crowed with excitement and punched his knee. "I'm so happy for you!"

"Don't be. I don't deserve it."

"Sure you do."

"I don't. It's only 'cause Luke is back on the dig and Trevan's a snookie. They only gave it to me because of seniority."

A "snookie" was a second year, a portmanteau of "second" and "rookie"—the implication being that you were still in the rookie phase until year three. In other words, you weren't a hotshot until they said you were.

"Well, it's not just about cutting, right?" I absently mirrored his butterfly stretch. "It's about leadership. You decide where the cut goes, how the line's gonna be placed. You're kind of in charge of the other sawyers."

"That's the problem! I *suck* at leadership. I'm not a leader."

I groaned and rolled my eyes. "You're being too hard on yourself."

"Yep." He grinned. "That's me. Big self-defecator."

I laughed dryly. I'd almost forgotten Eddie's chronic self-doubt, and it was a helpful reminder to put my hormones in check: this guy had a lot of growing to do. His new flame, a gorgeous and sun-kissed twenty-three, was probably perfect for him.

Addison texted that she'd arrived, so I rolled up my mat. "I'll see ya later, dude."

"I'm glad you came back this year, Kelly." Those eyes. Those stupid dimples.

Me too.

I took the path through the trees to the far side of the station, where several low-slung houses served as dormitory-style barracks. I was excited to see Addison and flop down on her twin mattress for girl talk. I felt ready for the first day of work and only a *little* nervous. You could never be prepared enough, but at least I knew what to expect.

I strolled up the trail, loose-limbed and light, a person restored to her rightful place. This would be, I was sure, a good year.

Later that week, I looked up at the familiar ridge, a rocky spine of uplifted earth splashed with brush and the odd ponderosa pine. The hand line, Brokeback Mountain, swerved through a jungle of poison oak before slicing up the hill, a streak of dirt that vanished over the first rise. Below us, the Middle Fork of the Rowdy River raced beneath a bridge and sledded around a curve, the peaceful sound of rushing water almost taunting.

"Line out!"

I fell into place with the dig. Addison stood a couple bodies ahead; I was a little concerned, because she'd struggled on French Hill earlier in the week—but then, so had I. Next came Englefield, a rookie with the wild-eyed, tousled look of Jack Black in his finest madman roles, and Bellomo, the former marine, a rookie with sleeve tats and smoothly parted chestnut hair. The other rookies, cheerful Orzech ("Shaggy," for his spot-on impression of the *Scooby-Doo* character) and deadpan Ender, were lanky types who'd proven their speed on French, so they took places near the saw teams up front.

I liked my company. Wink and Scotty were nearby, and Luke stood in front of me with a Super-P in his hand.

"Does it feel weird hiking without a saw?" I asked.

He waved the tool to demonstrate its weightlessness, grinning. "Best decision of my life, Kelly."

"Movin'!" Fisher's towering body led us onto the trail, and we began. Twenty male bodies, two female. Twenty-two pairs of leather boots, heels hitting the ground in staggered unison. Forty-four legs in green Nomex pants, a yellow shirt tucked into every waistband—some barely yellow, grayed by sweat and ash and bar oil and diesel and smoke.

A space began to yawn between two bodies—*Close the gap!*—then zipped shut. The crew was a churning, breathing, green-legged centipede, stretching and contracting as it inched up the hill.

As we left the switchbacks, I tucked my head, keeping pace. This was one of the worst pitches, and I was wholly focused on not falling behind. Soon the person in front of me—Englefield—began to lose ground, the gap between him and the man ahead widening. I stayed on his heels. Four feet, five. Six feet—good to go.

"On your left," I mumbled, and skirted around him, legs barking at the extra effort it took to gain speed and pass.

On a high that I had something over a couple rookies about my size (but, I noted with pride, ten-to-twelve years younger than me, and boys), I also passed Bellomo.

"This hill sucks," he gasped.

"I know. You got this, bud," I breathed as I stepped to his right and dropped into the line ahead of him.

Within a few minutes, though, I had slowed, and Englefield caught me. "On your left," he coughed, and pushed by, rivulets of sweat cutting down his face.

Oh, hell no.

The rest of the hike was a battle. I made it my job to catch Englefield. Then he caught me, and at the knob where we stopped, we were neck and neck; I can't remember who finished first (but I think it was me. Let's say it was me). I noted that the guy's competitive streak didn't switch on for his fellow male rookie—only when a woman, five foot six and nearly forty years old, passed him. I made a mental note of that.

Of course, I had my own competitive streak. The part of me that had never been an "athlete" felt proud of this new ferocity, while the part of me that wanted to remain "nice," grew concerned. Was I becoming an asshole?

But ultimately, competition was currency on the crew. To prove yourself, you had to outwork someone else.

So saintliness be damned. I'd bring the fight.

The buggies rolled along the 199 through fog that hung in torn sheets over the river. Pale ghosts of mist drifted across the empty highway, and we could've been the only people in the world. I was beat from digging line the day before, back clenched, hands blistered and raw.

Up at Low Divide, we were working a piece of practice line on the slope below the road. The dig lined out—Luke, me, rookies, Scotty, Wink. Addison wasn't with us today. Despite her struggles with hiking, she'd campaigned to get her hands on a saw, and I smiled as I saw her buckling the chaps around her long, lean legs. She hefted the chainsaw to her shoulder without effort and took her place in a line of large men. The guys glanced at her: curiosity, skepticism? Who knew what they thought of the woman among them, holding their symbol of virility, a dick with an engine. Even the phrase "power tool" seemed to mean *masculine* power, and in her hands, the story changed. I was excited to see what she could do.

We tightroped along the narrow, underslung trench to where our line petered out in a tangle of brush, and I fell in behind Luke. This year, I didn't need instruction. He set the line, and I chunked it wider, our bodies moving in seamless tandem. Englefield, who came behind me, was a solid digger, too, and by the time our three Pulaskis had passed over the knotted forest floor, the line was close to complete. Bellomo looked unmotivated, but Shaggy compensated, each muscular swing of his Chingadera sending dirt flying. The group was genial, cheerful, and the line progressed well despite a thick network of roots in the damp, red soil. We soon caught up with the saws, who were moving slowly. Mac, who was giving new sawyers a chance to cut, stood nearby, hawk-eyed, evaluating their skills. BJ would almost certainly be on a saw this year, to my relief.

"Hey Luke," Mac called. "Back 'em up. We're gonna take a few trees."

"Copy." We moved twenty or thirty feet backward along our line.

Haines stepped forward and smoothly dropped a tree, followed by Ender, one of the rookies, who was more than competent. Then I saw Mac point Addison toward two Douglas firs, sixty-foot trees about ten inches in diameter wedged in a cluster of timber. Mac gestured; Addison pointed out the proposed lay, telling him where she planned to drop the first fir. The crew stood still, watching her.

Addison fired up the saw, nodded to Mac, walked to the tree. She put in a quick face cut. She was wielding a Stihl 461 with a twenty-eight-inch bar, no lightweight saw, and she held it with competence and ease. From what I could see, her face cut looked clean and correct. But Mac reached out as if to say *Wait*—as Addison, wholly focused on her task and, I imagined, aware of all the eyes upon her, flipped the saw over and moved to the other side of the trunk, positioning herself for the back cut.

In slow motion, the crew panicked.

"*Go*—" Benjy was saying, as Fisher shouted, "Get back!"

At once, everyone ran in our direction, and we stumbled backward to make space for the incoming sawyers. At the same time, Addison's back cut connected with the hinge, and the tree fell—*directly toward us*. It landed across the line, clearing the place where Trevan and Haines stood by just ten or fifteen feet.

"What the fuck!"

"Jesus Christ."

"She sent that thing right at us!"

Fisher glanced back at the dig, shaking his head. "That was careless. Fuckin' *cavalier*." He turned, shouting to her, "HEY! D'you see what you did there?"

Addison didn't turn. Probably couldn't hear him between the ear plugs and the rumble of the saw itself.

Luke glanced at me. "Jesus! Coulda killed us."

True. Even a six-inch diameter tree could kill you. Yet I frowned, muttering, "Yeah." Surely every one of these guys had dropped a tree in the wrong place. Surely, too, the level of scrutiny upon Addison was higher than that faced by the average male sawyer. I wanted to defend her. At the same time, what had happened was dangerous. So I kept quiet, biting my lip.

If Addison noticed the guys' reaction, she didn't let on. Saw idling, she moved on to the second tree. Again, she put in a quick face and an immediate back cut, zip-zip-zip. She definitely knew *how* to cut. This time, the fir fell away from us as intended—but got hung up in a nearby tree.

The guys let out a collective groan.

They were dismissing her too easily, I thought. Who performs well under so much pressure? That's why I seldom ran saw—I was terrified, sure I couldn't "learn" under the watchful eyes of twenty opinionated dudes. She needed more opportunities and less of an audience.

I hoped she would do better next time and pave the way, because I did want to run saw eventually. Maybe if I proved myself *again* on the dig, improved my hiking, worked up to swamper . . . then maybe by my fourth or fifth season? I could see the labor unrolling, season after season of performing under relentless surveillance and ruthless judgment. Was it like being pressed into a diamond or more like being ground under the heel of a boot?

We were moving again. I shoved the rest of a protein bar into my mouth and picked up my tool. As we began to dig, I knew it was only a matter of time before the deployment drill began. Sure enough, there was Mac on the radio, simulating the ultimate emergency. "Hey, uh, we're seeing some increased fire activity below. Must've been a spot we didn't see, down low in the drainage."

We dug, ears pricked. A few minutes later, Mac again. "Yeah, I'm not liking this. She's really picking up some steam. Let's start getting out of there."

"RTO!" Fisher said, and the dig silently turned and began to pick our way along the cup trench. The saws soon caught up with us. We were quiet for once, no jokes or snickering.

"This is getting hot," Mac said.

"Double-time!" Fisher called, and we began to walk twice as fast. A few people broke into a jog, and Fish barked, "Hey, we're not running yet."

The crew slowed to a stride. Waiting, ready.

"Get 'em out of there!" Mac yelled. This was scarier with my own radio, his voice close to my ear. The urgency felt so real. "Fire's comin! Go. Go!"

"Drop and go!" Fisher echoed. "Up that cut!"

The saws had created—I think for the purposes of an escape route—a six-foot-wide cut through the brush, a corridor leading to the road. As we wheeled into this green alley, we unbuckled our packs and flung them to the ground, ripping off the Velcro that held our fire shelters in place. The shelters were jammed in tight, and the process didn't go as smoothly as you'd hope: you were supposed to bring, along with the shelter, a bottle of water, gloves, your shroud, a radio if you had one, and your tool, in the event you needed to clear brush to create a safe deployment spot. The sawyers had to bring their saws, in case they needed to cut open a clearing. For this exercise, we had preselected a "safety zone," a hundred-yard gravel bench at the end of the ridge.

Gathering these items took precious time, and I had the thought that if a real fire were coming, I'd end up with a shelter and little else. I wondered what they found on people after they were burned over.

"Go! Run," Fisher was yelling, exasperated. "Come on!"

I yanked the shelter free, and it sprung open from its accordion folds. Mashing it into a bundle, I tried to stuff it into my yellow as I moved up the hill, radio and Pulaski in hand. We were anything but orderly now. We tripped and staggered up the cut, arms full of loose objects. When we reached the gravel road, we sprinted for the safety zone. My legs felt impossibly heavy in fourteen-inch boots. The sawyers jogged clumsily with chainsaws on their shoulders. I thought of how the fire in the Happy Camp had raced uphill at sixty miles per hour. No hope of outrunning that.

"Not much time," Mac was shouting. "Let's go!"

We reached the safety zone, chests heaving. Mac was waiting for us, and Fisher went to stand beside him.

"Two lines," Mac said.

"Make it tight!" Fisher added.

We formed two lines of ten; the idea was that you could take fire better as a cluster of aggregated lumps. Again, though, in every photo of a real-life deployment, the bodies were scattered. I joined the front line between Luke and Miguel. We shook out our shelters, which unfolded like wrinkled tinfoil parachutes. Miguel and I exchanged a smile as we stepped in: feet in the bottom corners, a hand in each of the top corners, grabbing the handles.

"Get down!" Fisher said, irritated. We lay on the ground, face down in the gravel. "Get closer. Y'all are a mess. Scoot in tight, come on!"

On our bellies, we wriggled until the sides of our shelters touched and our feet pressed together. It was hot under the plasticky chrysalis, the sun a filtered green. Sweat beaded my forehead and dampened my heavy leather gloves.

"Fire's comin'!" Mac said. "Hold those shelters down tight. Here it comes!"

I pulled on my shelter, attempting to stretch its edges taut to pre-

vent air from leaking in. We were reminded every year that most firefighters died not from the flames themselves, but from asphyxiation by
toxic gases. If necessary, they said, dig into the dirt, and put your face
in the hole. The pocket of fresh air might just save your life.

"Fire's on you now," Mac said. "It's bending right over you."

I couldn't help it: chills covered my body. Goose bumps, as if this
were real.

"Hold on tight," Fisher shouted.

Mac and Fish came around grabbing our shelters, shaking them to
imitate the high winds and convective pulses of heated air a fire would
generate. If they were able to move your shelter, you weren't holding
tight enough. We lay there for several minutes, breathing shallowly.

"Okay," Mac said at last. "The fire's passed. Don't come out yet. I
want you to check in with each other."

We wriggled around, asking the person on each side how they were.
You good? "Muy bien," I said, and Miguel's laugh came back through
the layers of fabric.

"Count off," Mac commanded. "Starting in the front left."

We began the count, each person shouting a number: *One! Two!
Three* . . .

"Six!" I yelled.

Seven! Eight! Nine . . .

As the numbers accrued, nearing twenty, my eyes stung. I knew
every voice. I thought about Miguel's four small children and Luke's
dream to return to a dairy farm in Minnesota. Mac's baby, Sonia, and
Fisher's wife, Jenny. Keller's mother, a middle school principal. Barrel
would turn twenty-one this summer. I thought of the lives we had
left to live, and I said a silent prayer that this scenario would never
be real.

At the end of the day, Van called over the second years—Haines,
Trevan, Barrel, Miguel, me, and Keller—and handed out stapled pack-

ets that read, "NWCG Task Book for the Positions of Firefighter Type 1 (FFT1), Incident Commander Type 5 (ICT5)."

"I'm opening Firefighter One for all you second years," Van said. "I'm not sure how many assignments you'll get this season. Depends what kind of year we have. But I'm hoping you can all get some ink this summer."

We thanked him, paging through the document. Inside was a list of skills with corresponding evaluation forms: preparing for an assignment, giving a briefing, supervising a group, using a radio, patrolling the fireline, providing a spot weather forecast. The last would be a given for me, since I was the assigned weather person for Bravo. We tucked the packets into our cubbies.

When I talked to Addison that night, she saw the chainsaw situation very differently than I'd expected. She was annoyed that the second tree got hung up but didn't mention the first. On the whole, she seemed to think she'd done well. And the saw boss, our most exacting Squadie, whom I'd never seen go soft on anyone, had confirmed her opinion.

"You know what Mac said? He said, 'I wish you were a faster hiker.'"

I groaned. "That's frustrating. But it's also, like, a reason to hope. It means that if you do get faster at hiking, there's a chance to get on a saw team."

"A *chance?*" Addison said. "It makes me so angry. I've been running saw for five years, and now I have to fight for a chance to get on a saw team *eventually?*"

"Yeah," I said slowly. "It's frustrating. But that's a hotshot crew." I shrugged. "You can only run the saw if you can hike the saw."

"It's fucking stupid."

I said *mm* or *yeah*, though I did not agree.

But I tried to put myself in her shoes. She'd told me on one of our preseason hikes that six years earlier, her brother had died in a car accident. I imagined being twenty years old, and entering this intimidating profession, and losing a sibling . . . I got the impression that Addison had help from therapy or a support group, and I was glad. But it seemed to me she carried a heaviness so palpable it was nearly a visible burden: the weight of unresolved grief.

If I had come to firefighting in my early twenties, the job would have destroyed me. No sense of self, slutty and needy and weak, I probably would've slept with half the crew, had a meltdown, and left before completing a single season. Yet here was this young woman building a career in fire, braving a culture that was often hostile to the presence of women.

But not here, not on this crew. Remembering how I'd been supported and accepted the year before, I hoped this would become a corrective experience for Addison too. Squeezing her arm, I thought, *This'll be a good place for her. I'll make sure of it.*

A few days later, sun sparkled on the river at the Forks, snowmelt-frigid and emerald-clear. I dove in and came up breathless. My hands tingled; lips went numb. Still, I treaded water for a minute, watching my friends onshore.

That day, I had tackled a hike we called Horrible Hill carrying half a jerry can of water, the 2.5 gallons adding twenty pounds (for sixty-five pounds altogether). I'd come in nearly last, a failure reminiscent of my rookie year. But what would have humiliated me before was just a bad hike now, a reminder to carry more weight more often. When I reached the top gasping and red, I had grinned, heaved the jug to the ground, and shouted, *Anybody thirsty?* I was too proud of making the guys laugh to care about much else.

"How do you do that?" Addison called.

"What, tread water?"

"No. Dive! I could never do it."

"Are you serious?"

She giggled. "Seriously. I never learned."

"Well, you're learning right now."

I scrambled onto the rocks, cold water shearing off my body. I had grown thick that spring, probably 165 pounds. I was muscular—stronger than I'd ever been—but a little flub pooched out around last year's two-piece. All my life, no matter my size (even when I starved myself to 115 pounds in high school), I had always felt like an elephant in a swimsuit. I longed for the time just three or four fires from now when my body would lean out by default—when weight loss would happen *to* me, like an act of god, while I ate everything in sight. It would be a stretch to say I loved the job because it starved me; there was so much else to love. But it wasn't an undesirable side effect.

"Okay!" I said. "Let's see if I can remember. I know you've gotta get low." I waved Addison over and showed her how to crouch, curling her body into a ball with hands steepled. We did several practice runs, "falling" forward in that position. Addison went in like a stone, shock of dark hair flashing like a raven's wing before she sank.

"You need more distance," Haines suggested. "More thrust."

"Yeah, more *launch*," Trevan said. "Just, ya know, launch it!"

"Stop!" I hissed. "Don't listen to them."

When we tried to advance to a squat with a push-off, she splatted into the water in a half belly flop, half banana. She came up gasping, giggling. I was bent over with laughter.

"Getting closer!"

"Ugh," she paddled over. "I think we're done."

We lay on the rocks, letting the sun dry our skin. With relief, I wrapped a towel around my waist, hiding myself. Haines's carved torso glittered, water droplets clustered in his chest hair. Eddie's dark locks lay in wet ropes on his smooth neck. Trevan was less skinny this year, more muscular. We told him so, and he said, "I know, turds. I told you. I was in the gym all winter."

The resource order came when we had forgotten how badly we wanted it.

On an early June morning, we hiked Brokeback to the bell. I did well, Addison had improved, too, and the crew sat at the top beneath the tree outfitted with a metal triangle, grinning as each person arrived and rang the "bell" in victory. A month in, the worst of training was over.

In the afternoon, we drove to an area called Three Ponds for a lesson on pump operation. We spread the equipment near the shallow pond: MARK-3 portable pumps, foot valves and lengths of hose, jerry cans of fuel.

"This would be a good place to meditate," somebody said.

"Great idea," Fisher said. "Ramsey, let's have a little sesh before we get to work."

A week earlier, Van granted me an afternoon of classroom time, and I taught a workshop on firefighter mental health, peer-to-peer support, and mindfulness meditation. To my surprise, the guys loved it. But I never expected *Fisher* to suggest we meditate.

"Okay, everybody, find a comfy seat," I said.

"Can we lie down?"

"Sure."

We settled at the pond's edge.

"Close your eyes," I began. Then ten radios crackled.

"Mac, Van."

"Yeah Van, go."

"Bring 'em back. We got the order."

We hurried back to the station, whooping and bumping fists when Fisher said the order was for Arizona. The Southwest meant travel and hotels. It meant cacti and sand, overtime and per diem, more burning than digging line, and a paycheck that would get us out of the red. *Hell yeah, boys. Southwest, here we come.*

Back at the station, people rushed in all directions—stocking bins, loading the ATV, grabbing cubies of water and cases of MREs. I strode around briskly, feeling tall in my boots and sure in my duties. They'd put more on me this year: the supply bin on Bravo as well as the weather, for which I'd been granted my own radio. On the dig, I would be second P behind Luke. I double-checked the stash of supplies, grabbed extra batteries, picked up a spare weather kit. I helped Miguel and Wink load water on the Supt truck. Like the men I'd envied last year, I, too, could be everywhere at once.

None of my responsibilities were huge, nothing glorious. I stood barely an inch above a rookie—and I liked the shelter and anonymity of the herd. But I had a place here, a role to play.

Eddie wasn't in Bravo this year, which saddened me, especially since Bao was away on a summer-long detail to a helicopter in Idaho. Two of my buddies gone. But Trevan sat beside me in the back row, and we still had Keller, BJ, and Luke. Odd-duck Englefield now occupied the captain's chair in front of me, loading a small grocer's worth of bizarre foods into his bin, including an entire tub of cottage cheese. *You plan to eat all that before it goes bad?* I asked, and he said, *Yeah. And I'm lactose intolerant too*, with a wicked smile. To his right was Shaggy, a young rookie with great music taste and an easy grin.

We snapped our line gear into the shelves.

"Y'all about ready?" Fisher asked impatiently.

"Almost!"

"What are you smiling about?" Shaggy asked.

"Just excited, I guess. The Southwest is fun. You're gonna love it, dude."

It would've felt silly to tell him the truth. *I'm smiling because I finally belong here.*

"Ready?" Fisher said, glancing over his shoulder.

I pulled the buggy door shut and Trevan said, "All in!"

"Here we go, boys and girls!" Fisher hollered, and we rolled out through the stone gates.

Chapter 14

The Telegraph

Bravo was broken. The swing buggy we'd borrowed had a CD player, and as we waited near a gas pump, Fisher discovered that it was loaded with the previous crew's music. Excited, he pressed the button for disc one, and a high-pitched wailing filled the buggy. *Bagpipes?*

Laughter.

Luke asked, "Is 'Amazing Grace' on there?"

"I doubt it."

But a moment later, a recognizable tune arose from the honking instruments. A forlorn melody, unmistakable. "Holy—" Fisher howled. "It *is* 'Amazing Grace.'"

"*Fuck* yeah!" Luke yelled, pounding the ceiling.

Fisher turned it up, and we rolled past Alpha with bagpipes blaring. I could think of no better invocation for the first travel day, a moment that felt like going off to war, than this cross between a blessing and a dirge. No better tune for a group of people headed into chaos and flames—hoping to be saved, to save something, or both.

*   *   *

We arrived the next day in Pinetop-Lakeside, Arizona, our prepo site. Prepo, or "pre-position," is when a module is ordered to an area because of a heat wave, wind, or any harbinger of increased fire activity. They place you somewhere central, and you wait for a fire. Prepo is notoriously chill: hotels, per diem, eating out, PTs . . . and volleyball.

Volleyball, the unofficial sport of hotshot crews everywhere—and the official nightmare of nerds; that noble, uncoordinated tribe of which I counted myself a member. I dreaded volleyball. That day, I played so poorly that even Wink took to bullying me, saying "It h-happens to the best of us," every time I missed a spike or a bump, until I grew frustrated enough to tackle him into the sand.

Later, as I settled at a picnic table with my book, Benjy ambled over to see if I'd proofread something.

"Sure," I said, honored to be asked.

When I sat in the passenger seat of Alpha buggy and opened his laptop, my heart fluttered. It was a personal and semi-legal document about some serious stuff going down in his home life.

He slumped in the driver's seat.

"Dude. I'm so sorry."

"Ah, is what it is," he said. He sounded gruff, but I wasn't fooled. His eyes were red. He looked like he hadn't slept in a week.

"Well. It sounds tough to me. It would be understandable to feel . . . upset," I said with a sad smile. "The good news is, I can fix up your grammar easily. No problem."

"Cool."

I knew I wasn't there to fix his writing, though it was a mess. Benjy needed a friend.

His brother had perished in an accident five years earlier, and he (understandably) wasn't over it. Benjy bore the twin burdens of loss and his difficulties at home like just punishments for a crime I could see no evidence of.

That night, he texted me an SOS, and I sat on the edge of his bed-spread and let him rage for fifteen minutes. Bitch this and crazy cunt that. But when I gave him a hug, he broke. His body shook with hot sobs that seemed to be wrenched out of him against his will.

"I'm afraid I'm a monster," he gasped. "I'm afraid I'm a bad person."

Aren't we all.

Tears filled my eyes. "You're not. You're one of the best people I know."

He mumbled thanks, trying to catch his breath. "I'm afraid I'll be broken by this. That I'll just break, and I won't be okay again."

I murmured words of comfort, and eventually his tears subsided. He seemed sheepish then, so I made an excuse to duck out. It was hard to know how to promise a guy he wouldn't be broken forever, when life's waves kept knocking the legs out from under him—this man who, on the hill near a fire, was sure-footed as a mountain goat and decisive as a general. It wasn't fire that was hard; it was ordinary life.

As I climbed the motel stairs, I remembered my own first round of "difficulties at home."

By the time our road trip ended, and we drove the bleak winter highways from Wisconsin to Pennsylvania, Matthew and I were nearly out of money and teetering on the brink of divorce. We'd drained our savings to see the country, fighting bitterly every step of the way.

We moved to Pittsburgh, where I'd been accepted into graduate school, and the next spring, just before my mom remarried, I left Matthew. It had been a long time coming; three years of me clawing to get free as he grasped to hold on.

Almost the instant I was cut loose, a baby-faced divorcée of twenty-five, I was back to my old wanton ways.

There was the male model (a month or so); we rode around on his motorcycle and got bottle service at downtown clubs, me feeling like a fraud in miniskirts and makeup. Then there was the writer who owned a house in Polish Hill (a year). A friend who was engaged to his childhood sweetheart (a whoopsie, now and then). The director of a local nonprofit, whom I seduced with a crooked finger on a dive bar dance floor (one night only).

Other women marveled (not without resentment) at my talents for seduction. I heard that the queen bee of the hipster scene in town said about me: "What, is her pussy filled with cocaine?" Friends would say, *I wish I had your confidence*, but my edge wasn't self-esteem. Quite the opposite. I was brazen, pretty enough to get what I wanted—and desperate. I craved the attention more than other women. *Needed* it.

Scenes linger in my memory: fucking in cars on highway shoulders, sleeping with someone's boyfriend, waking up unsure how a stranger from the wedding ended up in my room . . . When those memories replay, the regret still turns my stomach. I thought I was getting love, but I was getting hurt. Correction: I was hurting myself. I put myself through heartbreak and loss again and again. Hope and despair. I threw myself at men like you'd throw yourself off a cliff. I wanted to vanish into them, become little more than their aftershave or evaporating sweat. This, like starvation, was a way to disappear.

One summer when I was dating a musician, we visited my dad's lake house. Sitting in his dining room, we played him a song, Mark on guitar. I took a verse now and then, throwing the high harmony on the chorus.

My dad sat enraptured, eyes half-closed, cigarette about to fall from between his fingers. He swayed a little, like he was keeling on an invisible boat—it was hard to tell if it was the music or the effect of whiskey number five. When we finished, his face was wet with tears.

"You have the voice of an angel," he said.

My latest boyfriend was a bona fide talent, but my dad didn't care about Mark's gifts—it was me he watched. It was as if, possibly for the first time, he saw me sitting across from him.

A friend and I moved to Austin after grad school, Mark followed, and when it fell apart, he screamed and threw the city trash bins across the yard. He told his friends that I was "Armageddon"; I had ruined his life. He wasn't the first to say something like that.

I waited stiffly for the tantrum to end. I already had the next guy cued up like a song. That was Charlie, a person whose entrance into my life marked a new phase—a better one—and the end of my desperate, lost, philandering, and ultimately sad twenties. Until I fell into Charlie's warm embrace, I hadn't noticed how tired I was.

Tired of long nights in bars, secondhand smoke, and the merry-go-round of friends and parties and shows. Tired of trying to figure out a "career" and the shallow solace of fucking a stranger. Tired of drunks. Tired of grief.

That was it: I was mourning. If only I could've worn black, donned a veil, and joined a convent. If only I'd gone to India to scrub floors and fidget through dawn meditation. If only I could've shrugged and said, "Sorry I'm a mess. My dad's dying." How I might have been understood then, and held.

But it wasn't cancer or Parkinson's, some obvious disease ebbing the life from my father. We don't acknowledge drinking as an illness, though it is, and we don't see an alcoholic's kids as orphans of a living ghost, though they are. I was left to witness my father's multi-decade decline on my own, sans six stages or support group. I was left to blunder in the dark, unable to even name it—*this is grief.*

It just felt like everything hurt.

*　　*　　*

But wasn't it great when everything hurt? Physically, that is. Sore muscles were the surest way to forget the past—or at least, that was the philosophy that got me into fire, the ethos that found me running uphill in the Arizona heat.

Our second day of prepo began with a six-mile trail run, the first three miles uphill. Squats, lunges, push-ups, planks. Down the hill, back into boots and greens, and out to the woods; Van had found us something to do.

As we rode out the dirt roads to the unit we'd be prepping, my head was pounding. The run, the desert air, the lack of sleep, and the stress of being Benjy's confidante—something was getting to me, and I felt sodden as old lettuce.

We parked in a pullout and readied our gear.

"Kellay!" Mac called, elongating my name in that affectionate way. He held a small, cute saw, maybe half the size of the Stihl 400-series we used on fires. A pint-sized Husqvarna. "You want to cut today?"

I hesitated. This was my chance to show I was a go-getter, that I wanted to be on a saw team eventually. But in the split second I had to decide, I faltered. There'd be nobody to mentor me, not like last summer when Ryan walked by my side and kindly told me what to cut, offered notes. Just go out there with this tool I hadn't touched in a year, and barely knew how to use, and get after it? Like, drop trees *on my own*?

"Um, that's okay. Not today," I said. "I have a headache."

"Oh. Okay," Mac said, stunned.

When I saw the look on his face, I wanted to take it back, to time travel and say, *Heck yeah. Thanks, Mac!* And then run saw just as horribly as you please and drop a tree caddywhompus, drop trees every which way, on my own head, anything to avoid that look. I would accept a week in the hospital over that disappointed expression on his lean, handsome face. But it was too late.

Mac turned away and offered the saw to Addison, who took it glee-fully, not a second's hesitation. Well, there was a silver lining. Addison would get another chance.

I joined a line of swampers near Scotty, whose easy smile always comforted me, and though it was of little solace, we only lopped and scattered brush and tiny four-foot-tall pines (trees, I noted with regret, I could easily have cut) for an hour before the call came in.

Load up. We've got an order.

We drove southwest on Highway 60, a remote pass made eerie by smoke that thickened as we drove, the air yellowing, trees and brush glowing like green neon in the hazy light. We followed the canyon of the Salt River, a narrow thread of water humming silently far below us, and passed a ghost town called Seneca. This was Apache territory, or it had been.

We were headed to the Telegraph, a new fire in the Tonto National Forest that promised to become the next big thing (three days old; 56,600 acres). This was its smoke, coloring the air a hundred miles away.

As we pulled into Globe, Arizona, I noticed two things. One, how the landscapes of American fire could become routine, how I'd end up with a mental atlas of the West just like Benjy's. Looking at a map, the town of Sunflower, where we'd put in line around Winkler's Ranch a year before, lay forty miles as the crow flies north-northwest of our destination for today, the town of Superior. Two megafires within fifty miles in under a year. If I were this patch of desert, I'd start to take it personally.

(To clarify: a "megafire" is a wildfire that consumes more than one hundred thousand acres, while a "gigafire" burns more than one mil-lion).

The second thing I noticed was the Telegraph's column, sheared and sloppy, pale gray at the edges with a dark, angry core. My heart picked up to a trot. Even if the sight of a new fire was a thrill laced with dread, it was most of all a thrill.

Oh shiiiiit, Keller said, watching the crumbling high-rise of smoke billow and foam into the hot desert sky. We reached Superior, had fire-camp dinner in the parking lot of an evacuated medical clinic, and drove at dusk through rock-cliff canyons studded with cacti and sun-bleached grasses. The fire's perimeter was pouring off the ridge, glowing and dripping like hot paint between sand-colored rocks. But this was just her flank, a twinkling red that spread quietly as oil. Her head was a different story.

At dusk, we came to a wide pullout to gear up, and there, on the jagged silhouette of the horizon, loomed a funnel of smoke like a raging tornado. The column was growing even as the day ended and the temperature dropped. Insane. That's not how it's supposed to go, but the Telegraph didn't care about the rules. The earth, brush, and trees were oven-baked from the hundred-degree day, and she had hit the right alignment of slope and fuels. From where we were, we could hear the howl—like the roar of a thousand lions, like a fleet of jet engines passing overhead—the sound of fire devouring everything. At the base of the thick and twisting column, flames shot up like fireworks, flared like the flash on an old camera. If we could see the flaming front at this distance, it was huge, taller than houses.

We watched for an hour or two; darkness fell. The column subsided and swirled away beyond the hills. "This is my last year in fire," somebody was saying, maybe Luke. They always said it like you'd say, *This is my last year smoking cigarettes.* Luke had already had three or four "last" years. Fire was a fickle partner you couldn't quit.

At zero thirty, we got the call: time to burn.

I was paired with Fisher and Luke, mostly as their fuel mule. No problem there: I loved playing porter of the woods, traipsing along with a steel can of ammo and a five-gallon jug of diesel and gas, flames on one side, cold darkness on the other. The weight—say, ninety or so pounds—didn't bother me anymore, especially in this flat terrain. And I'd found that if you were an attentive, obsequious mule, some fun stuff might be thrown your way.

Dawn found us firing rounds into a bowl, a hollow in the earth carpeted with green bushes. We had lit off the edge of the dirt road with drip torches, but as the sun tinged the horizon gray, the air remained too humid, and the fire wouldn't move. So we traded off the pistol— "Firing!"—and shot, the flares taking with a *pffffft*! Soon the bowl filled with a constellation of merry little blazes.

"Good enough, folks," Fisher said. "Sounds like we're hikin' out."

We trudged uphill the way we'd come. The sky was splashed with orange and pink behind tatters of clouds, a perfect desert sunrise. Lizards scuttled away from our boots, and we joked quietly as we made our way to the buggies. A twenty-five-hour shift, and I felt great. I had been of use.

I joined Addison on the elevator to our room. We'd been awake for nearly thirty hours, and now we'd scored a day's sleep in the Four Points by Sheraton in Phoenix, which had the dream bed, a mattress of holy softness. It cupped me like a cloud, like the kindly hands of an immortal mother. I thought briefly of Josh, with a pang of guilt about already feeling distant from him and the passing thought, *I should call him when I wake up*. And I was out.

After several more night shifts (burning, huddling by warming fires while babysitting a burn), we flipped back to days, the sun howling out of a cloudless sky, the desert glinting beneath it like hammered metal.

We prepped a property that we'd been told belonged to a man named Jack. Houses, horses, barns, a canyon full of overhead brush. A doomed place, but we tried. We cut all around the pad where the home stood, chaining great bundles of greenery into the hole below. As we sat down for a snack, I mentioned how pleased I'd been with dinner the night before. It wasn't every fire where you received a Thanksgiving feast.

"Turkey? That was ham, Kelly," Trevan said.

"No way. That was definitely turkey."

"It was pink! Like a *ham*. And circular. Like ham!"

"You don't put gravy on ham."

"Who's with me?" Trevan said, looking around. "Who knows that was ham?"

"I could see ham," said Keller, almost apologetically.

"I vote turkey," Luke said.

"How much you wanna put on it?" Trevan asked me, a gleam in his eye.

"Twenty."

"Really? Sure you wanna do that?"

"Yeah," I said calmly. "I know I'm right."

By the end of lunch, we'd recruited teams. Meat debates raged through the afternoon, a welcome distraction from the heat and sun that pursued us everywhere, leeching water from our skin as we scraped meager fire line in the sand.

Near the end of the day, I saw a text from Josh that his crew had an assignment: they were headed to the Joshua Tree area. He was on prepo, but surely they'd get a fire down south . . . or enjoy two weeks of hanging out with cacti. I was happy for him.

His assignment did mean, however, that when I returned from this roll, he'd be gone—which increased the likelihood that he'd get back from *his* roll, and I'd be gone. Chances were, we'd spend a month apart, maybe more, before our R&R days aligned. I had just missed his birthday for the second year running, and now it looked like a long haul before we'd celebrate. I was bummed, but not that bummed. Then, in a pattern that was becoming common, I felt guilty about my lack of bum.

Luke was one of the guys assigned to pick up our meals. In camp, he asked the caterers about dinner the previous night. What meat had that been? Back at our spike camp, as I ate, Luke came by and whispered—as if dropping a gift in my ear—"It was turkey."

Oh, did I gloat. I found Trevan in the buggy and leered in his face. "Did you hear?"

"Ah," he waved me away.

"I WIN," I said. "I was right, you were wrong. Come on. Say it."

Trevan shrugged. "I'm still not sure."

"Oh come on, can't you just say it? I was right! This is, like, the one and only time. Give me this."

"Can we really trust Luke?" Trevan raised an eyebrow. "I'm not convinced."

He never gave me the satisfaction of admitting I'd won, but the next day I found a twenty-dollar bill in my cup holder.

Chapter 15

Denali

Day ten, I woke covered in ash. Feathery gray chunks of it spangled my sleeping bag and lay like dirty snowflakes on my boots. When we'd fallen asleep in the parking lot and baseball diamond of a municipal park, we could see the fire backing down a mountain just outside of town. An apron of char with a ruffle of flame, it poured down the hill. The sight of fire in the darkness as I drifted off burrowed into my mind, and I startled and tossed, dreaming flames would overtake us in our sleep.

Fisher was on the phone with Jenny as we climbed into the buggy, groggy and struggling to shove our sock-fattened bags into the bins. He was telling his wife that today felt like the end times.

"Okay, love, I'll call you later. And if I don't, you know what to do."

Her laughter on speaker phone. His deranged yodel-laugh. "I'm kidding," he said, hanging up. But he turned to us to finish the joke: "Shoot the dogs and sell the house."

"Pretty dark, Fish!" I yelled, and he grinned over his shoulder. "Yeah, well."

By afternoon, some fresh Armageddon was indeed upon us. The Telegraph blew up near the town of El Capitan, where we'd prepped the house.

Fire was pushing Highway 70, and if it jumped the road, it risked merging with a smaller fire called the Mescal. We drove to a staging area, a football field–sized dirt lot where buggies and dozer transports, water tenders and engines waited. Waiting, with good reason: as we piled out of the trucks, we looked back and saw an army of flames marching across the hills.

We strung out in the shade of the buggy, leaning against the vehicle's cool green metal, and someone pulled out binoculars and passed them down the line. When they got to me, I cinched them to fit my face and gaped at the scene in the magnified sphere. The flames stood at least fifty feet tall, running shoulder-to-shoulder like Olympic sprinters through the brush and juniper. The licking, seething edge of the fire raced for a cluster of houses on a rise above the highway. We could feel the heat from here, like the hot gust from an opened oven. The wind carried chunky black clots of smoke to the south.

"It sounds like the ocean," BJ said. He was right—this vegetation made a different roar than our California timber, high and clean.

I got a lump in my throat. "You think Jack's place is okay?" I asked softly.

"Doubt it," Trevan said.

Standing in front of the forward-march of flames would be death. As the guys liked to say when a fire was unstoppable, and you could only get out of the way, *There she goes. She gone.* Fire was always a woman to them; some people took offense, but I found the comparison flattering to my gender. What force, after all, was more mysterious and powerful than wildfire?

One by one, the engines who'd lingered to spray water on the houses withdrew. They crawled like ants down the hill and crossed the highway to join us. I said a silent prayer that the people who lived in those homes had grabbed their family photos and gotten the hell out.

*   *   *

The next day, we went direct for ten hours on a squiggly black edge around El Capitan. Our tools were hardly necessary in the thin, sandy soil; you could practically kick the ground cover aside, leaving bare earth. I carried a rake in addition to my Pulaski, so I joined Wink on team power rake.

A guy named David had met up with us for this roll, a former hotshot who now worked in the Fuels department (as in fuels reduction, responsible for forest thinning and prescribed burning projects). While he certainly had the qualifications to substitute as Bravo's Captain until our official detailer arrived in July, years had passed since his time in operational fire. He was very kind, but since he was also academic and not overtly muscular, much of the crew regarded him with thinly veiled disdain. *That's not a fuckin' hotshot.*

We climbed a cut bank off the road. David carried his Rhino tucked in his pack, so the wooden handle stuck out behind him like a stinger. Wink was behind David, while I followed Wink. As we scrambled up the loose embankment, Wink looked down, watching his footing.

David, losing his balance, took a half step back. As he righted himself, his tool handle swung upward, catching Wink in the face. I heard the sound—*crack!*—and put a hand on Wink's back. "Whoa. You okay?"

"Yeah, fine bud!" He turned and smiled. My eyes went wide. Confused, he brought a hand to his mouth. Blood ran through his fingers.

David turned. "Oh no. I'm sorry!"

"Oh my god," I said. "Let me see your mouth."

"What?" He opened wide.

"Wink. Your *tooth*."

One of his front teeth was gone. Broken clean off, nothing but a shallow stump remaining.

The following minutes were organized chaos. Someone got on the radio, someone on the phone to find the nearest dentist, and someone on the UTV to pick up Wink. Meanwhile, a guilt-racked David began to build a case for his defense.

"He was following too close to me," David said. "I didn't know he was right there."

I blinked at him. *Bogus.* We followed close on each other's heels; we were trained to. But we also carried our tools in our *hands*—for this reason.

"W-what if I was to keep working?" Wink was asking, as Scotty—who had arrived with his EMT kit—examined his mouth, quickly deciding that, yep, this was a job for a dentist.

Poor Winkler. He was in debt, a hole he dug every winter, and this was only the first roll of the season. He needed money—couldn't afford to miss even a few hours of OT and H (overtime and hazard pay, which nearly doubled our hourly rate). Yet here he was, face smeared with blood, afraid to leave the line.

"I think they'll still keep you on H-pay, buddy," Scotty said, trying to comfort him.

"B-but what if I was to go to the dentist t-tonight?"

"No, bud. You gotta go now," Scotty said with his gentle smile. "We'll get this taken care of and we'll get you right back to the line. I promise."

With that, they loaded Wink's tools and line gear onto the UTV while he climbed dejectedly into the passenger seat. As they pulled away, he gave me a bloody, gummy smile.

The air temperature was at least a hundred and ten, so even with the easy "dig," we had salt rings on our yellows, perspiration matting our hair. After a while, you ran out of sweat and the salt dried to a crust on your cheeks. Van hiked in with one bag full of ice and another of cold Gatorades. He made his way down the line, pouring ice water on everyone's necks. So kind.

By the time the sun began to sink, distant thunder shook the sky, and Wink returned with a fresh, temporary tooth, white as a chunk of marble.

I sent Josh a series of texts when we got into service. He sent back one response, a "hey I love you" that gave no indication he'd even read what I'd written. I thought, *If I weren't out here busy and tired, this would suck.* Then I thought, *No, it still sucks.*

All this time, I'd been blaming myself for communicating poorly or not trying hard enough, and Josh had seemed to blame me too. But when he responded the next morning with another text that didn't acknowledge what I'd said, I thought, *Aha.* So it wasn't just me. He got distracted on assignment and dropped the ball too. I felt like he also failed to try.

It wasn't a comforting vindication.

Day twelve, we were going direct again in the punishing sun. We took an afternoon break in the shade of someone's evacuated house to hop on Zoom as a group. Wink had won Firefighter of the Year (for the previous year) for the entire Six Rivers National Forest, not just our station or district. A major award, and they were hosting a ceremony in his honor that he obviously could not attend.

We stood beaming at Wink as various bigwigs speechified on-screen about Wink's years of service, his selflessness, his quiet way of *being* there, ready to lend a hand. Van spoke, too, calling Wink "the heart" of Rowdy River Hotshots. Then the honoree himself was given a chance to speak. I could feel the people beside me stiffen. They, too, were worried that he wouldn't be able to spit out a single word. But he didn't hesitate.

"Th-thank you to my friends and f-family. Thank you all—" he looked shyly around the circle, at us—"for helping me and t-teach me so much."

What a guy. The humility, the beauty of his gratitude, when so much was owed to *him*. I wiped my eyes, and I wasn't the only one. But Wink's other best quality was his sleeper wit. His speech wasn't quite done. "And I got a n-new tooth yesterday!" He opened wide and pointed to the fresh cube of shiny white enamel.

Applause, cheers, and a chorus of the Rowdy River hoot.

At the end of shift, I saw a text from Sarah, who was pet sitting for us back in Happy Camp. *Denali isn't eating,* she wrote. *And she's having a hard time getting up to use the bathroom. She's kinda just peeing where she is. Not sure what to do?*

My stomach bottomed out. I thanked Sarah and called Josh. This was his dog, his baby, the animal he'd shared life with for nearly fifteen years. Who was I to say?

I didn't hear back from him, not before I passed out at nine thirty in the gravel shoulder of the road behind the city park. Sarah had texted that eventually Denali ate a little bit, but I went to bed anxious and angry. How was it that even when I was on a fire, and Josh was on a cover assignment with cushy hotels, it seemed like I was the more available one, the front line of communication for our shared domestic life? I thought of how my friend Emily said that her kids' daycare only ever called her, though her husband's schedule was more flexible. Was this *women's work?*

The next few days, Denali did a little better—well enough that Sarah and I decided she could hang on until I returned from Arizona. Then I'd take her to the vet myself. It was a dark cloud in my periphery for the remainder of the fire. Maybe whatever ailed her could be cured. But she was a very old dog, and she'd been slowing down all year. This might be the end.

On day thirteen, at morning briefing, the IC emphasized that it was too hot for everything. The aircraft were overheating, and the dozers were too hot to function. It was "probably not a day for crew work," he concluded.

And yet. Somehow—always, somehow—we ended up taking an epic UTV ride deep into the hills and going direct on a hot edge of the fire on an utterly exposed, scabby ridge where the earth was pure rock splashed with slippery pink fire retardant. And we were going under-slung (digging line beneath the fire on a slope), forced to construct a cup trench in sheer granite.

Digging that day was like being swaddled in an electric blanket and asked to perform calisthenics inside a sauna. There was no hiding from the sun, a punishing tyrant that baked our skin through the Nomex. The rocks were secondary suns radiating heat upward, so we were seared evenly, top and bottom, unhappy steaks.

So it was going really well. Then the fire beetles arrived.

Melanophila acuminata, or the "fire chaser beetle," contains highly sensitive infrared receptors that—via a small pocket of water in its abdomen that expands in response to heat—can detect heat up to eighty miles away. The half-inch, narrow black beetles flock to the scene of a forest fire to lay their eggs in smoldering wood, where their offspring are unlikely to be disturbed by predators.

Literally *born from fire*: How metal is that? I would've admired the species for their resourcefulness—except that they bite. And it *hurts*. Less of a sting, more of a chomp like a black fly bite, with an ache that lingers.

As we worked to chip and pry rocks to build our trench, the fire beetles swarmed. They alit on our scalps, gnawed our necks, crept into the folds behind our ears. They crawled up our sleeves and bit the back of our arms. They flew up our pants, clamping down on the tender flesh of the inner thigh.

"Ouch!"

"Jesus."

"FUCK!"

Luke swatted his neck, Shaggy jumped, Scotty slapped his sleeves, and Englefield swore. I reached up my pant leg, grasping for a beetle that had latched onto my knee pit. We were getting mauled.

"Back off!" Scotty called, and we retreated a few yards into the green, still swatting away the beetles' shiny black bodies.

"What are we doing?" Bellomo asked. "Why are we doing this? It doesn't make sense."

I remembered the days when I had asked those questions. No longer. Now I had fully accepted the concept Eddie taught me: *It never makes sense, Kelly.* On this day, our task defied logic—the fire had already jumped this line elsewhere, and a bulldozer was pushing out ahead of us. So Bellomo wasn't wrong to ask. But there was nothing we could do about the pointlessness of the day's work, and as his questions turned to whining, our replies turned to grunts.

We dug and dug. The heat of the day kept rising, now at least a hundred and ten. The fire beetles kept biting. Finally, Bellomo snapped. I'm not sure if he threw down his tool or if he just had throwing-his-tool-to-the-ground energy.

"This doesn't make any fucking sense!" he yelled. "What are we DOING? I don't know why the hell we're out here, but it's too hot, and there's no reason for this. I don't know why Van thinks we have to get after it, but we don't. This is dumb. This is so STUPID!"

Bellomo wasn't wrong, of course; it *was* stupid. But the rest of us had learned to accept it.

"Come on, man," Luke tried to console him. "We're all strugglin'. But this is the job."

"This doesn't have to be the job!"

Bellomo was briefly inconsolable.

When our chainsaws started overheating and threatening to geyser fuel in the searing heat, Van finally gave the word to hang dow. We "hooched up" under a few tarps lashed to limbs of palo santo, huddled together in a pocket of shade. For the fun of it, I spun a spot weather report. We called it "spinning weather" because you literally twirled a device called a sling psychrometer, essentially two thermometers on a chain, to determine the humidity.

Telegraph Fire, Division X (in the phonetic alphabet, "X-Ray," which I loved), June 17, 1530 p.m., Elevation, 3100 feet, on a Western-facing slope with sparse stand density. Temperature: 116 degrees. Relative humidity: 8 percent. Winds 1–2 miles per hour out of the West. Dew point: 39. Probability of Ignition, or POI: 100 percent.

Holding the radio near my mouth, I keyed it up and read out the data. I relished delivering these updates, clarity and precision of speech being a rare easy task for me. I reported the bonkers POI, concluding, "How do you copy?"

Laughter, both under the tarp and in the background when Van came on the radio. We'd witnessed uncanny fire behavior at 90 degrees with a POI of 75; this weather was *beyond*. "Good copy. Thanks, Kelly."

That season, Wink's favorite catchphrases were "might as well" and "which is nice." Scotty and I had taken to using them almost more than Wink did, and now we joked, "Want to get after it?"

"Might as well."

"It's 116 degrees."

"Which is nice."

When we hiked out and stood on the road waiting for the UTV's to shuttle us out, Shaggy and Barrel came along with cold bottled water, which they poured on everyone's necks. You could hear each sigh of relief as they moved down the line. *I bet it's not every crew that does this,* I thought. *What a sweet and loving act. WE are sweet.*

I thought it again when, back at the buggies, Bellomo made his rounds, apologizing for losing his cool on the dig.

"Ah, no big deal! It happens," Luke said, his hand sweeping it away. "We've all been there."

And Scotty said, "I get it, man. I get it. We just . . . the work is hard enough. We've gotta keep it positive."

Bellomo promised to try, and soon we were rolling through the town of Globe, where Van surprised us by authorizing a stop at—wait for it—DAIRY QUEEN. And oh my sweet baby Jesus, how amazing it feels, when a day like that one is done, over and done with, though maybe never forgotten, and you're sitting in the cold, humming air-conditioning in a slick booth with a DQ blizzard in your ash-stained hands.

I was sitting next to Englefield. Eddie slid in across from us. We watched in mingled horror and admiration as Englefield destroyed mountains of food: multiple burgers, fries and tots, and two types of ice cream.

"Wow," Eddie said. "You're an animal."

"Never forget it," Englefield said, a rascal's grin around a mouth full of burger.

The next morning, up at dawn, I was heading to the bathroom when I spied Eddie on the lawn. The municipal park in Globe made extensive use of sprinklers, and that morning they sang in rainbowed arcs across the grass, crisscrossing streams of water winging in every direction. Eddie, in boots and greens, walked under the spray. He spread his arms wide and turned up his face to receive the rain. Watching him, skin golden in the early light, eyes closed in bliss, I thought, *I love that guy.*

The thing is, I wasn't even alarmed to admit I loved him. He was taken, I was engaged, and I reasoned, you can love someone this much as a friend. Didn't I love my friend Lindsay, an artist who dragged me into icy creeks in April, in just this way? What was the line between platonic and romantic love, anyway? If I never touched Eddie, which I never intended to, I'd have an amazing male bestie.

I was lying, of course. But I'm telling you, I did it so well, I believed myself.

*   *   *

Heading home, the heat oppressed us, heavy and smothering. As we waited in line for an oil change for the buggies (federal policies about vehicle maintenance were so stringent, we often had to stop mid-assignment to perform some routine buggy task), the stifling air in the back of the truck made breathing difficult. We were being boiled alive.

We snuck into the Valvoline waiting room for a moment of respite in the air-conditioning, which achieved only a meager triumph over the weather, cooling the room to about eighty-five.

We had donned the clean cotton crew shirts we saved for travel. Still, we reeked of smoke and ash and body odor, of fourteen days without a shower. Sweat slimed our flushed faces. We took turns at the water fountain, cupping water in our hands, splashing our cheeks and necks.

Fisher burst in.

"Are you bird-bathing in that water fountain?" We froze, guilty. "Get the fuck out of here!"

"Easy for him to say," Trevan grumbled as we filed back to the buggy. "When he's up front with the A/C."

Shaggy said, "Dude, I wouldn't leave my *dog* in that vehicle in this weather."

As we drove across hundreds of miles of desert, into Nevada and then California, I wondered if fourteen hours in a 105-degree vehicle could be considered a form of torture. I had started my period, too (of course), so I could feel the blood dribbling out as the sweat drained off of me, a human sieve. The old dehydration headache began to throb.

Music didn't help. I couldn't read, couldn't think. Texting with Josh to confirm my plans for the dog and the vet was a Herculean effort. All I could do was stare out the window, holding my hand at an angle to divert the hot wind into my face.

We were so drained by the end of the day that we no longer spoke, no longer even looked at one another, miserable and mute. We would do it again tomorrow, stoic as soldiers, because we knew that complaining wouldn't change a thing.

Someone didn't know that yet.

When we piled out of the buggies at a hotel, Addison was fuming. As we rode the elevator to our room, I agreed that the lack of air-conditioning in the buggies was ridiculous. I tried to console her, hoping she hadn't let everyone know how she felt.

But the next day, I heard from the guys that she had "thrown a tantrum" about the heat. They told me hesitantly, unsure if it was okay to talk about Addison. Like they hoped I could intervene. Because it wasn't just this moment of anger; we all had our moments. In her first assignment, she had made a mistake that left two guys stranded on the line, had been short-tempered with people, and didn't hustle sufficiently at her chores, in their opinion. Of course, a hotshot's idea of what constitutes "trying" can be extreme—but it was an opinion I shared. And hustling was the hotshot way, our identity, the whole freakin' deal, right?

I reminded myself of how young Addison was and how much she'd been through. And I remembered how hard my first roll in Arizona had been, how much grief I'd been given over the performance of *trash*. So triage was my instinct, too. I had to help. But intervene how? Say what, exactly?

I tried. I pulled Addison aside and suggested as gently as I could that she try to go above and beyond, to be the most awesome, helpful, positive, *uncomplaining* crew member—I didn't say "assimilate" or "in order to vindicate all women and earn the men's trust," but she knew what I meant, and she pushed back.

"Why do I have to work so hard to be accepted?" she asked. "Why couldn't I just be a mediocre crew member, like any man can be? Why do we have to be extraordinary?"

I let out a bitter laugh. She was right; I had seen milquetoast men accepted into the crew—even promoted. I recalled Westbrook's dispassionate leadership on the dig, Bellomo's recent heat fit, Hayes's lackluster hiking the previous spring. Most of our male colleagues hustled and strove, but even those who didn't were tolerated with little more than an affectionate eye roll.

Here again was the age-old double standard, and I couldn't disagree with Addison. It wasn't fair.

On the other hand, it worked for me. The high-performing, self-sacrificing, never-good-enough hotshot mentality fit tongue and groove with my default settings. Why be mediocre when you could be extraordinary? Even forgetting the guys, I loved excellence for its own sake—and for *my* sake. But that didn't mean everyone had to feel the same way. Was I only interested in "diversity" on the crew if it looked like me? Had I clawed out a place for myself, only to pull up the ladder behind me?

I should have worried more about those questions. And I should have defended Addison, or at least shown I wasn't the person to come to with gossip. But I was exhausted, and my thoughts drifted toward home and the problems that awaited me there. So when they talked about her buggy tantrum, I said something like "Really?" or maybe even, "Wow, that's not cool."

Hence, without realizing, I began to ally myself with the boys.

Denali didn't rise from the porch to greet me. She looked happy, and her tail wagged weakly, but when she tried to stand, her legs trembled, and she collapsed. She lay in a stinking puddle of her own urine, fur matted and damp. I was in tears.

"Oh, sweet girl," I murmured, stroking her pretty land-seal head. "I'm so sorry. We're going to take care of you. We're gonna get you whatever you need."

The next morning, Sarah and Dylan came over to help. Denali was a substantial Labrador Retriever, heftier in her old age, and strong as I was from work, deadlifting an eighty-pound animal into my truck as she squirmed and resisted was a struggle. My friends helped me lift her into the passenger seat, then hugged me.

"Let us know if you need anything else."

My *thank you* was almost a whisper, my throat raw with fear.

I made the two-hour drive to the nearest vet in Fort Jones. Our vet, on the cusp of retirement, couldn't see Denali on short notice, so I had to take her to strangers. She lay in the lobby, panting heavily. The staff must have noticed my distress, because one of the ladies offered me a glass of water.

The vet, an older man with impossibly kind eyes, took just a few minutes to complete his assessment.

"Cortisone shots might buy you some time," he said. "She's healthy for her age, except for her back hips giving out. But ultimately, you might only buy a few weeks, maybe a month or two. And she's very uncomfortable."

She would continue to be uncomfortable, and we would continue to be gone on fires, leaving her to suffer without her family. Leaving our friends, possibly, to make this call on our behalf. It wasn't fair, not to anyone.

"It's so hard," the vet said gently, patting my shoulder as the tears fell. "It's completely up to you. We will do whatever you want."

"I need to make a call," I said, and stepped outside.

Luckily, I got Josh on the phone. I told him everything the vet had said.

"I don't know what to do, babe." I said. "I think it's the end, but it doesn't have to be. We can try all that stuff if you want. I'm just afraid we'll be back in the same spot in a few weeks, and neither of us will be around for her." I took a shaky breath. "She's yours. This is your call."

"I think we call it," Josh said.

"Are you sure?"

Silence. The little hiccups of his tears. The quick inbreaths of mine.

"Yes."

"I don't know how to do this," I wept. "I've never done this."

"I'm sorry I can't be there."

"Me too."

"Tell her I love her? Tell her she was always so loved—" He broke off, sobbing.

"I will." Tears rolled onto my neck.

In the end, her death was peaceful. The vet led us out behind the clinic, to a green lawn with a pool of shade under a sprawling oak tree. The office faced a flat rural road through farmland, and when I sat down beside Denali, who lay on a towel in the grass, I had a clear view of Mount Shasta's white peak in the distance.

The vet gave Denali the injection, then left us alone. I stroked her head as her breath slowed. She fell asleep. Her chest rose and fell, softer and softer. I held my breath, waiting for hers to stop. When her chest stilled, her eye drifted open and its pupil, eerily wide, stared at nothing. She was gone.

I pulled my hand away, but I couldn't get up. My face wouldn't stop crying. I couldn't catch my breath. I was sad for the end of Denali's life, sad for Josh. Sad for our other lab, Chief, who'd lose his friend, and sad for myself. *I didn't want to do this alone*, I kept thinking. *Why am I here alone?* It seemed like no matter who I found to play house with me, when it came to the hard stuff, I was on my own.

I sat on the lawn for a long time before I found my feet and put them under me. With the watchful, snowy eye of Mount Shasta looking on, I went into the lobby to swallow hard and talk about cremation, about urns. About ash.

Chapter 16

Tangle Blue

During a surprise station day at the end of June, Eddie gave a talk on South Canyon, a 1994 fatality fire in which fourteen firefighters were killed—burned over—attempting to escape a fire's upslope run. The infamous incident, often called "Storm King" after the mountain in Colorado where it occurred, always left us unnerved. Those who died were hotshots and smokejumpers, the most highly trained wildland firefighters. *Just like us.* Strength and experience, we knew, didn't make you immune to risk. Instead, being "elite" only put us more at risk, because we often took on sketchier assignments. So we studied the mistakes we hoped to avoid: "on a hillside where rolling material can ignite fuel below," and "terrain and fuels make escape to safety zones difficult."

Eddie had been nervous to speak. A smart kid who'd chosen to hang with the skaters and blow off studying in adolescence, he had come to think of himself as neither intelligent nor well-spoken. But that didn't seem true to me, and he did well. The crew was eager to jump in with noisy overlapping opinions, making Eddie's job as referee easy.

After work, I drove to Crescent City for takeout, and as I headed back to Baudelaire, the text appeared: *Order to the Plumas. 0600 tomorrow.*

Copy. Last day of June, fires beginning to pop, no surprise. I shot off the "got an assignment" message to Josh, who called as I pulled into the parking lot. We were having an easy chat, dinner plans and favorite podcasts, when the conversation turned to my assignment. It had come on a Wednesday, just a shift away from my weekend, and Josh had come home just after I'd left for the week. He bemoaned that we'd spend a month apart.

"You know," I said. "The guys pointed out that next time you're on R&R and I'm up here, you could always drive up and visit me. We could hang after work." Despite being invited many times, Josh had never come to Baudelaire. He had never met any of the people I worked with.

"Why would they say that?"

"What do you mean?"

"Were you complaining about me?"

"No! I was just saying it's hard that we keep missing each other."

"How is that their business? Who are they to judge me?"

"Nobody was judging you, babe. They were trying to help."

"I don't like you talking to them about me."

"I'm not talking about *you*. I'm just talking about my life."

"Well, I don't like them acting like I didn't do enough."

"What are you talking about? No one said you didn't do enough!" *This is crazy*, I thought, because Josh had gone from zero to sixty. What I saw as quick anger blindsided me.

"In the future," he said icily. "I would prefer if you didn't talk to the guys about our relationship."

"I wasn't 'talking about our relationship.' But *copy*." I sent the ice right back at him.

Josh stiffly wished me a good assignment, and with a brittle voice I wished him a restful R&R. As we shuttered the conversation, Eddie shouted something taunting across the parking lot. "What was that?" Josh said sharply, and I said, "Just the guys," and he said, *Oh.*

"I love you," he said. I echoed him and hung up with relief.

Was this love?

I had a fleeting thought, terrifying. *What if this relationship is a house of cards?* When I was away, though things were great professionally, things between us quickly deteriorated. A month into the season, and Josh was hard to recognize, a man I felt was prone to volatile outbursts and spasms of jealousy. He looked less and less like the person I had promised to marry just a few months before.

But another fire awaited; this conflict would have to be worked out over R&R—if we saw each other. So I shook it off and strolled back to the bay to eat noodles and joke with the boys that they were in trouble with my fiancé.

My *second* fiancé.

Charlie and I met waiting tables in a restaurant in Austin, Texas. He was athletic, blue-eyed, mischievous—a guy who pranked the female servers and joked in Spanish with the cooks.

He was twenty-five (to my twenty-eight) and came from a large family who grew fruit in Maine. He had that farm wholesomeness, that big brotherly warmth. When I met his parents for the first time, and they learned that I had a master's degree, they teased Charlie that he was "out-chicked," i.e., that I was out of his league, but I knew the opposite was true. There was no way, with my "broken" home and checkered past, that I deserved someone so good.

But, somehow, he loved me. He gave love easily, lightheartedly, without desperation or grasping or the alcoholic's maudlin pronouncements. He didn't drink much. He loved me as if commitment were a foregone conclusion, and his security was confusing but wonderful, like a cozy sweater someone else's size. I had never known anything like it.

We fell into a sweet romance. Riding our bikes to live shows, road trips to the mountains of West Texas, beers on porches. Twelve months of endless summer.

After a year, Charlie confessed that he wanted to be back on the East Coast, closer to his family. I couldn't comprehend the urge (I wanted to get as far from my family as possible, ideally overseas, maybe outer space), but when he said we could spend the summer on an island where his aunt and uncle ran an oyster farm, I heard "island" and thought, *Why not?*

Three years later, we had made ourselves a life. We created an artist-in-residence program on the island, bringing painters and musicians and poets to stay for six weeks, free to make creative work while we tended to their every need. In turn, the artists shared their work in open studios or readings, had a little wine and cheese with the island residents.

After a few years, Charlie and I were paid as co-executive directors. We had a board of directors, a house near the harbor, a studio building. The waves of Long Island Sound lapped at the island's wild rocky shores; mossy paths wound through the forest to secret beaches. Sunset found us at a bonfire on the sand or fishing from a boat near the lighthouse. We were interwoven in the community and Charlie's large, welcoming extended family. It was, as far as anyone could tell, the dream life.

But I left him.

I had my reasons—over time, I felt that he had begun to tune me out; we were more coworkers than lovers. When we finally did get engaged, it was because I badgered him into asking me. *We've been together for four years, Charlie, what are you waiting for?*

Those things did happen, but they weren't the real reasons. In truth, I had found a life—partner, community, work—and it looked like if I stayed, I would be staying for the rest of my earthly days. The thought was terrifying. The idea of living on this five-square-mile speck of land buffeted by frigid waves for the next thirty years made me feel like I was drowning in open air.

That wasn't all of it, either. I think the real problem was that I'd found a nice family, and I didn't believe I deserved them.

So I went back to Austin, only seeing my mistake when it was far too late.

During this time I neither saw nor spoke to my dad. I saw some of the family—Courtney and Renee came to visit, and Evan spent a summer with us, working landscaping on the island—but I kept the "father" part of my life so deeply buried, I could almost pretend it wasn't real.

I didn't want Charlie to meet my dad. I didn't want to know how bad my father's drinking was. And, living in such a fancy place, I didn't want to admit where I'd come from. I didn't want these people with their homes in Corfu and their private planes to see that I wasn't one of them. But of course they already knew; class markers are almost impossible to fake.

One time, I tried to describe my siblings to a relative of Charlie's, a venture capitalist who'd made millions (possibly billions?) as an early backer of a prominent social media platform. He was a fox-eyed, sharp-tongued man. His wife, chair of our board, was a dear friend (to this day one of my heroes), and they'd been generous with us. But he scared the shit out of me. At dinner in their house on the harbor, I fumbled in response to a simple question about what my family was like.

"They're kind of, um, different from me," I stuttered. "Like, they didn't go to college, their lives are more . . . rough? It can be hard to relate—"

"So you think you're better than them." It wasn't a question. His eyes needled into me. *Hypocrite.*

"No!" I said quickly.

Charlie's Aunt Elizabeth, a lionhearted matriarch, rose to my defense, chiding her brother, "Oh, lay off it!" She smoothly changed the subject, but my face was hot with shame. *Was he right? Did I look down on my own family?*

No, certainly not. I wasn't better than anyone. I was the lowest of the low, an interloper, an impostor living among these whippet-people in their loafers and tennis whites. The truth was just that I preferred to keep my family and past at arm's length, where it was safer. Where it hurt less.

But when I left the island and found myself alone again, it all came rushing back.

First of July, my second year of fire, I was anything but alone. The buggies hummed down the I-5, headed for the Plumas National Forest. South of Yreka, smoke obscured the hills, and I thought it must be from the two fires already ripping near Mount Shasta: the twenty-three-thousand-acre Lava and the nine-thousand-acre Tennant. The former generated a pyrocumulus cloud that reached thirty-eight-thousand feet. Like a bigger Mount Everest made of pure white smoke.

Along with a few of the boys, I loved intel—a document called the "SIT Report" that tracked large fires by acreage and region, and the Sit 500, which showed which hotshot crews had gone where. Several websites hosted data and/or rumors about new fire starts; I liked one called Wildfire Intel.

I'm not sure what drove my information obsession. Maybe the desire to possess a whiff of foreknowledge in an unpredictable job. A semblance of control. But I also liked maps for their own sake.

The Preparedness Level, or PL, is a measure of how ready a given region/nation is to confront a major wildfire. A PL of 1 indicates that many resources—engines, crews, tankers, helicopters, dozers, skidgeons, incident commanders, smokejumpers, logistics people, etc.—are ready and waiting, not yet committed to a fire. It goes up from there, with PL 2 and 3 representing slightly fewer resources available, and so on. At PL 5, the highest, almost all resources are committed to existing fires, so if a new fire happens, managers will be hard-pressed to find firefighters without pulling them from another incident.

Each region hits PL 5 at a different time—the Southwest in May, Alaska in June, California in July or August. You can have multiple regions at PL 5 while the nation remains at an overall 3 or 4, but at some point every summer, usually by August, the whole nation will go to PL 5. At that point, good luck getting the crews you need for a fire.

That day, as we drove south, the National PL was 4, while Northern California still sat at a PL 3. We arrived at a small fire called the Dotta, which lay skunking about in a dry creek drainage below cliffs of chiffon-like rock, the kind of place you might call pretty, if you weren't there for a fire.

The first day we went direct and dug line in rotten root-bound earth and caught spots downhill below us and never had lunch. My stomach howled, and my head throbbed. Part of the afternoon found me with Fisher, trying to set damp ground cover alight with fusees (when short on torches, we broke out the red signal flares we all carried in our packs). When they didn't take, we resorted to pouring saw gas on the edge of the line, flicking a lighter on it, and jumping back before the rush of flame burned our faces. A thunderstorm stomped in out of nowhere at dusk, and between the lightning and the fire, it was hard to say which felt angrier, the earth or the sky.

Day four, I learned to run the MARK-3 pump. A Bureau of Land Management engine had posted up on the flat below the cliffs, so I was left with them, and the portly, genial captain taught me how to start the pump's engine, troubleshoot its inevitable problems. The red machine thrummed so loud you couldn't hear anything, especially with earplugs in. I answered the radio calls—"More pressure!" "Less" "Hey, pressure died"—and wrestled the machine back to life, drawing water from a pop-up tank that looked like an above-ground pool and pumping it to the hose lay along the fire's edge, where the crew sprayed and stirred the black.

At the end of the day, no fewer than five people said I had done well at running the pump. I felt I could stay forever in that slippery little drainage, lolling like a tick, fat with pride-blood. *Bury me here*, I thought, and write on my grave: *They said she was good at something once.*

We had a new Captain on Bravo now, Jesse Hale. He was "detailed," or assigned to cover Salomon's permanent position while Salomon detailed elsewhere. Hale came to us on loan from Wolf Creek Hot-shots in Oregon, but he had worked on Rowdy for years, back in the day, so a lot of the guys knew him. Some, like Eddie, considered him a mentor and friend. Fisher, who had an old beef with him, regarded him warily, a near nemesis.

Hale had a shaved head, tattoos, a chiseled jawline. He wore a douchey brand of sunglasses, maybe Heat Waves, and he didn't remove them to shake my hand. *Oh, another bro*, I thought. *Fantastic.*

On day six we were reassigned to the Tangle Blue, a small fire on the Shasta-Trinity National Forest. Eddie's birthday was approaching, and as we drove, I copied a poem and made him a card, my writing erratic as the buggy jerked and swayed over the rural roads.

Heading west on the 299 past the quaint town of Weaverville, we chugged up a steep grade into the mountains, following a gravel road with a sheer drop-off on one side and enough large rocks to make the buggies lurch periodically toward the abyss. We entered the Trinity Alps Wilderness at high elevation, the pines and firs stretching up to graze the sky, their hundred-foot tops bending in an unseen wind. Cool, clear air, no sign of fire.

That was because, as it turned out, the fire was pretty much done. A handful of smokejumpers had jumped the fire a day or two before, and they'd efficiently wrapped the couple-acre blaze in clean, narrow hand line, then strung a hose lay around the thing. Now it smoldered calmly, requiring nothing but mop-up.

At last we pulled off the rutted road, but my heart climbed into my throat when I saw where Mac and Fisher were parking the buggies. *What are we doing?*

When we hopped out of the vehicles and stood in a circle for briefing, I waited for Van to finish speaking, my pulse hammering. All those years in school, and still I got nervous to speak.

"So go ahead and get comfortable. You can set up tents, settle in a bit," Van was saying. "I think we'll be here a few days. Pretty nice spot, right?" Everyone nodded, smiled. We were far from civilization, sounds of birdsong and a trickling creek, and the map showed two or three promising high-alpine lakes within walking distance. Yet we stood— I cringed at the feeling of my heavy, booted feet crushing the tender grass—in a *meadow*. "Anybody got anything?" Van asked.

"Yeah," I croaked, raising a shaky hand. Van nodded the go-ahead.

"This is obviously, uh, a meadow," I began. "Meadows are sensitive, protected ecosystems. They're easily damaged. I hate to be that person, but . . ." I trailed off, self-conscious. "You're not supposed to *walk* on a meadow, let alone park or sleep on it. So if you guys could set up your tents not on this grass, but around it, that would be really good."

I watched Van consider his response, as if grabbing his tact hat and carefully fitting it over his balding pate. "Thank you, Kelly. I appreciate the sentiment."

Right, I thought. *But?*

"But—" There it was. "We try to do what's right, you know, MIST and all that. But sometimes there's no other flat place to sleep."

MIST stood for "minimum impact suppression tactics," an acronym the feds loved to throw around but seldom regarded as a true priority. I could feel my face begin to flush.

"Yeah," I blurted. "But sometimes it *is* avoidable. And here I think we could, you know, stay out of this meadow without much trouble. I mean, we work for the Forest Service. Protecting the land is kind of our job."

"Thank you," Van said evenly. "Everyone, let's try to keep that in mind and, uh, stay off the meadow if you can."

He released us to set up camp, but not before I had noted the crew's reactions: a proud smile from Addison that said *Hell yeah*; a nod of agreement from Trevan; a sardonic grin from Mac and a mischievous one from Barrel; a reflective look on Benjy's face; and though I didn't know Hale yet, I could've sworn his expression might be called "admiration."

When my tent was assembled, sleeping bag tucked inside, I stood and stretched and realized that while several of us were camping in this grove, my tent stood right beside Eddie's, just a few inches between where I'd lay my head and where his feet would be. I had started to camp several yards away, then discovered a soft-serve swirl of suspicious feces (human?), which drove me out. Now our tents stood almost *too* close, their position suggesting something untoward.

But it would be awkward to move now, and there wasn't much flat ground to choose from. Oh well. Separate tents, separate worlds. We *were* good friends, and the guys lay side by side like kids at their first sleepover party all the time. Was this so different?

I knew it was. And as I later heard, this was when the guys started to speculate about us: *Those two are fucking.*

Oblivious to the gossip, we lay in our separate tents and talked until darkness filled the space between the trees and stars flickered on in the velvet abyss above. These were slumber party admissions, soft-voiced and sacred: my worries about the tension between fire and my home life, Eddie's doubts about his new relationship. You know—girl talk. But when we said goodnight and I realized I was close enough to hear the deepening of his breath, the small, anxious sighs he uttered as he drifted off, longing swept me like a wave. When I masturbated that night—an act I had mastered performing in total silence—it was him I imagined, the weight and warmth of his body on top of mine.

Okay, so I couldn't pretend I wasn't attracted to Eddie. But I told myself, as always, that everyone has their crushes. It was harmless.

The next day the smokejumpers, who'd been released upon our arrival and were waiting for their ride home, lounged in a clearing below the fire with their long hair and open-chested shirts, casual muscles and ash-lined smiles. Jumpers are the surfers of fire, cooler than you and giving of almost no fucks.

Most of the crew hiked up the hill, with Keller assuming the lead on mop-up as Firefighter I trainee. The fire itself lay on the edge of, but not inside, a designated wilderness area. If it had been true wilderness, protocol was to let the wildfire burn, and we wouldn't have been there in the first place.

I was sent downhill to the creek, where the MARK-3 and another day as pump operator awaited me. Hale joined me, and once we had the pump running, he grabbed a spare piece of cardboard and drew a diagram of a two-stroke engine in Sharpie.

Fuel (24:1) -> Carb (jets>)/Choke -> Intake Port -> Spark Plug/ Compression Chamber/Piston/Crank Case/Crank Shaft -> Pump Head/Impeller -> Intake (H2O)/Output (H20)

And so on. If you're looking at that and it makes no sense, *same*, but Hale sat beside me and patiently explained the interplay between fuel, oxygen, and spark that—much like fire itself—produces combustion and powers an engine.

"That's so cool!" I said, sincere. "Thank you."

It was rare that someone took the time to teach in this job. Usually the approach was "just go try something," an attitude typified by the acronym scrawled in the back of Alpha buggy: FITFO, for *Figure It The Fuck Out*. The irony, as I later learned, was that Hale—the old Hale, the rowdier and possibly cruel one—was the person who coined the term.

When he had gone up the hill and left me alone with the pump, I crouched by the creek. Blue sky, clear water, yellow wildflowers. Butterflies circled, frogs sunned themselves on the rocks, and small fish held in the pools. This was the most life I'd witnessed so close to a fire.

My thoughts ran to Josh, the wedding, the hypothetical baby . . . and then wheeled back to the line of pines on the ridge, the wind bobbling the reeds. I was happy here, right where I was. I struggled to imagine that the following summer would find me stuck in Happy Camp with an infant. Is that what I wanted? Hadn't I said so?

The pump hiccupped, and I rushed to refill the fuel before it died. Soon the day was done, and I scrabbled up the hill and fell in with the crew to hike to the meadow, where Van had remembered to bring cake for Eddie's birthday. He lit the candles, and we sang as Eddie grinned.

Then, the well-known chant: "May you live a thousand years; may you drink a thousand beers. Happy birthday, ya hammer ass!"

Cheers and applause. Rowdy River hoots. Ed was a favorite, so seeing him happy made everyone happy. Cake for all, shift done and hours of daylight left, we changed into shorts and sandals and set off for the lakes.

That night, I handed Eddie an envelope as he climbed into his tent. "Here."

"For me?"

I nodded.

Inside was a simple note that said I appreciated him, loved him as a friend, and *Happy Birthday, Turd*. I had also copied a Marge Piercy poem called "To Be of Use" that mentioned, in passing, putting out fires. The poem had spoken to me, about all work, but most deeply about what it meant to be a hotshot, to labor in smoke and ash, in danger and hardship, to be worked to the bone . . . and love it.

As he read, I could see the poem making its mark. He reached the last line—*The pitcher cries for water to carry, and a person for work that is real*. He was quiet for a moment. I thought he might be crying, and my eyes welled.

He looked up through the tent mesh. "Thank you," he faltered. "This is—thanks, Kelly."

"You liked it?"

"I loved it."

We didn't say much else, and soon we went to sleep (separate tents!), but something subtle had shifted between us. Whether we stayed friends for life or fell out of touch by the following fall, it didn't matter. A new truth stood between us. A genuine, mutual understanding.

Sex was fleeting. Marriage, I had found, could prove unreliable. But to feel known? To feel known was forever.

Late in the roll, we spent several days on a small fire called Bradley near the town of McCloud. There, I succeeded in running a "short squad" to chase down spot fires, but Barrel and I failed to earn the crew's respect when we tried to supervise mop-up. That day, I had my first episode of dehydration-induced full-body cramps, a phenomenon I'd seen the guys suffer often. My body seized, legs curling, arms in spasm. It was kind of like transforming into a praying mantis, except that it could be cured by electrolytes.

On our day fourteen, July 14, the nation hit a PL of 5 (the preparedness level indicating that fire resources were committed, stretched thin), the earliest PL 5 in a decade. Vicki Christiansen, the Chief of the Forest Service, sent out a memo ordering wildland firefighters to take three days of mandatory R&R, instead of two, after each fourteen-day assignment. Most of us were thrilled for an extra day of recovery and time with our people, but some were upset about the lost income.

As R&R approached, I grew nervous. I hadn't seen Josh since late May—nor had I longed to. Our relationship felt virtual at best, and since I'd missed his birthday (again), I was under the gun to make it up to him. What was wrong with me? I knew I'd been excited to marry him a couple months before . . . yet now I felt ambivalent.

Falling asleep on the ground the last night of the fire, I felt as though my life, my real life, was out there, under a sky that was deepening blue, out where I was wild and dirty and "one of the guys" in the way that one might be one of the wolves. I loved it. I loved it beyond the level I thought possible to love a thing. I was tired, but part of me wanted to stay on the fire and never go home again.

On R&R, Josh and I took the telescope to Shinar Saddle, along with a large pie from the Pizza House, a bottle of wine, camp chairs, and three dogs. Denali's absence seemed to chill the warm summer night.

The saddle was a broad flat spot on the ridge that led to Slater Butte, near where the Slater Fire had begun less than a year earlier. Almost every tree along the road was stripped to coal-black sticks.

The day before, I'd gotten home early enough to bake a cake and wrap Josh's presents before he returned from the station. I came home to a filthy house, the floors crunchy underfoot—he had warned me, but it was never pleasant—and began cleaning before cooking and baking. The next morning, the water pressure had slowed to a dribble, so I hiked up Benjamin Creek to check that the foot valve for the intake on our water system was correctly placed. It was not. The creek had dropped as the temperature rose, and the foot valve was now half-suspended in the air. I dug out the creek bottom to deepen a pool and half buried the valve, then hiked back home to see if pressure was restored. Thankfully, yes. After that, I vacuumed large drifts of dog hair from every corner of the house, did dishes and wiped the kitchen, scrubbed the toilets, watered the plants, fed and let out the goat, played with the dogs, and tossed my ash-crusted yellows and greens and the sweat-hardened mounds of fourteen socks and fourteen underwear into the washer. The laundry reeked of smoke; so did my hair. I'd need more than one shower to get the fire off.

I was exhausted from the assignment and wanted nothing so much as rest, but these were the obligations of my domestic life. I felt surly as I tidied and swept. How was it that every time I came home, I cleaned the house top to bottom, leaving it perfect for Josh, but every time I came home again, it was filthy? I said nothing, though, because we'd been ships passing for six weeks. This was not the time to pick a fight.

As we climbed out of Josh's truck and put the telescope together, he grinned like a kid. He wore a hat, a plain T-shirt, and jeans that didn't quite fit his thick legs. He had grown a beard in our time apart, and I wasn't a fan.

He was handy and made quick work of assembling the instrument. Then we sat on the tailgate eating and waiting for darkness.

"Thank you," he said, taking my hand. "This is perfect."

"Happy birthday, babe." I smiled, thinking: *Thank god. I finally made him happy.*

We even had sex that night, though it felt a little mechanical to me. Obligatory. Still, his happiness didn't last.

The disagreement was my fault. Instead of staying home from Thursday night to Sunday afternoon, as our R&R allowed, I was driving back to Crescent City on Saturday evening for Eddie's birthday party. As I stacked clean socks in my PG bag on one side of our bed, Josh stood on the opposite side, arms crossed. The wrinkles between his eyebrows deepened, twin angry crevasses.

"It feels like you're choosing them over me."

"I'm not! You're working all weekend, so it's only tonight that I'm missing with you. I've been home the last two nights! I'm not choosing them; I'm choosing them *and* you."

"But I'm your partner."

"Yes, and they're my friends. Last year I missed Eddie's party, and they never stopped talking about it. I always miss the bonding that happens outside of work."

I folded my yellow neatly like I'd learned in my one brief stint in retail, arms and sides tucked back to make a rectangle of the pocketed chest. Even clean, the shirt was stained, faded, softened by heat and sun and sweat. My fingers grazed it, almost affectionately.

"You just spent two weeks with them! I've barely seen you, and now you're *leaving*."

"I've come home multiple times in the past month, and *you* were never here! This is my job. Our job."

"It's your job to party with the guys?"

I looked up from the heavy wool socks I was rolling, one inside the other. I didn't have a good response. I resented his jealousy and his pinched, angry face. But I knew Josh wasn't wrong, and I *really* knew it when I got to Crescent City that night, and the "party" was more of a casual hang. Nothing special. With a guilty inward cringe, I realized that I'd blown off my fiancé for a forgettable evening with people I saw all the time. And I even knew the reason: Eddie. I had come back, more than anything, for him. I just wanted to be around him.

As I sat on the floor while Fisher and Eddie fell asleep on the couch watching *Super Troopers*, I noticed that my shoulder rested against Eddie's leg, and I thought, *Girl, what are you doing?*

Chapter 17

Yellow Butterflies

I left the island and moved back to Austin, leaving Charlie behind. We told each other this might be just a break; maybe we'd work it out, and he would join me in the city where we'd met five years before. But deep down, I think we both knew it was over.

I settled in a lofted garage apartment on the East Side behind the house that my best friend shared with a roommate. I took a job as a nanny for a family in wealthy Tarrytown—two girls, ages three and eight, and a schedule that never started before noon or ended after six. An easy job, I figured. An easy life with time to breathe, ride my bike, see live music. An ideal setup for a single early thirty-something.

But my grip on stability was tenuous at best. I moved through the world unsteadily, hollow and crisp as a cicada shell. A home without Charlie was much emptier than I had imagined, and single life was less thrilling now than it had been at twenty-five. I sat in my echoing apartment and wept. I drank wine with friends wearing a brave smile, came home, and wept. Perhaps this had been a terrible mistake. Maybe leaving an engagement, a career, and a charming small-town home wasn't a triumph of independence and self-actualization after all. Quite possibly I was nothing more than a runaway and a coward.

Luckily (stupidly?) I'd bought a plane ticket to Lima, Peru, on a whim before moving. So there I was, in the Andes, all alone. I had three weeks. My mother was petrified. My phone didn't work, I couldn't be reached. Perfect.

I met a man from Portland and convinced him to hike to Machu Picchu. We backpacked, taking a remote route called Salkantay and camping on families' lawns in tiny Andean villages. We climbed an eleven-thousand-foot pass, picked through ancient ruins, marveled at a meadow of a million yellow butterflies, and made out in a tent. After the hike, I lingered in Cusco on my own, walking the cobblestone streets and becoming a regular in a local cafe. It was the happiest and freest I'd ever felt.

Back in Austin, I managed to stay single for eight months, my longest run yet. I was like an addict staying off the sauce, but this time abstinence was less a matter of willpower and more of an intolerance. A dude allergy. I saw men, even hot ones, and a sick feeling twisted my stomach. Who could say you wouldn't invest five years and end up shattered, a sad little corn husk raising other people's children? I wasn't ready.

At the same time, the Peru trip had lit a spark, dredging up a feeling I remembered from a childhood in the forests of rural Kentucky. Silly as it sounds, I recalled how much I loved . . . the earth? I learned, or rediscovered, that I was happiest outside, at home in the woods and mountains, by a creek or lake, on any kind of trail. The outdoors liberated me from my neuroses and relieved the pressure to perform. Nature *was* an unconditional, accepting mother; you could show up a hot mess, and she would take you in.

Over the next several years, I became a solo traveler, bouldering gym girl, avid backpacker. Caves in Central America, a ridge in Zion, a glacier—bring it on. The farther I ventured into the world, the better I felt.

At the same time, something troubling was happening to my dad.

One May, I flew to Wisconsin for a family wedding, and my sisters and I went to see him. They had warned me that something was up— *He's real sick*—but that in no way prepared me for what we found.

We pulled up at a white house set close to the street. Some of the windows were boarded up, the others had ratty blinds drawn tight against their sashes. Weeds rioted from cracks in the driveway. The house looked strange, I thought. What was so weird about it?

Oh. My stomach bottomed out. It looked *abandoned.* "What happened?" I asked. "What's he doing here?"

"You haven't been back in five years, that's what happened," Courtney said.

"Fair enough."

"His friend Dan is letting him stay until he gets a new tenant," Courtney added. "Dad's supposed to do some work on the place in exchange."

Translation: Dan owned an uninhabitable house, and he was letting our father squat. Interpretation: Dad could no longer afford a place to live.

The kids had fallen asleep on the drive. Madeleine's daughter Avea's dark curls were damp against her sweet-smelling head. Courtney's son Ezekiel, a toddler, slept heavily, face creased in a dream frown. The weather was cool, so we cracked the windows and left them sleeping in their car seats.

"Dad hates kids anyway," Madeleine muttered as we waded through weeds to the back door. "I don't know why we brought them."

"He needs to know his grandchildren before he fucking dies," Courtney snapped.

"Hey," I said. "Nobody's dying."

We made our way up the back steps and through an empty sun porch with blistered linoleum. We entered the unlocked house—peeling paint, slant of light into empty rooms—and as we passed through the kitchen, Courtney called out, "Dad! Your daughters are here."

He didn't come to greet us. "Can't even fucking stand up," my sister grumbled, and led us into what must have been a dining room. The house had almost no furniture, so a room could be whatever it wanted. A sagging, overstuffed chair sat in front of a cheap plastic desk that supported an ancient desktop computer, several brimming ashtrays, and a Big Gulp cup with a lid and straw. The large front room was empty. Through an open door, I spied a folding cot with a single, flimsy blanket. Chair, desk, cot. This was what he called home.

I saw the smoke rising from the cigarette in his hand first. Then he turned to us, and my breath caught.

My father's body was bones. It's an awful comparison, but all I could think of were the images of men in concentration camps during the Holocaust. I'd never seen a human being in this condition. His limbs swam in his clothes. His cheekbones were hard knobs that pressed against his skin like they might push through. His flesh was a dark, sallow shade. His eyes rested in hollowed-out caverns. He was a walking corpse.

"Can't even stand up, huh?" Courtney said, shit-talking, seemingly unfazed. "I brought you a sandwich. You need to fuckin' eat."

"Hi, Dad," I said softly, feeling small and timid. My eyes stung.

"Hi!" he said. "Oh my goodness, look who it is. Hi!" Looking genuinely pleased, he tried to rise, succeeding in pushing himself only half out of his chair. I leaned down for an awkward hug.

"How are you?" he said. A minute later, though I'd already replied *I'm pretty good, I live in Austin now*, he asked it again, "Well, how are you?"

I repeated my earlier answer.

"Austin," he said absently. "That's great. That's just great."

As we tried to chat normally, he seemed confused. He mixed up the births of his children, saying that Courtney had been born in Sugarland, Texas.

"No, Dad," we reminded him. "Courtney was born in Boston. *Evan* was born in Sugarland."

He couldn't remember where I lived or how old any of us were. Yet he claimed to have a few irons in the fire, a few very exciting projects in the works.

"One with an A-rab," he said. "And one with an African guy."

"That's great," we said, though we knew full well there were no projects. He had no work at all; he could barely get out of this chair. But he seemed less to be deliberately lying than to believe in something we couldn't see, as if his delusions were a kind of Narnia and he'd gone through the cupboard for the last time.

"We're worried about you, Dad," Courtney said.

Oh, so we were addressing the elephant in the room, then? I jumped in. "Have you seen a doctor? I think you should."

"You look like you haven't eaten anything in weeks," Courtney added. She'd handed him a sandwich after we arrived, and he had roused himself with impressive effort and shuffled into the kitchen, saying *I'm not hungry now, but I'll have some of this later, thank you.* He put it in the fridge.

"You need to eat, Dad," Madeleine said timidly.

"You look sick."

"You women!" he erupted, his lethargy yielding to anger without warning. My sisters and I instinctively flinched. "Always telling me what to do! Always trying to *control* me."

We were silent. I wanted something to grip and considered taking my sister's hand. But Courtney was stone-faced.

"Mind your own goddamn business," our father hissed. "I am *fine*. I'm not sick! It's all of you telling me I'm sick that's making me ill."

"Dad, we're just worried," I said as gently as I could, though I was torn between the desire to call an ambulance and the impulse to run from the room.

"Well, I am *fine*. I'm totally fine. I don't need *nothin'* from *nobody.*"

My father, though blue collar, was capable of flawless grammar. He read books, listened to National Public Radio. The redneckism was something he put on for effect, and it almost gave me hope that he was capable even now of this small degree of artifice. But the lower half of his jaw moved, unconsciously, as though he were chewing over some old bit of food. His lips smacked together. It was unnerving.

Courtney kept arguing, trying to insist upon the hospital. Madeleine had gone silent. She wiped tears from the corners of her eyes. Why was she crying as if we were at a funeral?

Oh. My slow, dumb brain finally caught up. Somebody *was* dying. This man in front of us. A man whose hands I knew like my own, because they were shaped the same. A man who had come to my backyard carrying half-melted Andes mints. I could picture how he held a drill, how he swung a hammer. I could see him striding ahead of me, running a hand through his thin brown hair, eyes shining with hope. *Let me show you, daughter of mine, this house I'm buildin'.* A man who had built everything, only to tear it all down.

Our father was dying. And since he didn't want our help, it appeared that his decades-long campaign to drink until he vacated this plane of existence would finally succeed. This could be the last time I saw him.

Time stood still. Grief crept over my skin.

Trying to take control of myself, I thought: *Maybe I should say something.* Like what, a goodbye? What was there to say? My sisters had gone to the car to check on the babies. Dad had run out of steam and stared blankly out the window over my shoulder. His jaw wobbled from side to side without his permission.

A thousand baby bunnies jumping out of a hole. A million yellow butterflies.

"Well," I began, hesitant. I remembered him crying an apology into my shirt at his house on the lake. I said, "I forgive you, Dad."

Those were not the right words.

He turned sharply. For the first time, he looked directly at me, through me, eyes darkening with rage.

"Forgive me," he said, spitting each word. "For *what?*"

Chapter 18

Shadow One

We were headed to the Dixie Fire, the biggest show in Northern California, forty thousand acres and ripping. On the map, its leading edge looked like three heads racing north, red Medusas.

Shaggy said sadly, "The Plumas keeps getting hammered! The fire scars are merging. Soon there'll be nothing left."

As we drew closer and the Dixie's column bloomed like a gray cauliflower in the sky, we drove through the scar of the North Complex, a fire we'd fought the year before. Mile upon mile of carbonized trees and denuded earth, a now-familiar scene of extinguished life. And the column growing taller, billowing, filling the sky above the burned world. Fire on fire on fire.

California's (and the world's) fire predicament isn't hopeless. Experts—fire historians, ecologists, foresters—have found proven solutions to the "crisis" of wildfire.

One, we can reduce fire severity by removing fuels, the densely overgrown trees and brush that built up over a century of fire suppression. Two, we must *burn* the landscape. Intentional fire, which includes prescribed burning and Indigenous cultural burning, is widely accepted as the best way to create a more resilient, wildfire-resistant forest.

Though it sounds counterintuitive, burning more on purpose equals less out-of-control fire. So when we utter the firefighter catchphrase, "Let her burn," we don't just mean *Stand by twiddling your thumbs and watch the train wreck unfold*—although sometimes it's unsafe to do anything else. We also mean *let* the world burn, as in burn deliberately, in order to prevent the next disaster.

Enacting these solutions is a matter of policy, money, and workforce: we need more invested in fuels reduction and intentional fire, along with separate crews—not the same destroyed bodies who suck smoke all summer—to get the work done. Because half the land in the western United States is federally owned, I'm looking at you, Congress. So is the narrowed, all-seeing eye of history.

We were part of history in the making, though we didn't know it; by October, the Dixie would consume over 960,000 acres and make a name for itself as the first fire to cross the crest of the Sierra Nevada. It remains the second largest fire in California history.

The camp in Quincy was a firefighter reunion. Red engines lined up in long rows, and men in pressed uniforms lounged on camp chairs. Rows of green buggies, too. I'd heard that Klamath Hotshots were on the fire, with an anxious twinge in my gut; that was the crew where Aaron, my first firefighter ex, worked as a Squadie. I was nervous to run into him. In a way, he was the reason I'd ended up here. Or *a* reason.

Soon, we were busy enough that I forgot to worry. Day two, we prepped dozer lines and roads. Day three, B buggy began to slowly perish. The dash showed a light that read "Regen," some sort of electrical issue. The engine lost power going uphill, and we shuddered forward, halting and bucking, as Fisher crooned, "Come on! Come on, *please*." When we finally reached the line, we laughed with relief.

I spent that day on lookout—a Firefighter I training assignment—with Benjy, watching the column grow. To pass the time, I thought up goofy descriptors for a smoke column: runaway cappuccino, fresh popcorn, overflowing washing machine. Cloud dragon, shaving cream, sky ejaculate. I kept these ideas to myself as Benjy told old war stories from crews past.

Day four, we took Bravo to ground support in Quincy, where they announced that the buggy's problem was above their pay grade. I was lookout again, this time with Hale. We discovered we'd both been married before, both divorced, both loved crossword puzzles and good books. His twists on cliché sayings cracked me up. *Rome wasn't burnt in a day*, he'd say, or, *We'll burn that bridge when we come to it.* The shift was the start of a friendship.

One day, we were shuttling out from the line on pickup trucks just as Beckwourth Hotshots were shuttling in. I caught sight of my former roommate. "Paige!" I shouted. She turned, gave me a wicked grin, and thrust two fists into the air—each with the middle finger firmly deployed. Laughing, I flipped the bird back at her. *I love you too.*

On day five, I saw Aaron. Klamath Hotshots were parked in the crowded lot at fire camp, and as he strolled past our buggy, I spied him through the open door. My stomach knotted. *Stupid*, I thought. *After all these years? Just be a grown-up and say hello.*

"Aaron!" I called, stepping into the buggy door and hopping down.

"Hey Kelly," he said with a casual tone and familiar grin, as if we'd only parted ways last week. Certain men always use your name, and when they do, it feels powerful, as though they're speaking you into being. "I thought you might be here. Heard Rowdy was around."

We hugged. He looked handsome, but he'd aged more than the two years since we'd last crossed paths.

"So." That appraising smile again. "You became a hotshot."

"I did."

"Suspenders and everything. How do you like it?"

"I love it," I said. "It's addictive."

"Yeah, it is. Look at me. I keep saying I'll leave, then it's one more year."

The sparkle in his eyes said that he was impressed to see me out here. And also, that I was still hot. *Count it!* as my friend Sal liked to say. *Still got it.*

"Always one more year," I said, thinking about whether I'd do a third.

"Heard you and Josh are getting married?"

"Yep," I said, knowing I sounded more confident than I was.

"Congratulations," he said politely. "He's a good guy."

"He really is," I said with a kind of squint.

We wished each other a good shift, a safe assignment, hugged again, and he loped off, his quick athletic body no less perfect than before. I climbed back into the buggy, and Keller and Shaggy said, "Was that him?" "How was it?"

"It was . . . fine," I said with a shrug. "He's just a guy now."

It was true. Sure, that rascally charm and troublemaker's glint in his eye would always be sexy. But now that I was in this profession, I knew a dozen Aarons. He was just another hotshot.

We had to give up Bravo to a service center in Reno that specialized in ten-person Crew Carrier engines. There were no spare buggies available this time, so the members of B-mod would be divided between three pickup trucks. I went with Hale and Jones to Redding to pick up the rentals. Jones, who'd joined us during the Dotta fire, was a reserved, almost painfully quiet Yurok man, the opposite of his cousin BJ. He'd taken a year off, so he was new to me, but this summer was his fifth on the crew. He seemed impossible to know, yet I instinctively liked him.

We each got our own rooms at the hotel, and the solitude felt luxurious. I was about to check out the pool and hot tub before bed, when I got the strangest text from Josh. He said he felt sad and missed me, that home was different when I wasn't there, that he hated how often I had to be gone for work, but we'd just have to suffer through it. He said he couldn't wait until I left hotshotting for good, so I could be home with him *where I belonged*. Then we could both have the "love we deserved," or something like that.

Hmm.

His words *sounded* sweet, and I knew it was hard being the one stuck at home. But his attitude felt unfair. For one thing, I wasn't the only one gone a lot. For another, he'd implied that when the season ended, I would be leaving fire . . . forever. Sure, I had suggested that this might be my last season, but had I promised that? Shit, maybe I had. Yet my feelings were changing, and he wasn't asking; he was *telling* me what I would do, how our life together would go. If loving Josh meant having to stay at home *where I belonged*, I didn't like the sound of it.

My pulse pounded in my ears as I tried to draft a response.

Hey babe. I miss you so much. But I think we need to talk next time I'm home—because fire season isn't something I'm just "suffering through." Being apart is hard, but I love this job. I hate that you're unhappy, but I want to go on assignment and know that it's ok to be . . . happy out here. Anyway, can we talk this through? I love you and I'm so excited to marry you. Sweet dreams.

I was seething with anger and feeling far from excited to tie the knot, which at the moment sounded like a noose. But I controlled myself and tried to use nicer terms than, *Don't ask me to be unhappy because you are,* or, *It's not my problem if you lack the inner resources to enjoy life when I'm away.* I lay awake for several minutes, breath shallow, awaiting a response. When none came, I nuzzled into the clean white bedding and went to sleep.

The next day, day six, we picked up three Dodge rental trucks from Enterprise and drove them back to the fire, a caravan passing through the Shasta-Trinity, the Lassen, and the Plumas National Forests. When we arrived, the crew spent the morning going direct on a hot edge in leaf litter. Tiny fire, with its slow-crawling, two-inch flames, was so adorable; you could pretty much stomp it out with your boot. Tiny scrape inserted to stop it, we set about emptying the contents of the buggy and distributing them into the trucks. Every bin and compartment became a bag thrown in the bed of a pickup.

Later that day, two fires merged, the Fly becoming part of the Dixie. On the radio, we heard that a firefighter had been trapped in a tunnel, cut off by fire on both sides, and that he was rescued by the rarely seen *fire train*—a train owned by BNSF Railway specifically outfitted to fight wildfires (and protect assets like train tracks, wooden railroad ties, etc.). It had two locomotives, a fire suppression car, and two water tenders able to hold fifty-six-thousand gallons of water or retardant.

"The fuckin' fire train, yo!"

"In fifteen years, I've never heard of the fire train showing up."

"Can we go see it?"

We were not allowed to go see this novelty, and at the end of shift, the pickups were a disaster. Our hand tools and chainsaws rattled in the truck beds, and the bags of gear quickly accumulated a thick layer of dirt. Beyond that, we felt unmoored without our home on wheels. Not one team, but three.

That night, bedded down in the brush, I fought to fall asleep in heavy smoke amid clouds of mosquitoes. How were these bugs still at it with so much particulate in the air? They usually vanished once the smoke burned your throat.

Josh hadn't replied to my text. I was getting the impression he might be angry, and when we'd briefly had cell service in fire camp, I had called him. No answer. I tossed and turned, the whine of mosquito wings echoing the nagging feeling that something was off in my relationship.

Day seven, we prepped roads far from the fire line, and Hale and Fisher figured out our pickup truck assignments: Fisher would take Trevan and Keller; Luke and BJ would take Shaggy; and Hale, who as Captain needed the freedom to roam without taking a saw team away from the group, claimed me and Englefield.

We had two gray pickups, and one dark red. Fisher and Hale commenced a battle over whose vehicle would be "Shadow One," whose "Shadow Two." Luke and BJ claimed "Burgundy" (and sometimes, in jest, "Ron Burgundy").

My two new companions had big personalities. Hale, midway through a transition from what he called "hood rat" to what I'd call well-read hipster, bore a tattoo just above his heart that showed a toggle switch with two settings: "on" and "on." Englefield had trained as a chef in a previous life, and his stories featured wild adventures like driving a suckling pig to a luau on a four-wheeler. The three of us drove around, that first week, in a constant state of chatter and shared music. I missed the buggy, but there was something special about getting to know two people so well.

Finally, I got a reply from Josh. When I opened it on a break, pulling off my gloves, my heart sank. *Your phone is transferred to the new account*, he wrote. Logistics about our shared cell phone plan, but nothing about my text—and no good morning, no have-a-good-shift. It was cold. Ernest Shackleton's final expedition cold.

Okay, so he was pissed. *Copy.* But what could I do if he wouldn't *tell* me—if he wouldn't take my calls? Without communication, we had nothing. It had already been two days. How long would he ice me out? Giving someone the cold shoulder for a day might generously be deemed "taking space," but beyond that, it felt cruel—especially when that someone was sleep-deprived, smoke-poisoned, and deeply stressed, and you knew it. As what I perceived to be his rigid hostility continued, my anguish began to sour like old milk. Gradually, it crusted over into anger.

On day nine, we were brushing out a road corridor, all those not on saws chaining out the swamp across the road. We formed lines to pass the limbs and armfuls of cut brush, playfully throwing a log or pushing sticks in each other's faces. An hour into the work, I noticed that Addison was following a sawyer and swamping on her own, carrying brush all the way across the road. This was inefficient and strange. Normally, people would naturally move to fill in the gaps and make the swamper lines about equal. Yet today, nobody moved to stand by Addison and help her out.

"Why's Addison swamping by herself?" I asked Miguel.

"Maybe because she's mean," Miguel said.

"Really?"

"Yeah, she snapped at me a few minutes ago. I wasn't doing *nothing*. But I guess I didn't take the brush fast enough. She's scary, man."

"Yeah, dude," Shaggy jumped in. "She yelled at me for how I was throwing the swamp."

"At *you?*" I asked. I could no more imagine yelling at Shaggy than striking a puppy.

"Yeah, and she's just, like, cold," Shaggy said. "She's got the sunglasses, then her face is just like—" He mimed a straight-mouthed, hostile frown. "You'll say something, and she doesn't say anything back. It's like she's looking through you."

Miguel laughed. "The guys are avoiding her," he said. "We decided we can't get in trouble if we don't work around her."

"Ah," I said. "Still kinda sucks she has to work alone."

"That's what she gets. If you're gonna be mean, nobody's gonna work with you." Miguel shrugged.

I supposed that was true. I didn't want to go help her, because we'd then become the *girls'* chain. But after a few more minutes of watching her frantically dash back and forth, I couldn't take it. She was gonna wear herself out. I walked over and stood at the road's edge and spread my arms wide for the next load of brush, wordlessly indicating that I was here to help. As she placed the bundle in my arms, she mouthed, *Thank you.* Though it was hard to tell behind the shades, I thought I saw the glint of tears.

I spent the day joking and goofing, trying to get a grin out of her, and by the end of the shift, she had marginally warmed. We smiled as we parted ways at the trucks. I stood by our pickup, where Hale had found a cup of nacho cheese, and Eddie had scrounged up some chips. Eddie and I stood crumbling chips into the cheese and scooping it out with a spoon.

"This is disgusting," I said.

"Yep, we're gross." He grinned. "What's that taste like?" He took a sip of my LaCroix, and I rolled my eyes.

"You know what it tastes like, turd." I shoved his shoulder.

But that teasing, brotherly thing got me every time, and stealing my drinks was a form of—the word wouldn't have occurred to me then, but I see it now—intimacy.

Dimples flashing, Eddie wandered back to Alpha. When I hopped in the truck with Hale and Englefield, the latter was raging. Apparently, Addison had bitten his head off at the end of the day: add his name to the list. Englefield echoed Miguel, saying the guys were trying to avoid her so they wouldn't get in trouble. By "get in trouble," he meant be accused of harassment.

It struck me that whether she knew it or not, Addison seemed to wield an inordinate amount of power within the crew. The guys were afraid to respond to her reactive (in my opinion, volatile) behavior because they feared retaliation, a weaponization of her gender into victim status.

On the other hand, if the men had been willing to respectfully confront her as they would each other, maybe the situation would've been easier to repair. Instead, they steered clear of her, which I imagine only made her feel worse. Hence the downward spiral into mutual hostility.

While I didn't relish the task, it fell to me to do something. As the only other woman, I was the one person in a comfortable position to challenge her.

I approached Addison the next morning. As gently as I could, I said that I'd noticed she seemed unhappy, that her attitude was sometimes negative. Such behavior had a dampening effect on morale. "Try keeping it positive," I suggested. "You'll have better interactions with everyone. Like a positive feedback loop."

Addison admitted that she'd been down on the crew. She complained again that she was miserable not running saw. I tried to be nice, but thought, *Can't hike it, can't run it*. She said she missed her old module. Hotshot culture was stupid, egotistical, difficult for no reason.

She wasn't entirely wrong; the culture was intense and sometimes inane. *But this is what you signed up for*, I wanted to say. *I thought you knew what hotshots did, how hard this would be*. Instead I said, "I know not running saw sucks. But you can still make a contribution and do work that's really fun. And they're more likely to put you on saw if you show a great attitude doing everything else."

Addison promised that she would try to be more upbeat, and I saw her make an effort. We began to burn that afternoon, and she was put on torch. I stood near the front of the line of holders because I'd grabbed a fiver of burn mix to fuel-mule. I was happy to be carrying something heavy again, the ninety pounds on my back a steadying, reassuring presence; now that we had new rookies, I rarely got the chance. Such a simple way to feel useful.

Addison smiled, playfully stuck her tongue out at me from the edge of the brush where she spilled flames in neon strips. I grinned back. All at once, I had a girlfriend again. When she was in a good mood, she was lovely.

It wasn't too late to fix this.

That night, lying down in ten days' worth of my own filth, scrubbing the grime from my thighs with a wet wipe, I sent Josh another beseeching text. *Please let's talk*, I wrote. *You're clearly upset, and I don't know why you won't tell me. I miss you, and I'm sure we can work out a better way to deal with the distance. How was your day? Please, this feels awful, can we talk it through? I'm literally begging you.*

Send. I wiped the ash from inside my ears, got a fresh wipe and rubbed at my face. My heart thudded nervously. Then the green bubble blinked on the screen, and I grabbed my phone. Josh said his day was fine, and goodnight. That was all.

I waited, staring blankly at the bright screen, which hurt my eyes in the darkness of the woods. Surely there was more coming.

Nothing.

I threw my phone to the ground, tossed the wipes, stood up, and kicked my boots to the side, heart pounding. A massive emotion reared up inside me, rising slowly, majestic and threatening, like the slow, hooded blossoming of a column of smoke, a dragon lifting its head. It rose to its full and terrifying height, a silent explosion over a darkened plain.

Rage.

It had been a week since our first tense exchange. All I'd said was that I was not as miserable as he was being apart. That I wanted to talk. Despite my repeated pleas, he had ignored my calls for *six days*, ghosted me, answered with terse hostility. Were we even together anymore? This was behavior I'd expect out of a very young man. These couldn't be the actions of the thirty-eight-year-old I'd dated for almost two years, who I was supposed to marry in four months.

I am DONE, I thought, throwing myself down on my sleeping bag. I was tearless, my anger frosted over like a winter windshield. This was how it always felt when I crossed the threshold from the chaos of battle into the clear air of finality. I felt nothing. I was stone. *I'm done trying. Fuck it.*

I may have thought, *Fuck it*, but I meant, *Fuck you, Josh.* Fuck you for punishing me and withholding affection. Fuck this insecure jealous garbage. Fuck you for making my time away even harder. Fuck you for acting like a child.

I told myself I was done begging for kindness from a wall, but I assumed we'd have it out next time I went home. Not willing to even entertain the possibility that it was over, I planned the conversation. I'd request better communication and "more space to be myself" in the relationship. I was ready, I thought, to ask for what I needed.

On day twelve, we were sent to a nearby fire, the Evans. The route to the black wound through private property, a ranch where squares of pasture were stitched with tidy fences. Bison calves, shaggy-furred and wobble-legged, sheltered against their parents' legs.

The fire was new and running hot. As we hiked in, I asked Engle-field and Addison to switch places in the tool order. In my mind, it was simple: the fire was moving quickly through flashy fuels, so we would need to move fast. I wanted someone behind me who could really dig.

Englefield moved into position behind me, Addison behind him. Neither said a word.

We reached the fire's edge. Flames were backing downhill through knee-high grass. We would come in under them. The saws fired up, and Eddie started mowing down grass and brush, setting the outer edge of the cut. He made a mistake, as we quickly realized. He set the cut too narrow, its perimeter only ten or fifteen feet off the burning edge. Since the fire was *trucking*, this meant that by the time the dig arrived, the flames had come downhill, narrowing the cut. Soon, we were putting in line with fire upon us, only a few feet between the flaming edge and dense, uncut brush. This left just enough space for the line to go in, but it pinched us, pinning us against the bushes, trying to scrape dirt as quickly as we could with fire licking our bodies.

Luke, who was digging in front of me, yelled back, "This is too fuckin' hot! Ed needs to cut wider."

Sweat rolled down my face.

Luke paused, reluctant to intervene. Then he shook his head. "It's too hot. I'm gonna say something."

He strode quickly along the fire's edge, lifting an arm to shield his face on the flame side. I tucked my head. If you kept your face down and squared to the fire as you dug, the hard hat would take a lot of the heat, but if you lifted your face for even a second, hot air scalded your skin. Breathing was difficult.

With Luke gone, I set the line and kept the pace. Englefield was a few feet behind me. I didn't look back, trusting everyone to dig fast and guard their skin until we reached a turn in the cut—which was coming, just a few more yards—where we'd have some respite. Mac, bless his heart, had started from the back of the saws and was digging toward us, catching the edge of the fire before it could crawl across the cut. This would be over soon.

Just as I reached the corner, though, I heard angry voices behind me.

"Move!" Addison demanded. "Let me get in front of you."

"No!" Englefield snapped. "I'm in front of you today."

"Well, you're digging too slow and leaving me right by the fire. It's too hot!"

"We're all fucking hot! Deal with it. That's how the job goes."

"Don't tell me about the job. I've been doing it a lot longer than you have."

"It doesn't show," Englefield spat.

"Go fuck yourself!" Addison shot back. "Get out of my way, you engine *fuck*."

"Whoa!" I spun around. "You two, over here. Come on, step out for a sec."

I gestured into the green and drew Englefield and Addison aside, away from the flaming front and the rest of the dig.

"Let's take a beat," I said. "Let's all get a deep breath. I know it's really hot. This sucks. But we've gotta keep our heads. Okay?"

They nodded, though neither looked like they agreed. Addison was stone-faced, dark eyes trained on the ground, tattooed arm crossed over the nearly bare one. Englefield glared at me like I was the one who'd done him wrong. I took a few steps back and told the rest of the dig to get away from the fire's edge, too. "Take five, water up. This is pretty crazy. I'll dig this last little bit."

"You need help?" Shaggy asked.

"Nah, I'm good."

I got them seated and sipping water, their faces shiny and red, and I moved ahead and scraped the last ten yards to connect with Mac's line. Without being asked, Englefield hopped in behind me, and the two of us made a quick, usable trench under the fire. When we tied in to Mac, he informed me that he'd tied in to another crew's line ahead—so we were done.

Just like that, what had seemed like a hellish day in the making, was over in twenty minutes. That's how the job was: you never knew what to expect.

Crisis over, I moved into damage control. I brokered a half-hearted apology between Addison and Englefield, and within an hour, as we cleaned up the line and did some light blacklining off the edge, even Addison's mood seemed to improve. I was shocked at just how ugly things had gotten, even if you chalked it up to working under intense heat (literally) and running on fumes at the end of an assignment.

We hadn't reached Dirty August yet, let alone Snaptember. This could be a long season.

Still, I felt proud of what seemed like a moment of leadership, and I was patting myself on the back for the rest of the day, still fluffing my feathers as we climbed into the truck. When Hale asked about the day, and I told the story, my conclusion was ascending to triumph. I was saying, "But I talked to her, and it seemed to get better—"

"You had to fix it because it was your fault," Englefield said flatly, looking straight ahead.

"Excuse me?" I sat in the back seat, Hale driving and Englefield in shotgun. Fields of bison scrolled by.

"You know." Englefield glanced over his shoulder, dark eyes flashing. "You knew just what you were doing. You put Addison behind me because you didn't want to deal with her shit, and you let that shit fall on *me*. You made the whole thing happen, pulling your little puppet strings."

"What?" My voice caught in my throat.

"You manipulated that whole thing."

"I didn't manipulate anything!" I began to tear up. "Why would you say that? I was just trying to make the dig work . . . better."

"Don't play innocent," he said punishingly. "I know, and you know, what you did."

"What—" My voice broke off as I began to cry.

"I think that's enough," Hale said, glancing sharply at Englefield.

I was silent. Englefield said no more, and Hale was uncharacteristically quiet. I sank down, turning my head as far as possible toward the window. The tears came in torrents. The loud music covered me, but Hale glanced back and knew. His eyes widened with sympathy.

Fucking *Englefield*. Maybe Addison was right about him. I hated him in that moment, despised his notion that women were always trying to gossip and manipulate. Those were surely his own issues. Still, I *had* moved Addison to serve my own purposes, to speed up the front of the dig. And she had annoyed me in recent days, digging behind me, offering unsolicited pointers about where to place the line. So it was possible that I'd moved her in part to get a break. Englefield may have been right that it was selfish, or thoughtless, but I wasn't trying to "sic" Addison on him. How could I have known the two of them would be such an explosive combination?

The tears wouldn't stop coming. I felt skewered. The progress I thought I'd made in brokering peace between Addison and the guys came undone in an instant. Things with Josh were a mess. My attempts to be a leader on the crew resulted in being told I was a monster.

I wanted to go home. But not to Happy Camp, somewhere else. My real home, though I didn't know where that was.

On day thirteen, I heard from Josh: his crew would be leaving for a fire the next day, so we wouldn't see each other this R&R. If the roles had been reversed, he would've sulked. Now, however, he was clearly ecstatic to get a roll after sitting in station for weeks, and suddenly—now that he wasn't stuck at home—his tone changed completely. He said he was sorry we'd miss each other but couldn't wait to see me when he got back. He told me he loved me, wished me a good R&R.

I stared at my phone in disbelief.

What the actual—? He continued to be friendly, even lovey. He sent me a photo of his newly shaved face and asked if I was happy (yes—that beard was nasty). I responded politely, but I was mystified. NO MENTION of the week-plus that he'd blown me off. No mention of my many requests to talk, which he had ignored. Now that he had a fire assignment, he moved on like the whole thing *had never happened.*

If only I could forget so easily.

The next two days, thankfully, remained mellow. Englefield and I made up, the sincerity of his apology a touching surprise. We dug an endless cup trench one day, mopped up another. Mac was shocked to learn that I enjoyed hallucinogenic mushrooms, which he claimed could cause permanent brain damage; he looked at me like I'd been sullied, no longer the sweet girl he knew. Hale and I exchanged a glance, rolling our eyes.

As we drove home on the fifteenth day, I learned that the road over the mountains to Happy Camp was officially closed—not the kind of closed you could talk your way through, but hazard tree-removal closed. Giant scorched pines falling over the highway closed.

Well, dang. I would have to drive home the long way, down the coast and over Bald Hills, which took at least four hours. I hated taking that road in the dark. As we finished washing the buggies at the station, I mentioned that I might stay the night in Crescent.

"Yeah, stay!" Eddie said. "You should get a room at the North Coast Inn. I'm getting one, it's super cheap."

"That's sounds fun," I said. "Maybe I will."

After we circled and Van thanked us for our work on the Dixie and we yelled "Day one" and broke up, Eddie and I sat on the tailgate of my truck and reserved our rooms. While we made this plan, Trevan walked by and gave us a puzzled look. Only in hindsight did I see how suspicious we looked.

In the parking lot of the motel, Eddie told me he'd broken up with Alexis.

"I'm sorry," I said, trying to suppress a blip of pleasure. "She seemed nice."

"It's okay. She was great; I just didn't feel it." He shrugged. "I feel bad, though. She sounded so sad."

"It's hard, dude. But she's young, she'll get over it." Alexis was twenty-three. In a decade, Eddie would be one on a list of exes and heartbreaks. She might not even remember his name. "Wanna get some food?"

"I could eat." I laughed; Eddie could always eat.

We walked to Port O' Pints. By the time we grabbed beers and settled in a booth, though, they'd stopped serving food, and when we looked up other restaurants in town, they were all closed too.

At that moment, Fisher called and invited us for tacos. Perfect. When we showed up at the Fishers' house, I was drunk on two beers. The empty stomach and quick succession of tequila shots Fish and Jenny pressed upon us didn't help. As I stood inhaling a shrimp taco from a paper plate, salsa water sloshed over the edges, spilling on the floor and my bare feet. I swayed unsteadily.

"You're spilling, drunky," Eddie said.

"I'm not drunk, you are." I grinned.

Hours passed like minutes. The four of us shouted over each other. *More shots!* Lime, salt, down the hatch. Jenny and Ed disappeared into the garage, came back. I stumbled, grabbing another beer. The Fishers weren't in the room anymore; they'd gone to bed. Eddie and I stood in the archway where the kitchen linoleum met the living room carpet. I remember talking, laughing, touching the soft cotton of his T-shirt. It was so soft, so soft—I felt like I could fall into him. *He reminds me of Charlie*, I thought. *He is warm, like Charlie.*

Then, for a while, nothing. I went dark, my consciousness drifting offline.

I blacked out for several minutes. When I came to, we were kissing.

Chapter 19

The Vessel

All the lights were on in the Fishers' kitchen, painfully bright in my squinty eyes. It was late, the house swaddled in the sticky, woolly air of a coastal summer night. And we were still kissing. It was a deep, warm kiss, perfect, even better than I'd imagined. Our chests pressed together, Eddie's hands moved over my back and waist, straying inside my overalls. My fingers played mindlessly in his long hair, pulling at the neck of his T-shirt. There was a forgotten but familiar tingling pressure, a warmth, my body begging for more. I pulled back.

Oh no. This was wrong, I knew it was wrong. But I liked it. I also didn't know how we'd gotten there. The world spun a little. Jesus, how did I get so drunk? I had no idea how long I'd been blacked out, or what else we had done.

I asked sheepishly, "Um, how did this happen? Like, how did we start . . ."

"You don't remember?" Eddie said. "A few minutes ago we were talking, and you started kissing my neck."

I groaned. "That sounds like me." For better or worse, I was a consummate first-move maker. Always have been. What's more, I knew that Eddie was not. He never would've jumped without me shoving him off the cliff. "Well, shit."

"We should stop," he said quickly. "We shouldn't do this."

"You're right, we shouldn't," I agreed.

Then I kissed him again.

We would've been fine if we left it in Fisher's driveway. We made out for hours—kissing like high schoolers in their parents' basement in the '90s—in the back of Eddie's truck. We slept a little, or at least he did. I lay wide awake, pinned between the wall of the camper shell and his broad body, which took up most of the twin-sized sleeping platform. He snored luxuriantly, and I watched him, thinking, *Oh god. What now?*

We had held a line—"clothes stay on." A drunken makeout without sex seemed like something you could reason through, maybe write off. Not that it was *okay*, but it was possible to "whoopsie" that, never repeat it, and move on with life. I might tell Josh and hope we could work through it, or I might never tell him. But it didn't represent a crisis on the level that sleeping with Eddie would be a crisis.

But at dawn, wide awake, we started to worry that the two of us sleeping in Ed's truck would look suspicious to the Fishers. That, and we had each paid $180 for lousy motel rooms, so maybe we should head back into town and get a few hours of sleep. Yeah. Good plan. Except that when we pulled into the lot, Eddie turned and smiled.

"Can I come to your room for a lil' bit?" he asked. "Just to snuggle?"

"Yeah, right," I said, and while it should have occurred to me that this was the time to say no and put a stop to this, my still-drunk, sleep-deprived head didn't bother rubbing those two brain cells together. "Okay. Just for a little bit."

The room was as drab and musty as I remembered. The bare yellowish walls were damp from the foggy breeze drifting in the bathroom window, left open to compensate for the lack of air-conditioning. We undressed down to underwear and T-shirts and climbed under the sheet.

Eddie's skin was brown and unbelievably smooth, like silk over his muscles. I ran my hands over them; his hands slid over my back, grabbed my ass. He was telling me my skin was soft; it was perfect. We writhed against each other ecstatically. His fingers began to pull at the edge of my underwear.

"Ah—" I said, a warning.

"I mean, the damage is done, right?" he suggested, breath on my neck. His dick pressed against me through two layers of fabric.

I moaned. "That's terrible logic."

"But you want to."

"I do."

"Then . . . might as well?"

I groaned again, desire overcoming rational thought. "Might as well."

The next morning, we sat facing each other at breakfast, pale and full of shame. I clutched a cup of coffee with shaking hands.

"That was . . . a mistake," I began.

"Yeah."

"I mean, it was amazing, but—"

"It *was* amazing." A sheepish grin from Ed.

"It really was. But—this is so bad. I'm a horrible person. Do you think I'm a horrible person?"

"No. I probably am."

"No you're not. I pretty much tricked you into this. I started it."

"That's true. I'm basically a minor you took advantage of." Rascally smile.

"Hey!" I punched his arm. "So what are we gonna do?"

"I don't know," he said sadly.

"We should never do that again, for starters. And I need to figure out what the hell is going on with me and my, um, relationship." I hesitated to utter the word *engagement*, a much heavier set of syllables. "I can't think right now. My head hurts. I need some sleep."

"Same."

"Fuck this town for not having any food after eight. If we could've gotten dinner, this never would've happened."

"Yeah. Definitely Crescent City's fault. *Fuck* Port O' Pints."

I laughed, though we both knew it wasn't true. Sure, we'd been hammered, but as any child of a drunk will tell you, alcohol is never an excuse. Whatever I had done while wasted was what I *wanted* to do; alcohol just pulled the goalkeeper.

Looking back, I could see the trail of breadcrumbs into this forest. The communication breakdown with Josh that summer, a growing closeness with Eddie over the past year. My fears about settling down in Happy Camp and becoming a wife and mother. All culminating in an action I regretted—a choice that would make me finally reckon with the question of marriage. This wasn't the first time I'd made a "mistake" that forced my hand. Once again, my body seemed to take the wheel, saying, *If you won't deal with this, I will.*

"Sounds like you want out," my friend Lindsay said over the phone. I stood in our yard in Happy Camp, throwing a ball for the dogs. Josh was on a fire, so at least I didn't have to face him yet. But R&R felt lonely and dark. I'd called several friends to confess my sins and seek help. The others took my stake in these two men seriously, weighing pros and cons while reassuring me that one unethical action didn't make you a monster. Lindsay took a different tack.

"Eddie is a boy. Probably not the love of your life, from how you've described him. He's just the vessel. Like a door you're using to exit."

I let out a hollow laugh. "You may be right."

For weeks, whenever we talked, she referred to Eddie like this. *How's the vessel?*

Was he, I wondered, anything more than an escape hatch? And did I really, truly want out?

The prospect of pressing the eject button was dizzying. Leaving Josh would mean leaving a community, a partner, and a house that felt like home. I had done that before, and I knew how such a choice could wreck you.

I clung to the safety of a stable situation, or even the illusion of one, with good reason. I knew exactly why "home" (and its opposite) were so important to me.

Unbidden, the memory came rushing back.

I was thirty-five. April had come to Texas, where spring rampaged over the hills. Bluebonnets crowded the highway medians and peaches ripened in the warm air.

Dad lost his truck, my sister wrote. *He's at the ER, but they won't admit him. Trying to get him into the warming shelter for tonight.*

Shelter? Sweating under the Austin sun, I couldn't comprehend her words. He needed a place to stay because . . . ?

The truth broke through with a kick. *Oh.* Our father had nowhere to live.

Sorry—warming *shelter?*
We had a snowstorm last week, my sister wrote.

Sure enough, the low for Neenah, Wisconsin, was forecast at twenty-two degrees, and a foot of snow covered the streets.

I see, I said. *Why won't the hospital take him?*

They say there's nothing wrong with him.

Hilarious, I wrote, adding weeping and laughing to tears emojis.

The last time I had seen him, he'd called my sisters and me "you women," refusing our help. But he showed up a week later, a contrite bag of bones on Courtney's doorstep, finally willing to be dropped at the ER. There, the doctors said his body was mere days from death by starvation. So we'd been right: he was dying.

A severe thiamine deficiency explained the delusional thinking. A hospital stint and rehab center later, he bounced back, put on a little weight. His mental fog cleared. And as soon as he felt better, he was drinking again.

He stayed in the basement of his former righthand man, Pablo, the one guy who'd held on through Dad's full series of bankruptcies. My dad called him Maestro. Mexican Americans and good Catholics, Maestro and his wife believed in family and couldn't understand why Bob's children wouldn't take their father in (again—my sisters had housed him many times). We only smiled. They hadn't yet been treated to the full Bob Ramsey experience.

When he started stealing from the liquor store and the gas station, they grew concerned. He got caught, spent a night in jail, and returned to their basement. When he stole from *them*, they understood, and Maestro kicked him out.

After that, he slept in his truck, parked on a quiet street or under an overpass, long limbs cramped from folding into the short seat. He had blankets, though, and whiskey, so he wasn't without comfort. A vehicle was still a place to call your own.

Then—driving drunk, safe to assume—he crashed his truck. He couldn't afford to pay the towing company to retrieve his vehicle from impound. Without work, he had nothing but what he stole (or what we—mostly my siblings—gave him, which was less and less). No home, no friends' houses, no truck. End of the line.

He called Courtney, who texted the rest of us. *Dad's homeless. What do we do?*

The five of us got on a conference call, which was a first. For a few minutes, we reveled in having the siblings together, laughing and catching up. Then Steve reminded us of the problem at hand.

"This is gonna be a brave new world for dear old Dad," he said. "He's gonna wake up tomorrow in a changed universe. What we have to decide is whether we're gonna help him."

Despite the heat in my apartment, cold stole over my skin.

"So when he wakes up tomorrow and sees that he's shit out of luck, that karma has finally caught up with his skinny ass, and he calls us, what do we do?" Steve took a breath. "I'd like to suggest we do nothing."

"I don't know if I can do that," Madeleine said.

"How many times has he asked you for money?" Courtney pressed. "How many times has he 'borrowed' your money, spent it on booze, and disappeared?"

"He can't live with me," Mad said quietly. "I can't have that around my daughter."

"He can't live with me, either," Courtney said. "I'm eight months pregnant. I've got two boys. I can't fuckin' deal with this."

"Evan," I said. "Are you on the call?"

"Yeah, I'm here." His soft, shy voice. "I'm just listening."

"Look," Steve broke in. "Dad has burned all his bridges. End of the goddamned line. These are the consequences of his choices. It's time for *him* to figure out what to do and whether he wants real help. We gotta let him do it. Tough as it is, I say we do nothing. See what he does."

"Yeah," I said. "I have to agree. I think Dad's a survivor. If we don't help him, he's gonna figure out a way to get by. Maybe he'll even stop drinking. But if we keep 'helping,' all we do is give him the means to drink."

"I know," Madeleine said. "It just makes me feel so bad. He's our dad. It's *cold* out there."

"I know." I could hardly breathe. "Bad" wasn't a big enough word.

"So how do we vote?" Steve said. "It sucks, but I think we all get it. Do we agree to do nothing?"

A pause. Five children breathing. I remembered a time when all of us could crowd into two bunk beds.

Swallowing hard, I said, "Yes."

"I don't like it," Madeleine said. "But yes."

One by one, five yeses rang out over the line. The voices of people I'd known since they were born, whom I'd held as babies and fed as toddlers and counseled as teenagers. *God*, I thought. *They're too young to go through this.*

But what about me? Was I old enough? At what age was it acceptable for your father to end up on the street?

We made the best decision we could. Still, I had a hard time falling asleep that night. I pictured him walking in the snow. I imagined him choosing a cot in the shelter, if he was lucky enough to get one. I saw his withdrawal from alcohol, his friendlessness, his fear. Did he know how much we loved him? What if he died without knowing?

I was glad I'd forgiven him, even if he hated me for it.

But who would forgive *me*?

I needed days, or maybe weeks, to reckon with what I'd done with Eddie and work out what to do, but I wasn't gonna get that kind of time, not until October at the earliest. August had descended upon California. We'd been swallowed by the whale, and its belly was fire.

Nationwide, seventy-eight large fires remained uncontained, twelve of those in Northern California alone. The names were my intimates, like friends or enemies: Dixie, MacFarland, Monument, Antelope, River Complex, McCash, Evans, Lava, Beckwourth Complex—burning a combined four hundred thousand acres in our half of the state.

We were headed south to the Monument Fire, which was ripping and roaring outside the town of Junction City on the Trinity River. Just over forty thousand acres, it had recently leveled four buildings in the tiny river bar of Big Flat.

We'd picked up a fill-in (a "fill" or a "scab") from one of the engines, a kid named Bradley. All of nineteen years old, fresh off the horse farm. When we met and he learned my age, he said, "Oh, so you're like the crew mom!" I cringed but smiled. "Um, not quite."

As we loaded up water and fuel in the Supt truck, I leaned into the tailgate to pass a heavy box. As I did, one of the guys, trying to move around me, briefly held my waist on both sides, kind of like he was grabbing me to maneuver me out of the way—or like he was just *squeezing* me? It lasted only a second, then he moved on.

What the—? I stiffened but didn't turn. Fawn in headlights. If I didn't react, it hadn't happened, right? I kept working. But unfortunately, half the crew was standing nearby. When the guy walked away, they turned to me, aghast.

"What the fuck was THAT?" Fisher said. "Ramsey, Jesus. That wasn't cool."

My mouth opened and closed. I looked at my boots.

"That was messed up," Trevan agreed.

"Um, yeah. I guess."

"You guess? No, man. That was fuckin' weird. You don't just touch a girl!" Fisher said.

"Right," I said, frowning. I thought I might cry. "Yeah, it was messed up. But I don't think he . . . meant to?" The way I saw it, the guy (who for obvious reasons I've chosen not to name) was lonely. I'd always been kind to him, and this was an unchecked impulse—a mistake. Didn't I, of all people, know what it was like to misplace your self-control?

"Doesn't matter if he meant to. You don't do that." Bless Fisher and his airtight ethics. "You wanna say something about it? You want me to tell someone? I'll take this to Van right now," Fisher offered.

"No!" I said, vehement. "I mean, not yet. Let me think about it, okay?"

"Sure. Let me know. But I'm sorry, Ramsey. That's fucked."

"Thanks, Fish."

I thought it over for two days. In the end, I decided not to say anything—not to the man in question, who would never act natural around me again, and not to Van, who'd be obligated to report it up the chain. The Forest higher-ups would initiate an investigation. This man would almost certainly lose his job, and hence, everything: his livelihood, his "fire family," and the retirement for which he had labored through *years* in smoke, in ash, in flames.

No way. I wasn't going to let a one-second lapse in judgment ruin the life of a man who, despite his flaws, I loved like a brother. I decided that if it happened a second time, I would address it directly with him, but it probably wouldn't; it had never happened before. I was right.

Still, it stung to swallow the incident in silence. As we slammed the buggy doors and pulled onto the highway, I thought, *Wow*—in a single day, I was the crew's mother and their sex object. The only thing I hadn't been was somebody's grandma. But there was still time.

Day one on the Monument fire, we prepped a house. Englefield ate angel fingers (Vienna sausages) from a can, shoving several weenies into his mouth at once, letting the juices dribble down his chin. He deliberately blew hot dog breath in my face, and I narrowed my eyes.

I hadn't heard from Josh in two days. While I knew they were spiked out without service on a fire, I had the paranoid thought: *He knows.* I held my breath, as if waiting for an explosion.

Day three we prepped an endless, steep dozer line through a hundred-degree afternoon. Hiking in, Addison began to fall behind. Then she dropped to her knees in the dozer line, gasping in the dirt.

"Hold up, folks. We lost one," Fisher said, irritated.

We looked down the hill. Scotty took a knee beside Addison, and I could imagine the soft words of encouragement he uttered as he checked to make sure she wasn't hurt. Meanwhile, another crew was hiking in, and they climbed past us, glancing curiously at the tableau.

"Sierra Shots are passing her. They're *passing her*," someone near me said.

"Won't she at least stand up? Get *up*. Don't let them pass you like that!"

There is no greater shame for a hotshot than looking weak in front of another crew. I probably should have been sympathetic, but I'll tell you the truth: that day, I wasn't. I had felt like collapsing in the line plenty of times. The work was so hard, and your legs wanted nothing more than to give out. I thought of the power hike on the North Complex the year before, and how I'd melted down. Still, I hadn't stopped until Salmon told me to; I hiked and cried. Something always kept me from stopping, some compulsion between "fear of shame" and "honor," or what we jokingly called "'tegrity." Why couldn't Addison dig deep for that inner grit?

I should have seen her kneeling in the dozer line and felt compassion for a suffering human being, but I couldn't muster it. I had my own shit going on, and it always seemed to be *something* with her. I rolled my eyes and turned away.

Day six, we skipped briefing to get an early start on a long burn operation. From the top of the ridge, we lit down a dozer line—me,

Hale, Englefield, and Shaggy—bringing the fire's edge to the Trinity River, the first time I'd tied in a burn to a body of water. Addison snapped a picture of me (in some dorky pose, as always, I never *ever* looked cool) beside the rushing river, flames on one side and green willows on the other. I appreciated having a woman there, someone who wasn't weird about taking my photo. The previous day's embarrassment quickly forgotten, I made a point of doing the same for her.

At the end of the burn, as the hillside smoldered and smoked, we posted up on a log deck in a wide clearing. I did a Zyn and let the nicotine buzz blur my brain. Eddie sat nearby, and though we could have talked, we texted—because what we had to say was private.

We had been texting a little each night. Intimacies, tender words, suggestive phrases. I knew it was a slippery slope (quicksand, high tide, crumbling cliff), but what were we supposed to do, blow each other off? We worked together sixteen hours a day. Yet I knew that until I figured things out and talked with Josh, I should avoid Eddie.

While I had an impulse to up and leave Josh, common sense went against it. We'd built a life together. And chances were strong that if I abandoned my engagement, this thing with Eddie would fizzle. He was almost twelve years younger than me, with no serious relationships under his belt. He was funny, warm, a compassionate friend—but if the responsibility of being first saw terrified him, what would he make of being a real partner?

Yep, the right thing to do was to pull back from Eddie and try to forget that night in Crescent City. But I couldn't bring myself to do it.

I was sick with guilt and dread. I couldn't eat. My stomach began to hollow. Though I grew lightheaded, I struggled to choke down the meals from fire camp, which—inconsistent quality aside—I normally destroyed. I was a terrible person, selfish and ruined and bad.

On day twelve I watched Eddie drop a snag burned to nothing but trunk, a charcoal obelisk, a giant crumbling chopstick. It stood over a hundred feet tall, so fragile that the top could easily break as it fell, landing on the sawyer. Watching Eddie operate the saw, I felt a rush of pride. Despite his fears, he had learned and improved dramatically, tapping the same tenacity that made him one of our fastest hikers. He cut the tree with ease, not a shred of doubt in his face or capable hands. The snag landed with a boom that shook the hillside.

No matter how I shamed myself, when I saw Eddie's broad, filthy figure in greens and graying yellow loping up the line, a smile broke over my face, a surge of love and desire I couldn't control.

Day ten, the fire blew up. We were furious because we'd been saying, *Let us burn. Let us light any* one *of these million prepped dozer lines.* A series of lines had been snagged and prepped and stood ready in ever-widening arcs of protection leading away from Junction City. But we hadn't been allowed to burn them. The Incident Management Team waited, for reasons that were over our heads, until the fire was too close.

Now the Monument was pushing the town. Flames gusted over the ridge and marched down the hillside, torching as they backed toward hundreds of vulnerable homes. The valley fell into pandemonium. Engines and crew hauls raced through town, pulled U-turns on the hill, crowded in the safety of a parking lot. Flames licked through the drainage just behind the fire station. The radio was overrun with urgent voices.

A house on the far side of the river had caught fire. Flames shot through the roof. Hale, who saw me wipe away a tear, knew I was thinking of Happy Camp. He'd been on a detail with my old crew when that fire came, so he'd seen the Slater's destruction firsthand. Like me, he knew people who'd lost their homes.

"I think about it too," he said. "Hard to forget."

"You never forget," I said, eyes wet, chills flowing down my back— the same chills I got every time I remembered that Labor Day. Hale gave my shoulder a squeeze.

"These poor people," I lamented. "We could've stopped it, if they'd let us."

"I know, dude. Hate to say it, but you're gonna see that in this job. You're gonna see it a lot."

I shook my head. "I'm not okay with that."

"I know."

We were sent to put hand line down a cut bank behind Main Street, a gully of trash and discarded tires. As we dug, the fire produced a noxious black smoke that tasted like burning rubber. We breathed it in, the only air we had, gagging, coughing and streaming tears, until Fisher came along and said, "What the hell, get out of here! Don't inhale that shit."

Some guys felt the tire smoke in their lungs for days.

Soon darkness fell, and without any discussion of rolling into night shift—a twenty-four was assumed, in this kind of crisis—we joined a burn operation on a dozer line just behind a row of homes. Lighting that close to structures was unnerving, sending flames into trees no more than twenty yards from someone's lawn. This wasn't the usual Forest Service purview; we were meant to work deep in the woods. But call it what you will: the Wildland-Urban Interface, forest too close to the houses, or houses built too close to the woods. Overgrown forests, hotter world. Here we were.

They started the burn while I took weather (spun the sling psychrometer, calculated the temperature and relative humidity, determined wind speed, etc.) in the cone of my headlamp, standing near a marijuana grow too obvious to be a secret. When I finished reading the weather over the radio, I rejoined Wink at the corner of two dozer pushes. We stood in the flickering orange light of the fire that covered the forest floor and climbed each tree in a flaming string. Wink told me that he'd bought a ring and was about to propose to his longtime lady.

"Oh my god, *Wink!* That's awesome," I crowed, punching his bony shoulder.

"Shh! Only you and Scotty be knowing," he said, finger to his lips.

Wink was notorious for his open secrets, and I had a feeling he'd told a half dozen people the same thing, but I promised. "I won't say a word."

Fisher strode down the dozer line, his face dark. "They said this piece was snagged by another crew," he said by way of greeting. Snagging was cutting down the standing dead trees, which would pose a huge risk once they caught fire; the other crew was supposed to have mitigated the danger for us before we burned. "Doesn't look snagged to me. You see this?" He pointed into the burn. "Snag, snag—there's another one. Snags every fuckin' where. And they're starting to come down."

He told Wink to keep patrolling the hillside part of the burn, but not to linger. "Don't stay up there. Feels sketchy."

"Sure thing, Fish. Y-you got it, bud."

"Be extra heads-up, you guys. These morons left us a minefield."

Fisher hurried away. As if on cue, a tree crashed into the dozer line on the hillside above us—a tall, spindly madrone with an eight-inch-diameter trunk. The tree landed with a "whump" in the pillowy dirt.

"Well," I said.

"Th-there you go." Wink shrugged. "We b-better get that out of the line."

Wink keyed his radio and called for a saw team. Hearing him, Luke loped out of the darkness to see if we needed help. The three of us approached the downed tree. Luke had turned toward the log on the ground when the second tree fell.

Another madrone maybe five inches thick tipped toward the earth, swift and clean, cleaving the air between Wink and me, the bole wood on a course for Luke's head. His back was turned, so he didn't see it coming. Wink and I opened our mouths, took half a step—*Luke!*— too late.

The tree slammed the top of his head. Glancing off his hard hat, the trunk struck his arm before landing in the dirt. Shocked, Luke placed a hand on his head and stumbled, trying to catch his balance. Then he tossed his hard hat away and fell onto his back.

"Luke!" we screamed. "Are you okay?"

He didn't answer. His face had gone white.

Time slowed. Like people walking underwater, Wink and I did what we were trained to do. *I'll call*, I said, and he nodded. *I've got him.* He knelt by Luke, placing his hands on either side of Luke's head, performing a hold called C-spine to keep his neck immobilized in case of a spinal injury. I keyed up my radio and spoke quickly. I probably should have called a Captain, or the Supt, but I called the first person I thought of, the one who knew how to save lives.

"Scotty, Kelly on Gray."

"Yeah, go."

"Uh." How to say this? I remembered at the last second that you weren't supposed to say an injured person's name over the radio. "A crew member has been struck by a tree. I need you here right away. Top of our burn."

"Copy. On my way," Scotty said.

"Hurry."

"I'll grab you on the UTV, Scotty," said another voice, maybe Van.

Trevan and Keller had just come around the corner, and when they saw us, they broke into a run, Trevan dropping his chainsaw in the dirt.

"I can't feel my arm," Luke said, face ghostly. "What *was* that?"

"It's okay, bud," Wink said, no trace of a stutter. "We's gonna take care of you. You just stay still."

"Is another one coming?" Luke cringed, lifting an arm as if to protect himself. "Is another tree gonna fall on me?"

My chest contracted. I'd never seen Luke scared.

Trevan and Keller reached us, along with a handful of EMTs from an engine parked in the turnaround below us. The UTV came around the corner, Van driving and Scotty in the passenger seat. Keller, also an EMT, joined the cluster of firefighters with medical training now surrounding Luke. Scotty ran up, eyes fearful but demeanor calm. He had worked on an ambulance, seen it all. Everything, I guessed, but his friend lying on the ground.

"Hey Luke," he said, dropping to his knees beside him.

Trevan looked at me. "Let's get the stuff."

I nodded, and we broke into a sprint down the dozer line. The Supt truck stood in a pullout less than fifty yards away, which was lucky; this wouldn't be a tough extraction. I thought through what to grab: backboard, straps, and the trauma kit, which included oxygen. Only then did I begin to register what had happened. Luke was down, and if his numb arm meant a spinal injury, he might not make it off this hill.

No.

Trevan's blond hair flew out behind him. God, he was fast, and he seemed so steady, so sure, not afraid at all. Better catch him. I dug in my toes and ran.

Chapter 20

Hail Mary

Two days later, Luke was back. In a small miracle, he had suffered little more than a concussion and bruised hand. The numbness, the ER doctor theorized, might've been a combination of impact and shock. "Got his bell rung," the boys said.

(Since Luke wasn't severely hurt, the Office of Worker's Compensation decided the government wasn't liable for his hospitalization. He received a bill for $49,000 and spent months with a caseworker fighting the charges. He did eventually win.)

Luke was back, but he didn't seem quite right, and neither were we. The day after the strike, while he was in the hospital, Van pulled us aside for an After Action Review. We stood in a circle in Junction City, within sight of the burned house, to go over what·had happened.

We felt pressured to burn because the fire was threatening houses. We didn't think we could turn down the assignment. The snagging wasn't up to our standards. Our egos said we could pull it off.

As we talked, it became less of a typical, practical AAR—"What could we do differently next time?"—and more of an opportunity to share our feelings. Of the several who burst into tears, Fisher was most surprising. "Fifteen years," he gasped. "It gives me flashbacks to other things. A buddy got his lungs crushed by a tree. Tops that fell out. Almost getting hit. When I think, I want to go home to my wife—"

He broke off, weeping, and Benjy cuffed him on the shoulder, his eyes also red. The other men in the circle looked at their feet, wiped their eyes. My face was wet.

To Van's credit, he prioritized the time to talk. The crew felt closer after the conversation, and for my part, I saw that these scary moments affected the men just as much as me. We were all feeling people who loved each other and wanted to keep each other safe. And we all knew—for me, for what seemed like the first time—that the risks were real. Were we willing to die for what we hoped to save?

The last few days of the Monument were quiet, although BJ and Luke tested positive for Covid and were sent home, while the rest of us were briefly quarantined and tested (all negative). One afternoon, brushing out a road, yellowjackets stung me eleven times, including in the lip, which swelled up like the blister from a second-degree burn. My face throbbed, and I swallowed a handful of Benadryl and felt groggy and sad and wondered if this was karma.

On the last day of R&R, I hiked to my river spot. I swam and sat and watched the clear green water.

The whole assignment, I'd been battling myself. First, there was the wrongness of what I had done, which was hard to get past. Next, there was a decision to be made, and I'd swung wildly between extremes: *Leave Josh / you can't leave Josh. Be with Eddie / Eddie is hopeless.* Every night of the roll, I had lain in my sleeping bag in the smoke, agonized, making myself sick. *You've really screwed yourself this time, Ramsey.*

Now, as I trudged along the trail, the sun warming the part in my hair, something shifted. The voice in my head, my "should" voice, had been telling me to work things out with Josh; staying was the most sensible course of action. Meanwhile, the animal in me knew exactly what it wanted, and that animal—call it the body, intuition, gut instinct—always won in the end. Looking back on my major life decisions, my gut had always been in the driver's seat. And now every cell, every follicle, every breath in my lungs spoke clearly: *Leave.*

I knew that when I went home, my body would betray me. I didn't want to embrace Josh, let alone sleep with him or live in his house. My arms and lips would refuse. The body doesn't just keep the score; it tells the truth, if you're willing to listen.

Back at the station that afternoon, I ran into Eddie in the bay. Leaning against the steel worktable with its vises and clamps, I asked him, "Hey, if I were to become single, do you think we'd give this a try? Like would we . . . date?"

"Um," he stuttered. He looked at his feet. "I don't know. I'm not sure, but I don't think so."

I might have said *Seriously?*

"I'd be so scared! Like, if you left your husband—"

"We're not married," I snapped.

"If you left your *fiancé* for me, that's a lot of pressure. I don't think I could live up to that. Like, what if it didn't go well? I'm not good at relationships. And then it would be so bad, I'd feel so bad, because you left him for me."

My friend Emily says you have to believe people when they tell you about themselves. *Especially* if they're telling you their shortcomings.

"Good point," I said. "Although I wouldn't leave him *for you.* Or not just for you. I'd be leaving him because this thing with you has shown me that I don't want to be with him."

"Yeah. Well." He shrugged. "I just can't make any promises. I'm sorry."

"Okay," I said. Fair enough—at least he was honest. But the tears were coming; I had to get out of there.

Leaving the bay, I collected my laundry from the engine building and drove out past the Grassy Flat campground to the gravel lot where some of the guys camped now and then. Luckily, I had the spot to myself tonight. I dropped the tailgate on my truck and sat folding fire laundry in the last bit of daylight. A sunset gold lit the cliffs above me. I could hear the river rushing through the slot canyon below and birds crying from the trees perched on the rocks. I sighed, relishing the place and my solitude. Nature was always there for me, at least. Nature didn't judge, control, or abandon you.

Crying a little, I thought, *Well, fuck it, then. I'll be alone.*

And all at once, the thought didn't bring me terror. *Alone*, I repeated silently, this time an incantation. My own home, my own things, my own time. No man in the house, no heavy footsteps or puddles by the shower, nobody to clean up after, no guilt for going off to fight the next fire, no one to report to but myself. Morning coffee in sweatpants. Traveling with friends. Crackers and olives for dinner. Settling into my body, finding a home in my skin—my flesh, my thoughts, my dreams for me alone.

I'd love to spend more time with Eddie. But if he turned out to be no more than a vessel, that would be fine too. *I* would be fine, sprung from the trap of Happy Camp and an impending marriage that felt like a sentence. I would be free.

I folded my pants and paired my socks, mentally preparing for the next day and a new fire, and for what I'd say to Josh. Oh god. Deeper dread, cold stealing into my bones. What on earth could I say to Josh?

I've fallen for someone else? I've fallen for myself? I just don't want to be here?

A white F-350 rumbled into the lot. I grinned, shaking my head. Leave it to Eddie to find me in my hiding place. He parked beside me and climbed out.

"How'd you know I'd be here?"

"I *know* you." He smiled. "And there's only like two places to go."

Laughing, I brushed a remnant tear from my cheek. He sat on the tailgate beside me, and I pushed the laundry onto my mattress in the bed of the truck. He was carrying two It's-It treats, ice cream pressed between oatmeal cookies and dipped in chocolate, the best product to come out of California—and yes, I am including all of Hollywood's creative output, the Beach Boys, and raw gold. He handed me an It's-It. We sat in silence for a minute, chewing.

"The mint really is the best," I said.

"Duh." Eddie turned to me with a look of deep concern. "Are we gonna be okay?"

That "we." That was it. He hadn't said we'd date, hadn't promised his undying love, hadn't pledged to be any kind of boyfriend. But the word "we" said it all. Whether we were meant to be or not, Eddie had placed himself on my side. Same team. He had my back, as a friend or otherwise—and he'd just demonstrated that when things were tenuous between us, he'd show up with a peace offering, ready to talk. He said he was afraid, but his actions looked like bravery.

Now we'd have to see how brave I could be.

Nobody was excited to go to the McCash, a fire that stretched from the steep, poison oak–filled crevasses of the Six Rivers (our home forest) into the steeper, poison oak–riddled canyons of the Klamath. The blaze was creeping toward Happy Camp, a place where none of us wanted to fight fire, least of all me. Josh would be home soon, and my dilemma would come to a head not on R&R, as I had hoped, but in the middle of an assignment.

The night before we left, playing a game in the bay, Addison had answered a never-have-I-ever style question—*Have you ever kissed anyone in this room?*—with a giggly, "Yes." Looking around the table,

I didn't see many options. Trevan (engaged), Hale (committed), Ed (mine-ish), Haines, and Ender. Though I sort of wished her conquest were Ender—who was in his late twenties and had a subtle, smoldering, witty appeal—I had a strong suspicion it was Haines. Hadn't he and Addison been flirting from the start? As we drove to the line, Hale and I speculated.

"It could be Eddie." Hale shrugged.

"I don't think so. I think it's Haines."

"He's a good-looking dude. But why wouldn't it be Ed?"

"It just wouldn't. I know him. He just . . . wouldn't."

"Why are you so protective of him?" Hale glanced at me, blue eyes piercing. I blushed. "He's not your little brother, you know."

Okay, so Hale hadn't caught on.

The fire put up a monster column that day. One flank made an uphill run, licking the slope like dragon's breath, and when we drove above the fire, Burgundy Two (Luke, BJ, and Shaggy's pickup) caught an ember under the hood. The fragment lodged in the air filter and set it on fire, like actual *fire* in the engine. We extinguished it quickly, but the motor was dead and, according to the mechanic from Fleet, "inoperable."

So we were down a truck. Shaggy climbed in the back with Englefield, and Hale and I were happy for his cheerful presence. That night, bedded down at a campground east of the river, I lay on my sleeping pad thinking, *Am I actually leaving Josh? Is this real?*

On day three, in camp, I chatted with Benjy as we waited for the rookies to grab breakfast. "Nice job torching the whole forest yesterday," he joked, knowing I hated being the lighter who made the woods burn hot.

"Ha!" I said, knowing better by now than to get defensive.

"Gets all mad defending a single meadow, then burns off half the Six Rivers in one afternoon."

"Oh, you're *funny*."

"Seriously, though. You're awesome. You're really killin' it this year."

"Dude," I said, floored by the sudden compliment. "Thank you. I'm trying."

"Yeah, it shows. You're one of the guys now. The dude!" That moniker, *the dude*, was one he'd bestowed upon his good friend, a woman he'd worked with for years in Oregon. Now he sometimes applied the term to me, and I knew it was his highest praise.

"I don't know about that." I grimaced.

"Well, I love ya. You're doing great."

"I love you too, Benjy."

Phew. I let out a long breath, walking back to the buggies.

Heart-to-hearts must've been in the air, because Addison pulled me aside near the UTV and admitted that the person she had kissed—more than kissed—was Haines.

"I knew it!" I crowed. "I love that for you, Addison. He's superhot."

She told me their liaison had begun during the R&R following the Dixie roll. If my calculations were correct, they had knocked boots on the same night Ed and I had kissed for the first time. Good old Dirty August. With a deep breath, I told her what had happened with Eddie.

"I'm not sure what to do," I said. "I feel like a terrible person."

"You're not." Addison wrapped me in a huge, warm hug. I'm sorry, guys everywhere, but there is no hug like a girlfriend's hug. It's just . . . softer, closer, squeezier. I was infinitely comforted by her touch, and by this exchange: a secret for a secret. I had told my best friends about Eddie, but most of them lived far away, so to have someone here who knew the truth was a balm upon the callous of my fire persona.

I gave her another squeeze. "Thank you."

Addison's secret didn't stay secret for long. On day four, she smacked Haines's ass, and half of Alpha saw it. Soon the whole crew was talking about them, and I was paranoid. Eddie and I had to keep it tight. If they found out, I wouldn't be Ramsey, second-year hotshot; I'd be reduced to "that girl Eddie fucked." It never changed anything for the man, but it changed everything for the woman. I started deliberately ignoring him at work, even being rude. A couple times I took it too far and hurt his feelings.

That day, day four, went down in the annals of Rowdy River history: the day we burned miles of line with no water, no crews or engines, no support. Legend.

The McCash was understaffed, and the edge of the fire had reached the bottom of a drainage below Titus Ridge, where it lined up to make an uphill run. This wrinkle of earth stood as one of the last good barriers between the fire and Happy Camp. Less than a year after the Slater fire, everyone was eager to keep a new blaze out of this half-burned, wholly traumatized town. So we'd been tasked with a Hail Mary burn from a wilderness trailhead called Johnsons Hunting Ground all the way to the Klamath River. The segment we'd tackle was seven or eight miles long.

I'd heard other crews brag about pulling off a *one*-mile burn in a single shift. To think we could do this successfully without losing our burn was madness. But we'd try. That was the Rowdy River way.

Early that morning, I stood at the trailhead beside Hale. I remembered hiking from here into the Marble Mountains as a wilderness ranger, camping at Ukonom Lake by myself, treading the blue water, sleeping on the pine needles. Would my home burn again?

"Ready?" Hale said.

"You know it."

"Eight miles of line, and we're left at the top with three torches." Hale grinned. While there were other lighters strung out along the ridge, the prospect of our smallness—gloved hands, little torches, twenty bodies—felt ludicrous, against this vast landscape.

"Perfect." I smiled.

An epic day ensued: lighters moving in two directions with blue fire spilling from their torches, firing across multiple teams; fire dripped off roads, off dozer lines; fire climbing trees and torching stands en masse, pouring down into the valley below; shooting the Veri pistol out the window of the truck, sparks flying . . . and smoke rising in thick billows, castle-like, all along the spine of the ridge.

By nightfall, we had covered the distance, and we stood on the far side of the river watching the orange glow in the dark. The miracle was that while the burn hadn't held perfectly, the losses were catchable. We could save the slopovers before they crawled away. Our burn would hold.

That night, despite the crew's big W, I lay on my sleeping pad feeling sick. Josh would be home the next day, and the crew would be moving to Curly Jack, a campground in Happy Camp. So Josh and I would be in the same town. I barely slept.

Day six was the first of September. That morning, Hale was doing lines of C4 from the center console of Shadow One's cab. Normally you'd mix pre-workout powder into a bottle of water, but Hale took it straight up, shaping the powder into lines and bending to snort the granules like cocaine.

As he did, he offered a rebrand for the month. "It's *Send*tember, bro!" he said, and whooped. "Full send."

"I want in on this," Englefield said, and leaned in for a line.

"Kells?" Hale asked.

"Not today." I smiled. Pre-workout could make me anxious on an ordinary day, and this was no ordinary day.

At briefing, a festive feeling prevailed. Van was proud of us, the team was proud of us, everyone was thrilled. We'd burned seven miles without support, then gone back and caught our own slopover, ensuring the burn would hold. In a sense, at least regarding the northern flank of the fire, we had saved Happy Camp.

As the circle broke up, Mac said, "Kelly, ya goin' home tonight?"

I grimaced. Mac and Josh were old friends. "Yeah, maybe," I hedged.

He gave me a baffled frown. "Go home!"

I tried to smile, wanted to vomit.

Patrolling our burn that morning, Englefield found a small spot fire below the road. We went direct and caught it, me leading a short squad of Englefield and Shaggy on the dig. As we slogged through a heavy load of bark plates and shredded wood, I knew that I was moving slowly. I couldn't seem to force myself to move on until I'd swept aside enough debris to at least catch sight of dirt.

"You can take less," Shaggy suggested.

"Yeah, leave us something!" Englefield grumbled.

"Okay, I'll try," I said, but I struggled to leave a task half-done. I had to see that dirt to know I'd done my part.

I knew my perfectionism was annoying, and my hunch was confirmed when I came up the line an hour later and overheard Englefield, BJ, and Shaggy talking about me. Just fragments, but I was clearly the subject. *She takes too much . . . too slow . . . won't fuckin' move on, even if she's holding up—*

At this point I was on them, my face a mask of fury. They fell silent, faces guilty. As usual, I could summon no snappy retort. I said something feeble and prim, like, "It's not nice to talk shit!" Then I turned and headed up the hill, trying not to cry in front of them.

I hiked up the road, looking for my place in the line of holders. By now, tears were pouring down my face. As I rounded the corner out of sight, I slowed, tear-blind.

This fucking job.

Last year I'd been weak, my digging not fast or strong enough, my inadequate skills the subject of constant criticism. But this year, I'd become a capable digger. Now I was *too* strong? No matter that every leader of the dig "took too much," Fisher most of all. Yet while Fisher was revered, a selfless leader who'd do anything to take work off someone else's hands, I was demeaned, my "taking too much" a form of greed or incompetence. "She's too slow; she's hogging the work." I couldn't win with these guys. I would never, ever win.

Just then, Eddie came down the line. We were alone, witnessed only by the swell and plunge of trees above and below the road. I collapsed against his chest.

"What's going on?" he said kindly, wrapping his arms around me.

I told him what had happened. "I can't get it right!" I cried. "I don't know what I'm doing here. Why do I keep doing this?"

He hugged me until I caught my breath. Then he drew back, brushed a hair from my face and smiled. "You should be really proud right now."

"Why?"

"You just pissed off a bunch of guys . . . because you outworked them."

I gave half a laugh. "I don't think that's it."

"I do! Think about it. They were talking shit because you did more than them. How embarrassing."

I laughed and quickly stepped back; Shaggy was loping up the hill. Ed withdrew to his spot around the bend as Shaggy came up to me and said, "Kelly, I'm so sorry."

"It's okay, Shag."

"It's not okay! That was so rude, and I didn't even mean it; I just got caught up in talking trash with those guys. It isn't fair, because you're a great firefighter."

I waved him off.

"You work really hard; you're basically in charge of the dig. You're one badass chick." His face turned shy. "I look up to you."

I blinked away tears and hugged his skinny, rope-muscled chest.

Somehow, I can't even remember with what excuse, I weaseled out of seeing Josh for one more night. The day had been enough, too much; I was beat. To offset my stall tactics, I promised I would go home the following night.

I tossed and turned on the pine-strewn campground floor, sweaty legs sticking to the sleeping bag, one foot straying off the tarp, attracting a curious ant. My mind rummaged through the past. *How did I get here, again?* I landed on my dad, on the image of his leg, as if a direct line of causation could be drawn between the moment of its loss and this moment, where I lay lost and coughing in darkness and smoke.

After he became homeless, things went downhill for my dad. He slept outside in a Wisconsin snowstorm, got arrested for stealing cigarettes from Walmart, went to jail . . . and by the time a doctor noticed the problem—frostbite—the damage had advanced too far. They took the leg at the thigh.

My sister wanted to go after the jail for negligence, but I knew better. When it came to my dad, there was only ever one person to blame.

Soon after that, our father became a candidate for a prosthetic. The appendage had already been made for him, but he didn't bother to keep the fitting appointment, so he ended up in a wheelchair instead.

Around this time, I went West.

California would be different. It had to be. And at first, it was. The best thing about my early time on the Klamath was that I was alone. Well, *single*, yet almost never by myself. It was a dream, summer camp for adults: hiking, rafting in inflatable kayaks, playing glow bocce at night on the beach, gossiping with the girls in the barracks.

But I screwed it up that summer when I fell in love (in "love," let's say) with my first firefighter. Aaron worked for Klamath Hotshots, and I remember asking, "What's a hotshot?"

Aaron was sexy, fun, politically conservative (my opposite, which made things spicy). He was blunt in a way that felt almost mean (but now that I've worked in fire, this looks normal). Once, calling out my tendency to intellectually condescend, he said, "I'm not just a meat stick, you know!" It didn't last. But when *he* ended it, I went into a tailspin. I spent the following winter in Ashland, Oregon, making lovely girlfriends, backpacking on Kauai, and fucking a string of dudes under thirty. Trying to vanish, numb myself with male attention. Ops normal.

The second summer on the Klamath, though, I loved my job. I ran a great crew of volunteer wilderness workers. I was fit, happy, fulfilled. When the women I lived with came home from fires, I'd think, *Maybe I could do that.* I begged to be taken on a fire, too. And at almost the same moment the crew finally picked me up, I met Josh.

He was a firefighter on a crew near Happy Camp. We crossed paths in the district office, and when I smiled at him, he blushed from collar to ears. I didn't usually go for short guys, but something about him was endearing. He was shy. He was *dorky.* His steady government job, throwback jeans worn unironically, the home he owned on some acreage, and the passel of animals he cared for: all of it bespoke security. Or maybe the word was *comfort.*

So I chose Josh—less for his sake than to prove to myself that I could pick a new type, the good guy, and a new life, the stable kind. Though he was handsome, I wasn't wildly attracted to him, but I figured I could learn, and in time I did. Josh came to feel comfy, sometimes even fun. Fishing together, hiking with the dogs, snuggling by the woodstove . . . I liked our life, and the alternative (which I saw as "dating jerks forever") was just too horrible.

The start of my relationship with Josh marked the end of my summer camp days on the Klamath. I see now, however, that I had a third option between "Josh" and "jerks," and that option was no guy at all. Life had presented a golden opportunity to live in a new way, remaining single and focusing on my work—myself—staying in a little cabin I had paid the deposit for in Luther Gulch, just a mile or two up Indian Creek. I could have become a hotshot—without anyone waiting at home.

But that November, when Josh suggested I move in with him, I said yes. I'm not sure why I agreed, when a part of me longed for solitude and my own little place. But I was closing in on thirty-eight, so maybe I was afraid that if I didn't hurry up and choose somebody, I'd never get married and have a baby (i.e., I'd fail to fulfill the unwritten but universal requirements of womanhood).

My mom and stepdad were over the moon. They came to visit and loved Josh, loved our property, loved rafting the Klamath River; they even talked about buying a cabin in Happy Camp. Here was the stability they wanted to see from me and I from myself: the symbolic repair of my parents' broken partnership. Everyone married off in houses.

Yet I thought of the cabin often over the following months, my "path not taken." Gradually I realized that Josh's nice-guy routine was a ruse, that what felt so comfortable was the resemblance to my childhood: a happy veneer that masked neglect in one hand and control in the other—that, and the truth that my authentic personality was far too wild, far too singular and headstrong, to ever belong here. Not for the first time, I sent my real self to ground, becoming what Josh wanted. And a year later, the Slater Fire raged up Indian Creek at sixty miles per hour and burned that little cabin to a pile of ash.

*   *   *

I woke in the campground clutching the same dread I'd snuggled into fitful sleep.

Day seven on the McCash fire, midpoint of the roll. We worked the south side of the incident, near a trailhead called Norcross. The fire burned all around us, and the valley of coal barely resembled the place I knew. Fisher and I went on a scouting mission on the UTV, driving a series of gravel back roads to see where we might reasonably put a line, or burn. After hours of driving, I confessed my doubts about Josh and my feelings for Eddie (or our feelings for each other).

"Yeah, duh," Fisher said dryly. "I know."

I laughed. "That obvious, huh?"

"Well, I might not have guessed, but Jenny picked up on it."

"Makes sense." Fisher's wife, sweet, clever Jenny, too gracious to call us out. "So what do I do about Josh?"

Fisher threw the UTV into park and looked at me. "Be an adult," he said bluntly, pale eyes stern. "Tell him the truth. Don't delay. Don't beat around the bush. Go home and be honest."

Good old Uncle Fishy, as we sometimes called him. His moral compass always showed true north.

The dogs were elated when I got home, a jumble of tails and yips, jumping on my truck before I'd even parked. Valentine leaned into my legs, Chief pressed his thick head against my hip, tail whipping, and Mouse jumped vertically, trying to vault the other two. The porch was a mess of dog beds and blankets, and the sliding glass door gave a familiar resistance to my hand: dirt in the tracks. Josh stood inside, grinning nervously. He had cleaned and made dinner. He was trying so hard, it broke my heart.

I paused on the threshold, glad that the dogs' demands for attention held me up a moment longer. I bent and nuzzled Valentine's face. As I stood, Josh crossed the room and took me in his arms. I tried not to recoil and hoped the subtle stiffening of my body wasn't noticeable.

Even without bringing Eddie into it, I had seen this person once in the past three months, and I felt he'd been a hostile, distant correspondent. He pressed his lips to mine and I pressed back briefly, neutrally, an assistant sealing an envelope.

"You hungry?" he asked, his smile overlarge, shaky.

"Always." I forced a smile. "Thanks for cooking."

"Well, it ain't fancy . . ."

We sat on the couch to eat because the table was strewn with fresh arrivals from Amazon, fishing lures and dog toys. I had spent a lot of my first season's fire money for that custom-built dining table—as well as the new flooring in the sunroom. I tried not to comb the house in my mind, cataloging potential losses. The TV was on, though at least he'd muted the sound. In a stilted fashion further impeded by eating, we tried to catch up.

He told me about the mountain lion they'd seen on the River Complex; I told him about the seven-mile burn, and he said he'd heard. Meanwhile, my mind was racing. How could I bring it up, and what did I mean to say? Was I expressing doubts or leaving? As much as I'd agonized about this, I hadn't come up with a plan. How wild that you can be almost forty years old and still not know what's going to come out of your mouth until you say it.

Josh was talking about our friends Gavin and Melissa, how excited they were getting for our wedding in Kauai. We had planned to marry on the island during a trip with two other couples in early November. The house was reserved, but the other details still needed sorting out.

"Speaking of Kauai," he said, treading gingerly. "You think you'll be ready to buy plane tickets soon?"

"Um." I frowned. Here goes nothing. "Yeah, about that. I think we should hold off on the wedding."

"What do you mean, hold off? Like postpone it, or—"

"I mean—" I paused, struggling to breathe. He had pulled away from me toward the corner of the couch, curling into himself. I drew a breath and plunged ahead. "I can't marry you. I don't— I have doubts about the relationship."

"What doubts?"

"I feel like I can't be myself. You want me home, but I want to be a hotshot. You seem miserable when I'm gone, but I *like* being away. I like the work. You want a woman who's around all the time. Even when I stop being a hotshot, I might not be that woman."

"That's not true! I don't need you to be home all the time."

"I just don't think I'm what you want. Before this, it was wilderness work. Who knows what it'll be next. I need someone who'll support my indep—"

"I do! I support whatever you want to do!" he said hotly. "Be a hotshot! Do whatever you want. I just want you to be happy."

"You say that, but when I'm off doing what makes me happy, you hate it. There's a difference between what you say you want and what I think you actually want."

He was silent for a minute. I said, "I'm sorry," and he said, "So that's it?" His voice broke.

He began to cry. I put a hand on his shoulder, but he shrugged it off. Then a thought seemed to come over him, a cloud darkening the sky.

"Is there someone else?" he asked, as if he already knew the answer.

I paused, aghast. I didn't want to tell him about Eddie for every possible reason: to protect Eddie from a man who owned a lot of guns, to protect myself from blame, to protect Josh from the heartbreak of betrayal. And, if I'm being honest, I didn't want to tell him because, in my experience, the "other man" conversation closes a door. If there was someone else, Josh got off scot-free. What *he* had done would be overlooked. This breakup would be on me.

At the same time, I'm a terrible liar. So I tried to split the difference.

"Well, not in a literal, physical sense," I said, grasping for words, the lies crumbling as they reached my lips. "But there's someone— emotionally. Someone I care about and would like to see if—"

"*No,*" he might have said, or he may have uttered only an inarticulate groan of rage. He stood and went into the kitchen, white as a ghost. Then rushed back to me and cried, "How could you?" He collapsed on the floor.

He seemed to be sobbing or gasping, maybe both. This went on for some time. I recall him lying in the fetal position. Then he stormed across the room to shout, breathing close to my face, "How could you do this? I don't deserve this! I'm a nice guy!"

I wanted to say, *No one deserves this.* And, *You aren't as nice as you think you are.*

But I had gone numb. Anger has always frightened me (which is, by the way, one of the hallmark signs of the Adult Child of an Alcoholic: "angry people scare you"), and while he didn't get violent in any way, I felt unsafe. I hugged my arms around my body and feebly repeated, "Can we talk about this?"

But he couldn't or wouldn't talk.

I'd been here before. When you're breaking someone's heart, you don't have the luxury of falling to pieces. If you want to go through with it, stay cold. You can fall apart later. Often, nearly three months will pass before you feel safe enough to exhale and begin your own long, quiet grief.

Frightened as I was, I had to go through with it. Because I was sorry for Josh, but I wasn't sorry for my choice.

To my surprise, Josh's reaction made for one of the briefest breakup scenes in my personal record. Within fifteen minutes, he seemed to be through with me and said, bitterly, "Why don't you go?"

"I want to stay and talk this through, if you're ready."

"I'm not. There's nothing to talk about. I'll ask Ginger to give you a ride back to the campground." Since I'd come to Happy Camp with the crew, my truck was back in Baudelaire; Hale had dropped me at our house. "Then you can be with . . . the people you really want to be with." The last with a thick frosting of spite.

"Um, okay."

"You've ruined my life, Kelly. I hope you're happy."

He went down the hall, said a few words to Ginger, and left the house without giving me a second look, slamming the glass door and peeling out, his massive truck's diesel engine roaring onto the highway.

Ginger, our roommate-dogsitter for the summer, padded out of her room looking scared. She must have overheard some of the fight, if you could call it that. "Josh said you need a ride?"

Back at Curly Jack, I tiptoed quietly between Shadow One and the picnic table and unrolled my sleeping bag in the dark, trying not to make a sound. I was shell-shocked, guilty, full of sorrow—with only the tiniest inkling of the feeling that would come later: relief.

As we drove along the river, I'd told Ginger that Josh and I had split, and she said, "I never got you and Josh together. It didn't make sense."

"Yeah, I guess not."

"You're a badass, though," she said. "I can't believe you just did that. You're brave."

Brave or stupid, I thought. *Only time will tell.*

Chapter 21

South Pebble

W̲hat was stupid was my assumption that Josh would handle our split like an adult.

We headed to the line on day eight listening to mellow music. I told Hale and Englefield what had happened, and they were kind. As we drove, however, I saw a text from Josh telling me again that I had ruined his life and that he hoped I could live with myself. *Ouch*. At the same time, a friend wrote to say that she'd seen something on social media, didn't understand it, and hoped I was okay.

A quick scan of the apps confirmed that Josh had resorted to the tactics of spurned fourteen-year-olds the world over: public shaming by meme. He had copied and shared a post about an engagement being a *promise*; another read, "I learned that people leave. Even if they have promised a thousand times that they won't."

I groaned and showed the guys.

"Ew, dude, I'm sorry," Hale said. "Did you know you were engaged to a child?"

That was the devastating part: I hadn't known.

I was firing with Hale that day, but I was hardly present as I wielded the torch, a phantom carrying flame. By the end of the day, more posts had appeared, and more friends had reached out to ask what had happened. Not only was Josh's public shaming turning our friends in Happy Camp against me, but he was informing *my* people before I'd had a chance. I would've preferred to tell my parents myself that I was no longer getting married.

By dinner, I was shaken and numb. Josh had turned out to seem so very small, and I was disappointed, even angry with myself, that I hadn't seeen it. Even as we broke up, I'd still believed he was the "good" person, and I the "bad." But the fights the previous winter, the jealous outbursts . . . what I had chalked up to temporary lapses in character now looked like signs of a deeper and more dangerous immaturity.

After dinner I sat at the picnic table, sadly mending a rip in my greens by headlamp with a needle and thread. Eddie strolled over and sat down across from me.

"Hey. So on the weekend, do you wanna go see Jesse Daniel in Portland? The guy who sings 'Trabajador.'"

A mutual favorite song. "Yeah," I said, surprised. "I'd love to."

"Good, because I already bought tickets."

I laughed. "So you *assumed* I'd say yes?"

"Yep." He beamed.

Hale was headed over, so we changed the subject to the big timber Eddie and Fisher had been cutting that day. But when I reached my tarp that night, where I'd left my phone tangled in the sleeping bag, I saw a text from Eddie: *Didn't want to say too much, but I know this can't have been an easy day. I hope you're doing okay.*

In one evening he had managed to become the man who screwed up the courage to ask me on a date, while remaining my friend through a breakup. No, it hadn't been an easy day. But despite the mess I'd created, and whether I deserved it or not, I went to sleep happy.

By day nine of the assignment, most of the guys had heard about me and Josh. I had expected—I don't know what, judgment? Disinterest? But they surprised me. "You let me know if you need anything," they said gruffly, with a hug or a cuff on the arm. "I saw what he posted— you need some protection?" Like brothers, they joked, but one after the other they said, *We've got your back. Anything you need.*

Even Mac, a friend of Josh's, merely shrugged and said, "Well. Sounds like you've got some stuff to figure out."

Oh, dang. Yeah, I had some big stuff to figure out. Like where to live. As we drove to the line, I scanned postings for apartments in Crescent City. If I was going to stay on the crew for a while, I might as well live near the station. I found almost nothing: dingy basements, wall-to-wall carpet, conspicuous black mold. There was one place—but no, it was too expensive. I handed my phone to Hale.

"Should I get this one?"

"Um, obviously!" he said, scrolling. "Wow, this is insane. But you can't afford that."

"Yeah, I doubt I can."

"Bro, you can't."

"I have a lot of savings . . ."

"Well, go look at it! Doesn't hurt to look."

I messaged the owner right away and set up an appointment for the first day of R&R.

On day twelve, Bellomo quit the crew and left mid-assignment. He could be a turd, but I liked him, and I felt a pang of failure or guilt;

he'd talked to me about some of his struggles. I tried to help, but could I have done more?

None of us had much time to ruminate about Bellomo, however, because on day thirteen, a tree fell on Barrel.

We were working in a nasty snag patch, putting in line. The saw teams moved ahead, felling the worst of the hazardous trees, but fire smoldered in the base of many remaining snags as we passed beneath them. Some of the overhead felt ill at ease with the situation, and Scotty, who was leading the dig, finally said, "Hey, I don't like it. Let's head back." We had turned to hike out to the road when the hundred-foot-tall, 18-inch diameter Chinquapin (a stone-heavy hardwood) began to fall.

The tree came down in slow motion. Barrel stood two people, and maybe thirty feet, away from me. People's mouths, in freeze frame, cried *Barrrellll!* Bodies leapt out of the wooden missile's path. Barrel turned to face the tree as it fell. He wasn't moving, and the falling trunk aligned with his head. We were screaming. At the last second, he took a half step to the left. The tree landed—*boom!*—and flattened him to the ground. He lay buried in limbs.

"*Barrel!*"

"Oh fu—"

"Get a saw! Call an EMT!"

In a moment, though, his slow, drawling voice came from beneath the cluster of limbs. "I'm fine!" He wriggled, crawled out from under the branches, and stood, dusting himself off.

"Not a scratch on me!" he proclaimed. "That was weird."

We were laughing, crying, embracing him. It was more than weird; it was a goddamn miracle. The bole wood, which would have crushed his skull or snapped his spine, had missed him by mere inches. The limbs took him down without breaking a thing.

Lucky as Barrel had been, this tree strike occurred only three weeks after Luke had been hit. So we weren't okay. As we stood in the dozer line awaiting orders, several guys took a knee. Eddie sat in the dirt and covered his face, his shoulders shaking. We kept going up to Barrel and squeezing him. *Glad you're okay, bro.*

The crew was collectively shaken enough that Van pulled us off the line. We made our way to a rocky beach on the banks of Elk Creek, where we tried to comfort each other, play cards, distract ourselves. Eddie was a mess. He blamed himself; he was first saw and should've noticed the snag—should've *cut* the snag. "Maybe so, but you're human," I told him. "You can't cut down every dead tree in the forest."

None of us were sorry that the next day was fourteen, our last. We left the McCash with relief, and as Happy Camp receded behind the truck, I thought, with a mixture of liberation and regret, *There goes home.*

The next day, though, I stood in front of another home. The duplex faced South Pebble Beach Drive, a scenic route that wound along a cliff above the Pacific Ocean. Succulents and flowers bloomed in the fog. The owner unlocked the door, and as I stepped inside, my mouth fell open. *Wow.*

The kitchen and living room had panoramic views of the ocean. Surf pounded boulders at the foot of a bluff on the far side of the street. The mid-century house, which had been split into two apartments, was immaculate, with polished wood floors and a fireplace. A few steps down, through a hallway, lay the bedroom, the size of two rooms. The entire front wall was a picture window with an unobstructed view of the Pacific. The place was lit by skylights, the windows admitting salt air and the distant sound of a foghorn.

The rent was $1,700 a month, but the landlord, who liked me, offered to drop it by a hundred dollars. The price was still more than I could reasonably afford without draining my whole fire savings in one winter. But I'd figure it out. I knew this was the place.

This was a place for me to heal, to cobble together the shattered fragments of what had been my life. I would do whatever it took, just to stay here and stare at the ocean, peaceful at last.

"I'll take it."

Eddie and I went to Portland over R&R, though the concert was canceled because of a Covid scare. We drove north along the Oregon coast, listened to music, joked, kissed—free together for the first time. We held hands, smiling at our twined fingers. In the city, we met my friend Nick for dinner.

Back at the hotel, after ecstatic sex that ranged from bed to shower to a sheepskin rug on the floor, I lay awake as a naked Eddie fell into easy, immediate sleep, snoring lightly. He looked beautiful, but I felt shaky and uncertain. There was a mental whiplash to lying beside someone new—disorienting, like one man had been switched out for another behind my back. I wasn't sure how to position my body on the bed, and my nakedness felt more bare than exposed skin, like someone had laid open my bones.

I was vulnerable, too vulnerable. I was already hurting, and now Eddie could hurt me too.

Back in Baudelaire, we got the order to return to the McCash fire for a second roll. We let out a collective groan. Had karma or Big Ernie the fire god chosen to punish me with a month in Happy Camp when I'd just left an engagement there? *Fantastic.*

The fire wasn't too much doing. Some snagging, light burning, a little "go here, go there." We worked with Chena Hotshots from Alaska; they had a female Superintendent, the first I had seen, and I fangirled hard. On day four, we put indirect line down a ridge, and Jones told me to "take the dig," then helped with pointers about setting line. Just a brief cut, nothing remarkable, but the gesture was an honor. On day seven, after we put in line around some slops, Luke said, "That's it. You're Lead P for the rest of the season." I glowed.

Though my personal life was in shambles, I thought, I could still crush work. At least I had that.

On day thirteen, we took a crew photo near the wilderness trailhead. I straightened my shoulders and crossed my arms. Now I knew how to stand, how to arrange my face—and when the photo was sent around, Shaggy pointed me out. "Damn, Kelly, look at you. You're hard as fuck!"

Some other guys leaned in to see, and they agreed. *Yeah, pretty hard. It's about time, Ramsey.*

I had finally stopped looking like whoever I'd been before, smiling and eager and soft. Now I looked like them, solid and strong, with a set jaw and grave eyes. No trace of a smile, arms locked over my chest, I looked for all the world like a woman you wouldn't mess with.

I had to move twice that month, each time on an R&R between fires: First, I moved everything out of the house in Happy Camp and drove it to Crescent City, where I put it in a storage unit for a couple of weeks. Then, in mid-October, I moved everything from storage to my new apartment.

Josh would only let me enter the house when he was gone at work, so I had to creep in and pack my boxes, feeling like an intruder. And I had to say goodbye to the dogs. I wept shamelessly, clinging to their necks, knowing Josh would watch me on the security cameras and no longer caring.

Between the first and second move, at the beginning of October, we went to a fire called the Knob outside Willow Creek, California.

The blaze was out cold by the time we arrived, basically a "suppression repair" assignment. I'd never done a fire rehab roll, and I wasn't a fan; I liked my fire with flames still in it.

We spread mulch, grass seed, and hay; removed hazard trees; and repaired hand lines by covering them with dirt and debris. We slept in a motel on the coast, which was comfortable but meant an hour's drive to and from the line. I shared a room with Addison.

On day three, Eddie posed a surprising question. We had been talking, or rather, *everyone* had been talking, about my new place. Pebble Beach had some of the best surf in the area, and the crew's surfers—Fisher, Scotty, Bao, Trevan—spent every weekend catching waves a few yards from my new home. So they started joking that my apartment would become the crew surf shack.

"I can't wait for our house," Fisher said.

"I'm gonna be there every Saturday," Scotty joked. "Bright and early."

"Good," I said. "I'll have coffee ready."

"Can we get a bean bag chair for our house?" Eddie asked, and I glared at him.

"You better watch out, or Ed'll become your permanent squatter," Mac joked, and I thought, *You have no idea.*

Eddie had been talking about finding his own apartment in Crescent City, and I loved the idea, because it meant we could hang out a lot but keep our own spaces. On day three, though, he texted and said he'd been thinking, and could he stay with me for the remainder of his season? He had converted to a Permanent Seasonal Employee (PSE), so he'd be working for a month or two after we regular temps were laid off. Could he stay—temporarily—in my house?

Hmm. Tough one. I'd enjoy having him around, and briefly sharing the exorbitant rent was appealing. But I had pictured the Pebble apartment as my own place, my sanctuary. I told him I'd think about it.

Hale was gone. His detail complete, he'd returned to Oregon. I missed him, and I texted him a picture of Englefield wielding a tub of cottage cheese like a threat. Hale laughed and said he missed us, too. Without him, Englefield and I were alone in a truck, two bickering children.

On day four, as we drove back from the line, I heard that a little story I'd written about the crew had been posted on a firefighting blog. Suddenly I felt nervous, remembering something less than complimentary I'd written about Addison, albeit without using her name. Maybe she hadn't seen.

But as we reached town, someone from A-mod texted that Addison had indeed seen, and she was *not* pleased.

"Ooh, cat fight!" Englefield crowed as we pulled into the motel parking lot.

"Stop it," I hissed.

But my hands shook slightly as I climbed the stairs and entered our room. Alpha wasn't back yet, so I hopped in the shower, trying to calm my unsteady heart. When I came out of the bathroom, Addison stood by her bed, face white.

"Hey," I said, wrapping a towel around my chest. "So you saw the piece?"

"Yeah, I saw it." Her eyes blazed.

"Addison, I want to apologize. I wrote that when I was angry, and I didn't know it was coming out now. I'm sorry."

"I appreciate that. But you have to take it down. *Now.*"

We argued briefly about whether an anonymous allusion to a person, one I'd described as a less-than-great crew member, could wreck her career. When she said what I'd written was libel, I balked, saying, "Not if it's true."

"You didn't tell the truth."

"Yes, I *did*." My patience snapped, and I finally let loose a stream of long-withheld opinions. "I think you're a terrible hotshot! You may be a solid firefighter elsewhere, because you're smart, but I don't think this is the job for you." Unable to stop myself, I vented the frustration I'd been carrying for months. "You can't hike, can't dig. You're not a team player. You seem to refuse to hustle at chores. You insist on running saw, even though you can't carry it up the hill fast enough. You whine until they give you a chainsaw because they're too afraid of you to refuse. I believe you're a toxic presence on the crew, like a—like a dark cloud."

Her face twisted. "What would you know about being a hotshot? It's your second fucking year!"

"More than you do! I can't believe I got you this job, and you've been nothing but a disaster. I regret it every day."

"You didn't get me this job! I got it on my own. They said I was the best-qualified candidate they'd ever had."

"That may be true. But you applied to this crew specifically because I encouraged you to. And then I vouched for you."

She had moved forward, and instinctively I took a step back.

"You think you vouching for me meant something to them? You don't know anything about fire. You can't even run a chainsaw." Her voice was heavy with disdain.

"Yeah, because I can't *hike* it, Addison! I respect the system and the rules. I have to earn that right! When I can keep up, they'll let me run it."

I had been standing there dripping in my towel, and now Addison coolly informed me—as if this were a show and she the director—that I could take a break and put on some clothes. I mechanically complied, shivering a little as I pulled on a pair of shorts.

"You know," she said, face darkening. "Not everyone likes you, either."

"What are you talking about?" I felt as if I'd been slapped. "Who doesn't like me?"

"I'm not going to tell you," she said, a cruel smile forming on her lips. "But they say you laugh at their jokes to make them like you. You're always giggling, sucking up, trying to be one of the boys. They see right through you. It's pathetic!"

"That's so—mean!" I cried, feeling like a child, helpless to find a comeback. I began to hiccup tears. "Why do you have to be such a *bitch?*"

"*You're* the bitch!" she roared.

I had to leave the room. I was still clutching the cheap white hotel towel, so I went into the bathroom and threw it to the floor. I sat on the edge of the bathtub, shaking, until I could breathe again.

I didn't know what to believe. She had struck wisely, where she knew it would hurt most: my relationship with the guys, my tenuous sense of belonging. *Did I really laugh just to ingratiate myself? Had I thrown another woman under the bus for them?* Maybe I was the monster here. I returned to the room and sat cross-legged on the bedspread, defeated.

"It's so sad that this culture turns women against each other," Addison said softly, after a little while. "That's what really happened here."

"Maybe you're right," I murmured.

In a way, I knew she was. I'd chosen to show my solidarity with the crew by siding against her. But I wasn't sure if that was more about gender or the tribe—more about patriarchy pitting women against one another or the demands of the job itself, which I truly didn't think she had fulfilled. I wasn't sure of anything anymore.

Addison requested her own room, and when I got back from the line the next night, her stuff was gone. I was alone.

I began to unravel. I couldn't sleep, and I imagined that the room had bedbugs and tore all the bedding off, pushing the mattress aside to scrutinize the specks and crumbs trapped against the box spring. I called Eddie to come and look. "Is this bed bugs?"

He hugged me tight. "I think you're losing it."

My eyes stung. "I know."

He was there for me that night, but Eddie didn't always have my back. When he first heard about the blowup, his primary concern was that Addison had been sleeping with Haines, so he feared that "girl problems" would cause tension between him and his swamper. He wouldn't even say that Addison was in the wrong, that she was the bigger jerk here.

That was Eddie, though. He was a hotshot through and through: crew above all. And he was a peacemaker, the guy who never took sides and rarely gossiped. In a way, I admired his diplomacy. Being "easy" was how he stayed a crew favorite. But in this case, it looked a bit like cowardice.

I would never be everyone's favorite. I might please and fawn, up to a point, but there was a limit beyond which my backbone showed through. When it counted, I could stand up—for myself, for a friend, for a wilderness meadow, for the truth. Of course, standing up could leave you standing by yourself.

Now, even with Eddie in a room at the other end of the motel balcony, I felt terribly alone. Who could I trust?

Sitting in the parking lot after dark, I called my girlfriends. *You're not an anti-feminist*, they reassured me. My friend Paige, also a second-year hotshot, said her crew had a girl just like Addison, and the two of them did not get along. "There are crappy girls in fire, just like there are dudes who suck," she said.

I asked my friend Lindsay if she thought I giggled to make men like me. She snorted. "Friend, no. You're just a fun person. People like being around you, and I'm sure she's jealous of that."

Their assurances helped, but you should always suspect yourself when you go looking for validation in more than one place. I needed friends to buoy me up because Addison's words had hit close to home. She was right: I was a pleaser, always had been; an expert in becoming what others wanted. An adaptive skill, it had often served me well at work and otherwise. But did the guys really think I was pathetic? And why was it the end of the world if they did?

Gradually, things eased a little. Addison and I had moments of being civil on the line, then almost friendly. One night near the end of the roll, when a beer pong game sprung up in one of the Alpha guys' rooms, Addison texted to invite me. Nervous, I figured I'd better show. When I did, she acted like we were friends—more than friends, *besties*. She giggled and hung on my arm, and one of the guys pulled me aside and said, "So you and Addison are cool again?"

I shrugged. "I guess so?"

But I accepted the unspoken truce. Her alliance was everything I craved. Because after the season, my breakup, and our falling out, I was in freefall. I'd rented a house near the crew, but did they secretly consider me a fool? I'd gotten into this thing with Eddie, but could I count on him? The problem with the "fire family" was that it wasn't your real family. That, and it could be just as broken and dysfunctional as the people you came from. The things I had established as the foundation of my new life felt suddenly unstable beneath my feet.

The last week of the season arrived. We worked thirteen shifts on the Knob, not fourteen, so we could take R&R and close out by our layoff date. The first day of R&R, I moved into my new home, with help: Fisher brought his old beater truck, the one he and Jenny called "The Murder Mobile," and Eddie brought his white Ford. With three trucks between us, we managed the move in a couple of trips, even if the well-heeled neighbors looked askance at our loud vehicles and the large, tattooed man who chattered nonstop as he effortlessly heaved boxes into the apartment.

"New element in the neighborhood, folks!" Fisher boomed, and I laughed but shushed him, telling Eddie to put on a damn shirt.

My jittery monthlong swirl began to calm just seeing the apartment. I remembered that these men were my friends, and nothing could sunder that bond. Watching Fish manhandle a bookshelf through the door, I could've wept.

When Fisher finished commenting on the surf and took off, Eddie and I stood shoulder to shoulder, gazing out my living room window. The ocean yawned, a shimmering blue pasture. An osprey landed in a tree on the bluff. Eddie took my hand, and we shared a deep, satisfied sigh.

"Will you admit it's amazing?" I asked. His running joke was that my oceanfront home was "just okay."

"Fine. It's amazing."

Later, apartment to myself, I threw open the windows to let in the damp air. I pulled back my hair and turned up the music, staring down a stack of boxes. I cut into the first one as the Rolling Stones sang, *I'll never be your beast of burden. I've walked for miles, my feet are hurtin'* . . .

I'd always loved the song, and now it made me think of fire—of the things we carried. We were often beasts of burden: for the crew, for each other, for the heavy pasts so many of us shouldered invisibly along the line, the dark histories and aching childhoods that had driven us to chase flames in the first place. I'd become a decent pack mule, hadn't I? But at some point, you have to stop carrying what isn't yours.

When I told my mom about the breakup with Josh, she said she was sorry to hear it. "But I know you'll be okay, sweetie," she added. "You always land on your feet."

What a season. The death of a beloved dog, falling trees, a quarantine. A breakup, a move, a farewell. Millions of acres of the planet I loved, burning before my eyes. Yet I might've been part feline after all, because here I was, for what felt like the thousandth time, landing on my feet.

The answer wasn't Eddie. He was great, but it was never the man. A new lover (and there was always another) wasn't the solution. Why was this so difficult to learn?

You are your answer. You are your own deliverance.

I paused, empty box in hand. Outside the window, high above the sparkling water, a flock of pelicans passed overhead, sturdy and weightless. The sun winked between their rapid wingbeats. I felt as if I, too, might finally let go, lift off, become and disappear into light.

On the final day of the season, Van handed me the two-year buckle. This should have been a triumphant moment, but it fell flat. Van uttered the same neutral words he said to all of us, "Great job this year!" And as Benjy gripped my hand in his massive paw, he said, "Hey, you're like the crew mom!"

I stifled a groan. While I knew Benjy meant well (truly—he was trying to name my place here, believing I had one), here was the classic stereotype: I had passed beyond innocent maiden, and for some reason I wasn't "the dude" anymore, so what could I possibly be? Not a regular, competent crewmember, but their *mother*. Ew.

Still, as the six of us stood in a line for a picture with our two-year buckles, I glanced at the men to either side of me and knew that I wasn't anyone's mommy. Nor was I their sex symbol, their savior, their boy—or even their girl. I was just another hotshot.

That evening was the crew party, a predictable night at Port O' Pints with Hawaiian shirts, rounds of free beers, karaoke, and shirtless dancing. But this year, I couldn't quite get into it. As some of the guys and Addison formed a circle to scream-sing in each other's faces,

I lingered at the edge of the room, sipping a glass of wine and talking with Ender.

When Eddie sidled over and surprised me by wanting to leave early, I found that I was ready. I loved these guys beyond the beyond, but I didn't need another night of debauchery to prove it. *Yeah, let's get out of here.*

As we climbed into Eddie's truck, BJ was weaving drunkenly along the sidewalk. His brow wrinkled, and he said, "Hey, why are you two leaving together?"

We howled with laughter. How had the gossip not reached him?

"We're leaving together because we're going to the same place," Eddie said slowly, spelling it out. "Because we are seeing each other."

"Oh," BJ said, and blinked. "Well, have a good night!"

We bade him good night and hit the road. As we turned onto South Pebble Beach Drive, Eddie took my hand. The moon was almost full, and it shone a silver path across the dark waves. Randy Travis's voice poured from the speakers, and Eddie sang along, glancing at me as he kept one hand on the wheel.

We followed the moonlit cliffs to my place, the ocean leading us home.

Epilogue

I planned to go back to the crew the following spring. When Salomon called in December, I said, *Yep, I'll be there.* And I was stoked. It was exciting to think about what I might learn in a third season; maybe this was the year I'd go for a spot on a saw team. When I wasn't staring at the ocean through the windows of my new apartment, I was training, running up and down the road above the beach and driving to Baudelaire to hike hand lines. It was old hat, the pain of climbing a hill so habitual by now, suffering was almost a friend.

But gradually, I noticed that my body was letting me down. Hiking was walking in irons, and my times didn't improve. I ran and ran, but my sprints only got slower, and my strength in the gym seemed to plateau, no matter how much I lifted. I was exhausted all the time. By afternoon, I could barely keep my eyelids open.

Thinking it must be overtraining, I added a rest day and carried on. Run, hike, lift. Sprints, pull-ups, lunges.

Then I got sick (ladies, think a UTI, yeast infection, and bacterial vaginosis *at the same time.* Best week ever?). The doctor ran blood tests, which offered an explanation for everything I'd been feeling: I had an autoimmune disease, Hashimoto's hypothyroidism, in which the body's immune system attacks the thyroid gland, gradually destroying it. You can take synthetic thyroid hormone to replace what the gland would normally produce, but you can't halt the body's attack or reverse the damage. Half the world has Hashi's (okay, about 10 to 12 percent of the general population will come down with it at some point in life, most of those people women). So I thought, *No biggie.* I filled a prescription and kept training.

But my symptoms were slow to improve. Always cold, night sweats, skin like parchment, hair falling out in clumps. My hands went numb in my sleep, as they had since the end of my first fire season; I had chalked it up to too much digging, but now I wondered how long I had been pushing my body through discomfort—or disease.

Part of me felt proud. Not only was I older, smaller than most, and female, but I'd been doing this job with a broke-ass thyroid slowing my metabolism and heart rate? Try that, boys. Take *that* crypt keeper's body and climb Middle Hell Line.

On the other hand, I was shaken. Autoimmunity can be triggered by many factors—viruses, pollution, stress. But a voice in the back of my mind wouldn't stop asking, *What if fire made you sick?* Smoke, sleep loss, poor diet, and a level of exertion that a recent study called the equivalent of biking a day in the Tour de France *every day* for six months. I read that the chemicals in fusees, which I could remember lighting bare-handed, were known thyroid disruptors. How many other toxins did we handle or inhale? Diesel, bar oil, stubbies and chuckers, fire retardant, chainsaw exhaust, burning tires . . . The exposure was incalculable.

There was no giving back a disease I already had. But I worried that by returning to fire, I might make myself sicker.

In March, I decided to take a year off. Van didn't love the late resignation, but he was understanding. I'd take a summer, I figured, to catch up on sleep, eat vegetables, experiment with the holistic measures some claimed cured the incurable—then I'd jump back in, a hotshot again.

But a year became three, and I haven't gone back yet. I miss fire all the time. Like a lover, like a lost limb. Like a home. Still, I don't go back.

At first, I didn't return because I thought that fire had broken me. The crises of that second season, from the dissolution of an engagement to the trees falling on my friends, had left me feeling unsteady, and I blamed fire: the job was too much. Firefighting destroyed families; hadn't I seen it again and again?

It took me months to see that the truth was far more complicated, and more of a paradox. I was reminded of what Eddie told me once on the line. *That's just fire. You love it, you hate it. You feel everything about it.* Fire had destroyed me, or destroyed some part of me. But fire had created me, too. Here was the secret I kept stumbling upon: that our deepest wounds were the fertile soil of our growth. New life tended to spring from bitterest ash.

A few years changed the crew, scattering most of us to the wind.

Fisher and Jenny had a baby, and Fish took a job in Fuels so he could be home more—though I've heard he still saunters into the crew bay to stand over some temp cleaning a saw and say, "The fuck you think *you're* doin'?"

Hale and his lady moved to Arizona, and Scotty switched to an engine to have more time with his family. Wink went to an engine, too, and his wedding is still pending. I can't wait.

Luke took a job in Oregon, then finally quit fire (though not cigarettes). Trevan went to Cal Fire, Shaggy to Montana, Keller home to Minnesota. Some guys, like Eddie, went on to become smokejumpers; others are arborists, foresters, city firefighters. I heard a rumor that Englefield is running heavy equipment, and I can't help imagining a tub of cottage cheese in the bulldozer's cup holder.

Addison didn't go back to the crew. I heard she got a job the next year with a module in Wyoming. I wish her well, and I even hope for her forgiveness, but I've never reached out, afraid my apologies would fall on deaf ears. In hindsight, I should have let her be the firefighter she wanted to be. Representing all women wasn't her job—or mine.

In time, the breakup with Josh, which first plunged me into shame—*all my fault, I'm bad*—came to look like something else. I had been attempting to find the line with someone who I felt didn't respect my independence. He saw a wild woman and hoped to make a housewife. I played into it, pretending I could stop being a "boy" in the woods . . . until finally, I snapped. By then, I had waited too long, so what might have been a polite adjustment months before was now an explosion. I handled things poorly; I defended myself by causing harm, which I regret. But now I can see that I was, however clumsily, learning to fight for myself.

The only people from my time who remained with the crew a few years later were Van, Benjy, BJ, and Bao, who finally stopped living in the camper and got an apartment in Crescent City. I visited him, surfboards covering the walls, the wine and gossip flowing. The characters on the crew had changed, but the stories sounded the same. Still, when I see a photo of the men—all men, again—lined up with crossed arms, there's a sense of disconnection and loss: it's my crew, yet these people are strangers. Almost everyone I knew has moved on.

A crew is always changing. Like a living forest, it's constantly in motion, never the same twice. One summer only, and it's gone, the rare alchemy among those twenty people vanishing like smoke. But we carry the crew inside us, each season's roster etched in memory, a family we knew. A place where we belonged.

*   *   *

Last winter, Eddie and I spent some time in Southern California.

One December evening, coming home from dinner in Ventura, we saw a wildfire in the hills. My mom had texted the usual, *Are you ok?* But we could tell (a quick calculation—wind direction, slope, how the fire was backing, nighttime temps) that the fire wouldn't even reach the farms in the flats. The nearby town where we lived would be fine.

Still, passing the fire, I pressed my nose to the window. My heart pounded at the familiar sight of flames orange against the night, the blaze illuminating the clouds like floodlights. I asked Ed how seeing fire made him feel.

"Nothing," he said. "I don't feel anything. Maybe happy that I don't have to go over there."

I laughed. "All I want is to get over there," I said wistfully. "Maybe dig some line."

I could almost feel the Pulaski handle in my hands. I remembered how to swing, the sensation of the tool connecting with the earth, the dirt flying.

"They don't dig *line* in SoCal, baby," Ed joked.

I rolled my eyes and punched his shoulder, and we drove home, the fire growing smaller behind us, the smoke flowing out over the Pacific, a white river in the sky.

For the rest of the night I was lost in reverie: night shifts, burning, the never-ending dig. Cup trenches and fire beetles, shooting the Veri pistol at daybreak with Luke and Fisher, running drip torch with Benjy and Hale, the billow of smoke into the stratosphere, the volcanic twinkle of fire on a darkened ridge. The excitement, the friendship, and fire itself, always taking my breath away. The love of my goddamn life.

Fire, I finally understood, had created *and* destroyed me—tore me down as it built me up. I would always miss it, but I didn't have to go back, because I found what I needed. I finally became strong—so strong, I no longer required a constant emergency, some fresh battle to

bring me alive. Fire made me strong enough to confront the flames—
and to face ordinary life.

My dad is still alive, as far as I know. But I don't know where.

My cousin Nathan tried to find him last year. He called around to
shelters in Neenah, Appleton, and Oshkosh, but legally they can't put
you in touch with a resident. Finally, he badgered one shelter into admitting that a Bob Ramsey *had* been there, and Nathan dropped off a note
with his phone number. My dad never called.

Though we all promised to stop helping, most of us backslid. For
months after our father became unhoused, Evan helped him with
money, groceries, a job—until Dad blew it all by drinking again. So
later, when my brother was driving through town and saw him sitting
on the sidewalk near the shelter, he didn't stop.

One by one, we've made our peace. Courtney told me that she
checks the obituaries from time to time, or searches Dad's name along
with "death." Now I do the same, turning up nothing.

Not knowing where he is feels different from watching him drink
all those years. My father's life has long felt unresolved, but now it
hangs in the ultimate limbo. He lives in a gray place, alive but not a
part of life. He often seems almost imaginary. My grief has no end, and
I live in parallel to it, mostly ignoring the pain until something triggers
a memory and suddenly I'm crying in the street.

When I picture my dad, I forget and see him whole, a tall man
leaning against the wall outside the shelter, the same man who waited
for me outside the Boston airport, gazing at some beautiful vision in
the distance of his imagination, cigarette pinned to his lip. Then I have
to correct myself: the leg.

In my mind, I remove one leg, though I don't know whether it's
the left or right he lost. The mental amputation feels violent, as if

I'm the one sawing through skin, muscle, bone. I can feel the terrible crunch. When the leg is gone, I fold him into a wheelchair. Now I barely know him. How does he pass the days? Does he have anyone, a friend? Does he think of me? I've spent my life wondering whether my dad missed me and had somehow forgotten to say so. Recently, I've decided that it's enough for me to miss *him*, that the love I carry is a fire I keep alive for my own sake.

Wisdom might be knowing which is the fire you keep, which one you fight, and which you have to let go. *Let her burn*, as the boys would say. *She gone.*

If my dad called, I would answer. Yet he doesn't call, and I don't go looking for him, don't go shouting down that dead-end street. Searching will only bring suffering. I've put my line in the sand. I've dug it deep, down to mineral soil; I know what to do. I stand behind it, arms crossed, legs braced, and watch the fire of my father's self-destruction consume everything in its path. I'm safe here. I've fought for my life, learned to survive, learned that I have a life worth fighting for. Flames climb a tree and lash the sky. The devouring rises to a roar. I stay put, watching the fire pull away from me into the dark. It's dangerous, but it made me who I am. I've hardly ever seen anything so beautiful.

Acknowledgments

This book wouldn't exist in its current form without my brilliant agents, Sam Stoloff and Sulamita Garbuz; thank you for believing in my work and urging me to make this a braver story. To my editors, Colin Harrison and Emily Polson, who have together proven that real editors *do* still exist—this book would be nowhere without you. To the whole team at Scribner, book wizards, thank you.

To the friends who read early drafts—Jules Fitz Gerald, Emily Testa, Alexandra Valint, Forrest Gale, Zach Rollins, and Stephen Trevitt—bottomless gratitude. To the Output: Art After Fire program (Kate and Alice especially), Mystery Ranch, and the American Wildfire Experience—thank you for your generosity and support.

Thank you to my parents, one of whom taught me to love books and nature, while the other gave me country music and storytelling. To my sisters and brothers—Courtney, Steve, Evan, and Madeleine—I'm so grateful to share this life and parts of this story with you, and so proud of the strong adults you've become.

To my stepparents, aunts, and uncles (especially Renee, Chip and Becky, and Uncle Bo). To my Nana and Opa (no longer with us), Don and Dolly, who stood at the end of the ice rink, smiling as if anything

I did was good enough. To Jessica and Martin Klemencic, for letting me write in your empty house, and for welcoming me into your family.

To Lindsay Blade, who answers my calls every time: thank you for talking me through this book, I love yous, now make more paintings. To my main ladies, Alexandra Valint, Emily Testa, Kate Megear, Lindsey Heddleston Smith, Christine Britton, Stacia Rodenbusch, Nina Vizcarrando, Liz Fraley, Stephanie Puckett, Alex May, and Erika Hurth: you inspiring women confirm the saying on my favorite dive bar wall, "Friends are the best part of life." Thank you to Miriam Bird Greenberg, Mike Agresta, and Greg Koehler for title ideas and serious laughs. Paige Quinn and Gabi Gomez-Wint, fire pals: I love and admire you ladies; keep kicking ass out there. To Amanda Monthei, fellow resident of the woman–former hotshot–writer Venn diagram, thank you for everything, and I can't wait to read *your* book.

To the amazing folks of Grassroots Wildland Firefighters—thanks for fighting for us. Thank you to "the boys" of "Rowdy" River, all of you, including the ones who aren't boys. You taught me so much.

To Dylan Cimbura-Hernandez for the deep childhood work and for saying this could be an HBO Max show. To Danielle LaSusa for helping me believe. To my teachers: Chuck Kinder, Lisa Russ Spaar, Nancy Smith, Charles Wright, and Rita Dove.

Special thanks to Brent (hellos), Twitch, Zach, and Anthony, and to one hell of a human being and friend, Christopher Puckett. To Forrest Gale for believing in me and being a f'real bestie.

To Rookie, finest writing assistant a girl could have. Last but most, Eddie, thank you—first, for friendship when I sorely needed it. Later, for bringing food and saying, "Keep writing, turd." For everything.

Resources

Further Reading & Listening

The Pyrocene: How We Created an Age of Fire, and What Happens Next / Stephen J. Pyne

Tending the Wild: Native American Knowledge and the Management of California's Natural Resources / M. Kat Anderson

Braiding Sweetgrass: Indigenous Wisdom, Scientific Knowledge, and the Teachings of Plants / Robin Wall Kimmerer

California: A History / Kyle Starr

We Are the Land: A History of Native California / Damon B. Akins

Granite Mountain: The Firsthand Account of a Tragic Wildfire, Its Lone Survivor, and the Firefighters Who Made the Ultimate Sacrifice / Brendan McDonough

The Big Burn: Teddy Roosevelt and the Fire that Saved America / Timothy Egan

Burnt: A Memoir of Fighting Fire / Clare Frank

Both Sides of the Fire Line: Memoir of a Transgender Firefighter / Bobbie Scopa

Life with Fire podcast

The Anchor Point podcast

To Support Wildland Firefighters

Wildland firefighters are killed in the line of duty every year. Meanwhile, when I joined the crew, federal firefighters were paid a starting wage of $13.32 an hour. They often face addiction, depression, PTSD, and high rates of death by suicide, all while struggling to support their families. To learn more or to help, check out:

- Grassroots Wildland Firefighters: https://grassrootswildlandfire fighters.com/
- Wildland Firefighter Foundation: https://wffoundation.org/
- The American Wildfire Experience: https://wildfire-experience .org/

Support for Children of Alcoholics

According to the American Academy of Child and Adolescent Psychiatry, one in five adults lived with an alcoholic relative as a child. If this is you, you're not alone. Here are some resources:

- For general info, check out the American Addiction Center: https://americanaddictioncenters.org/alcohol/support-recovery /child
- The Al-Anon family programs, specifically groups for Adult Children of Alcoholics (ACOAs), can be very healing. Search for a meeting in your area.
- Melody Beattie's books really helped me; I liked *The Language of Letting Go* and *Codependent No More*

About the Author

Kelly Ramsey was born in Frankfort, Kentucky. She studied poetry at the University of Virginia and fiction writing at the University of Pittsburgh. She worked for the U.S. Forest Service as a wilderness ranger and wildland firefighter. Her writing has appeared in the *Washington Post*, *Sierra*, *Electric Literature*, and the anthology *Letter to a Stranger*. She lives in Northern California with her partner, their daughter, and a dog named Rookie.